100 Hikes in™
ARIZONA

100 Hikes in™
ARIZONA

Scott S. Warren

THE
MOUNTAINEERS

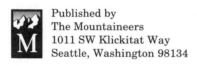
Published by
The Mountaineers
1011 SW Klickitat Way
Seattle, Washington 98134

Published simultaneously in Canada by Douglas & McIntyre, Ltd., 1615
Venables Street, Vancouver, B.C. V5L 2H1

Published simultaneously in Great Britain by Cordee, 3a DeMontfort Street,
Leicester, England, LE1 7HD

8 7 6 5 4
5 4 3 2 1

Manufactured in the United States of America

Edited by Miriam Bulmer
Maps by Mel Matis and Scott S. Warren
All photographs by Scott S. Warren
Book design by Marge Mueller
Typesetting by The Mountaineers Books
Book layout by Michelle Taverniti

Cover photograph: The Grand Canyon
Frontispiece: Pinnacle Balanced Rock in Chiricahua National Monument

Library of Congress Cataloging in Publication Data

Warren, Scott S.
      100 hikes in Arizona / Scott S. Warren.
        p.   cm.
      Includes index.
      ISBN 0-89886-375-9
       1. Hiking--Arizona--Guidebooks.   2. Trails--Arizona--Guidebooks.
3. Arizona--Guidebooks.   I. Title   II. Title: One hundred hikes in
Arizona.
GV199.42.A7W37   1993
796.5'09791--dc20   93-44622
                                                CIP

CONTENTS

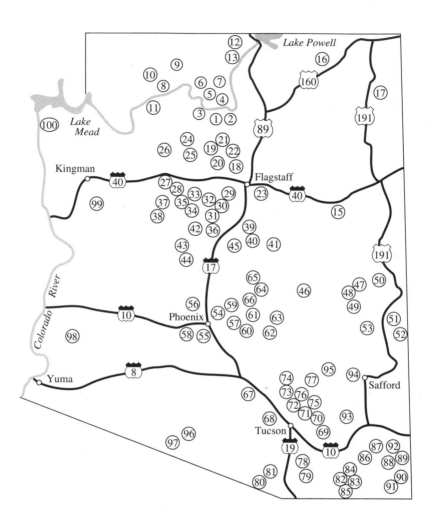

SOUTHEASTERN BASIN AND RANGE

WESTERN DESERTS

Map Legend

Main trail		Boundary	
Secondary trail		Start of hike	
Intermediate stream		Spring	
Perennial stream		Saddle or pass	
River		Building	
Paved road		Summit	
2WD gravel road		Campground	
4WD road		Picnic site	
Canyon rim		*Tank, pond or lake*	

City Creek flows out of the Mazatzal Mountains.

Introduction

Few, if any, states can match the variety of backcountry terrain that Arizona has to offer. From arid deserts and lush riverside thickets to tall stands of conifer and alpine tundra, Arizona has it all. For the hiker and backpacker, this diversity, combined with the many trails that have been established in Arizona's outback over the years, translates into a vast and interesting array of backcountry excursions from which to choose.

Topography

Undoubtedly, it is Arizona's topography that accounts for its greatly varied terrain. Geographers identify two primary provinces in Arizona: the Colorado Plateau Province and the Basin and Range Province. Stretching across the northern and northeastern third of the state, the Colorado Plateau Province is an expansive uplift that extends into Utah, Colorado, and New Mexico. This is a land sliced by deep canyons and spiked by red rock mesas and a few scattered mountain ranges. Carved over millions of years by the Colorado River, the Grand Canyon cuts across the northwestern quarter of the province, while the San Francisco Peaks reach dramatic heights near the town of Flagstaff. The somewhat gentler White Mountains rise along the Arizona–New Mexico border to the east, and a grand escarpment known as the Mogollon Rim borders the Colorado Plateau for hundreds of miles along its southern end. Elevations in the Colorado Plateau Province range from about 1,200 feet in the bottom of the Grand Canyon to 12,643 feet in the San Francisco Peaks.

South and west of the Mogollon Rim is what is known as the Basin and Range Province, which features expansive desert basins that are repeatedly interrupted by rugged mountain ranges. Changes in topography are rather sudden here. Climatic variations are equally impressive, as some of the continent's most arid deserts quickly give way to cool, tree-topped summits. Known as "sky islands," these mountain ranges often feature a biological countenance typical of more moderate latitudes to the north. Among the most notable of these ranges are the Mazatzals and Superstitions near Phoenix, the Santa Catalinas and Rincons near Tucson, and the Chiricahuas and Pinalenos in the southeastern portion of the state. Elevations in the Basin and Range Province extend from 70 feet in the southwest corner of the state to nearly 11,000 feet in the Pinaleno Mountains.

Climate

Because Arizona's topography extends from nearly sea level to above 12,000 feet, the state features an incredible diversity of climates. Throughout the year, temperatures can range from below zero degrees Fahrenheit in the mountains to well above the century mark in the lower basins. The highest temperature ever recorded in Arizona was 127 degrees, reached back in 1905. Similarly, precipitation may be a scant few inches a year on the desert floors to more than 25 inches in the higher mountains. Typically, most of this precipitation falls at two different times of the year. Winter brings periodic snowfall in the higher terrain and gentle rains in the desert, while summers feature frequent afternoon thunderstorms throughout the state.

Flora and Fauna

Because of Arizona's wide range of climate conditions, the state is home to an impressive number of plants and animals. These species of flora and fauna typically find niches within certain parameters of temperature and moisture, which are, in turn, dictated by elevation and latitude. Saguaro cactus, for instance, mostly grow below 3,000 feet, where temperatures rarely drop below freezing, while Engelmann spruce prefer a much cooler climate found above 9,000 feet. Similarly, elk live mostly in the cooler forests north of the Mogollon Rim, while javelina inhabit most desert regions to the south. Having recognized entire groups of plants and animals that share similar climate needs, scientists have identified specific biological communities or life zones. Corresponding to elevation levels, these life zones can be identified in the field by the dominant plants that grow there.

Extending from nearly sea level to about 4,500 feet is the *Lower Sonoran Zone*. Covering roughly one-third of the state, the Lower Sonoran Zone is home to Arizona's famed saguaro cactus. Other plants include cholla and barrel cactus, ocotillo, palo verde, creosote bush, saltbush, and mesquite. Wildlife within these arid lands includes javelinas, desert bighorn sheep, ringtail cats, coatimundis, coyotes, jackrabbits, rattlesnakes, Gila monsters, and a variety of birds.

Saguaro cactus in the Estrella Mountain Regional Park

The *Upper Sonoran Zone,* which extends from 4,500 feet to 6,500 feet, often features stunted forests of pinyon pine and juniper but may also include manzanita and a variety of oaks. Unlike oaks of the eastern woodlands, Arizona's various species of oaks (about a dozen in all) range in size from shrubs to small trees. Identifying these species is sometimes made difficult by the fact that they often interbreed. Animals that prefer the Upper Sonoran Zone include mule and white-tailed deer, black bears, pronghorn antelopes, and rattlesnakes.

Reaching to elevations around 8,000 feet, the *Transition Zone* includes the impressive forests of ponderosa pine found in many parts of the state. The largest stand of ponderosa pine in the country, in fact, stretches from the Williams area to the New Mexico border. Other tree species include Douglas fir, Gambel oak, and juniper. Mule deer favor this zone, as do elk, black bears, tassel-eared squirrels, and wild turkeys.

The *Canadian Zone,* which extends from 8,000 feet to 9,500 feet, is next, with its cool, wet timberlands of Engelmann spruce, blue spruce, white fir, subalpine fir, and aspen. Fauna that live here include elk, mule deer, black bears, and a variety of squirrels.

Stretching from 9,500 feet to timberline, which in Arizona is around 11,500 feet, is the *Hudsonian Zone.* In this harsh environment, dominant plant species include bristlecone pine, gnarled spruce, and fir. Weather conditions are harsh at this elevation; strong winds and snow are quite common. These stunted and twisted trees are collectively called krummholz forests.

Extending above the 11,500-foot mark, the *Alpine Zone* is found in only one location in Arizona—the San Francisco Peaks near Flagstaff. Because conditions are so harsh at these lofty elevations, no trees grow here. Instead, these areas support meadows of flowering annuals and perennials, many of which are found in other alpine areas of the world as well.

While elevation plays an important role in plant and animal distribution in Arizona, so does the presence of water. Perennial streams and rivers, and even those intermittent ones that flow with some regularity, are the foundation of what are called riparian ecosystems. In an arid state like Arizona, riparian ecosystems are incredibly important in maintaining ecological diversity. They are also wonderful places to explore. Characterized by thick and leafy canopies formed by cottonwoods, ashes, alders, Arizona sycamores, and other deciduous trees, riparian areas usually include thickets of shrubs, vines, and ground cover as well. In comparison to the surrounding desert or arid forestlands, these junglelike environments can be quite refreshing. Adding to their allure is the presence of a great variety of insects, mammals, and birds. Especially in southern Arizona, riparian areas constitute the best birding areas around. A third of the hikes in this book visit riparian areas around the state.

One additional factor that adds to Arizona's great variety of flora and fauna is the state's proximity to Mexico. As bird-watchers will tell you, a number of Mexican bird species regularly fly north of the border to nest or just escape the heat. Trees such as the Chihuahuan pine grow in the mountains of southern Arizona, and some species of mammals have filtered north too. Occasional reports have even placed jaguars in the southernmost wildlands of the state.

Using This Book

This book sets out to describe in detail 100 of the best hikes in Arizona. All of these hikes follow either designated trails or, at the very least, established routes of travel such as canyon bottoms. Cross-country excursions are avoided so as to lessen impact on the environment. Most of these hikes either access a particular point of interest or follow a loop route. Attention has also been paid to representing the variety of terrains and ecosystems found in Arizona and to providing as wide a geographical representation as possible. This is why many urban-area hikes have been included in this book, along with classic wilderness walks. Two regions of the state are underrepresented here: the expansive Navajo Indian Nation in the northeastern corner of the state and the basin and range deserts to the west. This is because both areas are lacking in established backcountry routes. Some of the hikes presented here are quite popular and should be avoided on weekends and holidays, but there are a great many other excursions that are not as heavily visited.

INFORMATION BLOCKS

Each hike begins with an information block designed to provide pertinent facts and figures at a glance. By scanning these headings, you should know right away what to expect during each hike.

In all but a few cases the *Distance* figure refers to the hike's round-trip distance. If a particular trail is 3.2 miles long, the distance figure will indicate "6.4 miles round trip" to let you know the total number of miles to be hiked. In a few cases where it is impracticable to retrace the entire route, the distance figure will read "one way." For these hikes a shuttle is required.

The *Difficulty* of each hike is calculated mostly by the trail's elevation gain and overall grade, and rated as easy, moderate, or strenuous. One short, extremely steep pitch may not necessarily bump a hike into the "strenuous" category, but continuous steep grades would. Hiking conditions such as the presence of deadfall, loose rock, and so on were also considered. Some routes that are not too steep may still be rated strenuous because of obstacles along the way. For the most part the hiking terrain involves established trails, although some short stretches may require scrambling skills.

The *Hiking times* presented are for persons of moderate hiking ability and strength who enjoy stopping occasionally to rest and take in the scenery. They take into account such factors as distance, elevations, grade changes, and trail conditions. These times will not fit every hiker's purposes, and are provided simply as a guide.

The *Elevation* entry shows the range in elevation that the hike covers. The first figure indicates the trailhead elevation, while the second is that of either the high or low point of the hike. In most cases this is also the destination of the hike. If this second entry is lower than the first, the hike descends in elevation (typical of most canyon hikes). If the second figure is greater, the hike climbs in elevation. In some instances, additional climbing may be required in the course of the hike. This added elevation gain is included in the hike descriptions.

The *Management* entry indicates which government agency or private group holds title to portions or all of the route. Entries include: the Bureau of Land Management (BLM), national forest (NF), national park (NP), national monument (NM), national historic site (NHS), national recreation area (NRA), national wildlife refuge (NWR), state park (SP), county park, or a city park; or owned by an organization such as The Nature Conservancy. These entities may offer additional information about a particular hike, including maps.

The *Wilderness status* entry indicates whether or not the hike enters an established wilderness area (WA) or primitive area (PA). Such information is helpful in determining what rules and regulations apply (see the Wilderness Etiquette section of this chapter).

The *Season* entry points out the best times of the year to attempt the hike. Where high mountain hikes are concerned, that means the months when the trail is free of snow. In the lower-elevation deserts, the optimal months for hiking are when the danger of heat exposure is not too great.

Many of the hikes in this book are possible year-round. Before setting out, however, you should check with the managing agency about the road conditions leading to the trailhead and the trail conditions beyond. During certain times of the year rainy conditions may, in fact, preclude access.

The *USGS maps* entry indicates which 7.5-minute topographic map or maps cover the hike. Keep in mind that these are often outdated in terms of trails. Some routes may not have been in existence when the maps were drafted, while other trails have since been rerouted. Nevertheless, topo maps come in handy, especially in combination with updated management-agency maps.

MAPS

Each hike in this book is illustrated by a map. While every effort has been made to include all pertinent information, the maps are actually meant to serve as an introduction to a particular hike. It is advisable to bring along more detailed maps.

HIKE DESCRIPTIONS

Each description begins with an introductory paragraph, followed by specific directions on how to reach the trailhead. This is followed by a running narrative of the route itself, which includes a description of grades, cardinal directions, possible hazards, and general trail conditions. Most major trail junctions are mentioned, as well as vegetation found along the way. Possible wildlife sightings are sometimes dis-

A raft on the Colorado River

cussed, as is the geology of an area. A historical perspective may also warrant mention on occasion. These discussions of the natural and human history of each hike are extremely brief, and additional research will only enhance your hiking experience. Each description ends with a summation of such technicalities as water availability, specific hazards, and regulations.

Wilderness Etiquette

Fortunately, much of Arizona's backcountry is now protected as wilderness. There are currently ninety-two designated wilderness areas across the state. These are included on National Forest Service, Bureau of Land Management, National Park Service, and national wildlife refuge lands.

As dictated by the Wilderness Act of 1964, a variety of regulations apply so as to preserve the natural character of the land and provide visitors with a true wilderness experience. Paramount among these regulations is that all means of mechanized travel are prohibited. This includes motorized vehicles, hang gliders, and all-terrain bicycles (ATBs). In Arizona, as in other states, ATBs, or mountain bikes as they are often called, present land managers with a particularly pressing problem. A few bicyclists either do not know that bicycles are prohibited or they believe that they are above the law. Although most users of this book will be traveling on foot, keep in mind that mountain bikes are strictly prohibited from all trails that enter wilderness areas. They are not allowed on most national park and monument trails either.

Of course, the Wilderness Act also prohibits such mechanized equipment as chain saws and generators. Commercial enterprises such as livestock grazing and outfitting are allowed under a permit system. Some areas have restrictions on fires and campsite location. Because dogs are disruptive to wildlife, some backcountry areas are off-limits to pets. In all other locations, pets should be strictly controlled, or, preferrably, left at home. Fishing and hunting regulations fall under the auspices of the Arizona Department of Game and Fish.

In addition to the regulations dictated by the Wilderness Act, all visitors should follow a number of commonsense rules having to do with no-trace camping and hiking. These rules should be applied not just to designated wilderness lands but to all backcountry areas.

- Do not build campfires—use a stove instead.
- Avoid camping in sensitive areas such as mountain meadows and around fragile desert plants.
- Camp at least 100 feet from the trail and use existing sites when possible.
- Camp at least a quarter mile from any spring or watering hole— state law actually dictates this to benefit wildlife that comes to drink at night.
- Never cut standing trees, dead or alive.
- Do not leave behind structures or nails of any sort.
- Do not dig holes and trenches, or level tent areas.
- Bury all human waste and use biodegradable soap at least 200 feet from water sources. Pack out or safely burn used toilet paper.
- Travel in small groups.
- Never cut across switchbacks or walk over sensitive ground such as microbiotic (cryptogamic) soil.
- Pack out all litter.

While these "no trace" rules certainly apply to the backcountry, they also make good sense when camping at a trailhead. Far too often, backcountry travelers forget to exhibit care for the environment once they are off the trail. The end result is trailhead areas that are trashed out and overused. In such areas, practice low-impact camping just as you would in any wilderness setting, and be sure to keep your vehicles on established roadways and parking areas.

Of course, it should go without saying that all plants, animals, rocks, and historical relics should not be removed, disturbed, or destroyed in any way. All natural objects and historical artifacts are protected by law in national parks, monuments, recreation areas, and wildlife refuges. Similarly, many species of cactus are protected by state laws, passed in response to an increase in cactus rustling in recent years. Antiquities of prehistoric or historic origin are protected by federal law. In recent years, artifacts, especially those of the prehistoric Indians, have been looted at an alarming rate. Prehistoric structures are also threatened by careless treatment. The simplest rule is also the best: look but don't touch.

Backcountry Safety

Backcountry hazards are numerous in Arizona, but if you take a few precautions the possibility of problems becomes quite small. This book outlines what some of those hazards are, but does not presume to represent the final word on treatment or prevention. The best prevention is knowledge and experience. Here are a few reading suggestions that may be helpful in giving you a deeper understanding of outdoor travel, the dangers you may encounter on the trail, and what you can do to make your outings as safe and enjoyable as possible.

Wilderness Basics: The Complete Handbook for Hikers & Backpackers, 2d ed., by The San Diego Chapter of the Sierra Club. Seattle: The Mountaineers, 1993.

Mountaineering: The Freedom of the Hills, 5th ed. Don Graydon, editor. Seattle: The Mountaineers, 1992.

Desert Hiking, by David Ganci. Berkeley: Wilderness Press, 1983.

HEAT AND SUN

Perhaps the most prevalent danger to hikers in Arizona is the heat, especially in the low deserts. Temperatures regularly top the 100 degrees Fahrenheit mark in the summer months, and sometimes reach above 120 degrees. Under such conditions the body can quickly become dehydrated. This, in turn, leads to fatigue, exhaustion, heat stroke, and even death. The best course of action is to avoid hiking during these hot periods. If you do choose to hike during hot weather, however, it is extremely important to carry plenty of drinking water: a gallon per person per day is the recommended amount. It is also important to remember to drink often. Surprisingly, many people fail to drink the water they carry at frequent enough intervals. To detect heat exhaustion, watch for cool and pale skin, headaches, dizziness, and lack of energy. Heat exhaustion may lead to heat stroke, which is very serious. Immediate treatment for both of these conditions includes having the victim rest in a cool, shady area. Give him or her plenty of water and seek medical attention as soon as possible.

In addition to the possibility of heat exhaustion and stroke, exposure to the sun can also result in severe sunburn. In addition to being uncomfortable, the severest cases can present specific medical problems, including third-degree burns. To prevent sunburn, wear a hat to protect your head and neck. Wearing light-colored clothing is also helpful. Use plenty of sun block (SPF 15 or above) on all exposed areas, and remember to reapply it frequently.

HYPOTHERMIA

Interestingly, hypothermia is a common hazard in many of Arizona's backcountry areas. Sudden changes in weather can bring on cold rain or even snow, especially in the high country. This combination of cold and wet can cause the body's core temperature to drop to dangerous levels. Symptoms include uncontrollable shivering, impaired judgment, deteriorating speech, drowsiness, and weakness.

Hypothermia can be an efficient killer, but it is treatable. As soon as possible, replace wet clothing with dry and place the victim in a prewarmed sleeping bag. It may also be necessary to huddle with the victim to help warm him or her up. Give warm liquids and high-energy food, and get the victim to a doctor as soon as possible. As with any backcountry hazard, prevention is the best course of action. Avoid getting wet and cold in the first place, carry spare clothing and rain gear, and eat plenty of high-energy foods.

LIGHTNING

Lightning is a killer in Arizona, and not just in the higher terrain. The Mogollon Rim, in fact, holds the dubious honor of having one of the highest rates of lightning strikes in the country. It is certainly best to avoid open terrain during electrical storms. This means keeping a watchful eye on the weather. Watch for clouds building up, especially in the afternoon, although lightning can occur at any time. If you should happen to be caught, retreat to a flat area or depression. Stay away from tall trees. Caves and deep alcoves are safe, as are cars. But shallow rock overhangs, ravines, and tents are not.

FLASH FLOODS

Flash floods are a common hazard in Arizona, especially in desert areas where bare ground tends to shed runoff rather than absorb it. If storm clouds are building, avoid washes, canyon bottoms, and creek beds. Also, do not attempt to drive across flooded roadways. Typically, such floods will recede within an hour or two.

WILDLIFE

As one might expect, the deserts of Arizona are home to a variety of venomous creatures: scorpions, black widow spiders, Gila monsters, and rattlesnakes, to name four. While the bite of any of these creatures can cause medical problems (and even death in some cases), the chance of your being bitten is actually quite remote. Rattlesnakes, for instance, avoid people just as much as people avoid them. To avoid unwanted encounters with venomous creatures, stay away from rocky areas where such species might be hiding. If bitten, seek medical attention immediately.

Other creatures in the forests and deserts of Arizona may also pose a threat, although the possibilities are, again, quite remote. In recent years a number of black bear attacks on campers have been reported, especially in the southeastern mountains. These conflicts have mostly arisen, however, because people have not taken the proper precautions. Be sure to store all food at least 10 feet off the ground, strung up in a tree away from camp. Many campgrounds are now equipped with bearproof trash containers, and signs have been posted warning visitors that they are in bear country. It is conceivable that mountain lions might pose a threat, although the chances of seeing one are extremely rare.

A danger recently discovered in the American Southwest is hantavirus, a deadly disease that strikes its victims swiftly. Hantavirus is

The West Fork of the Little Colorado River near Mount Baldy

thought to be transmitted through contact with rodents, particularly deer mice, or their droppings. Hikers and campers should avoid contact with rodents and rodent burrows, stay out of rodent-infested structures such as abandoned cabins and shelters, sleep in a tent (not on open ground), and store food in rodent-proof containers.

GIARDIA

Although not deadly, *Giardia lamblia* is a real hazard that plagues most parts of Arizona. A microorganism that is now found in most open water sources (streams, pools, ponds, and lakes, for example), *Giardia* can cause digestive tract problems if ingested. Symptoms include severe diarrhea, which may not appear until a week or two later, and treatment requires a doctor's attention.

Prevention is the only sensible means of dealing with *Giardia*. Essentially, you should not drink any surface water without first treating it properly. This means either filtering the water with a specially designed filter system (*Giardia* cysts are very small) or boiling it for at least three minutes for every 1,000 feet. For day hikes, simply bring along all the water you need.

GETTING LOST AND FOUND

For even the most experienced hiker, the possibility of becoming hurt or lost is real. First-time hikers should not travel alone, and seasoned veterans should consider taking a companion on more difficult hikes. Regardless of your ability, however, you should always let someone know where you are going. If you do become injured or disoriented, above all remain calm. Hopefully, another hiker or a backcountry ranger will happen along.

Before You Go

When planning a hike, a little preparation not only goes a long way to help make the trip fun and successful, it is also necessary to insure that you return safely.

A good place to begin is with your selection of clothes. Sturdy shoes with good soles are important, as is comfortable clothing. Weather conditions may warrant short pants and a short-sleeve shirt when you start out, but always come prepared with warmer clothing, especially when hiking Arizona's higher terrain. In the desert areas, light-colored, long clothing is helpful in preventing sunburn. A wide-brimmed hat is also a necessity. For hikes of any length, bring along rain gear—either a poncho or rain parka and pants—in your pack. Two pairs of socks are a good idea, but experienced hikers have no doubt worked out their own best solution for footwear long ago.

In addition to proper clothing, experts have put together a list of Ten Essentials which they deem necessary for a safe and rewarding adventure.

1. Extra clothing—more than is needed in good weather
2. Extra food—so that something is left over at the end of the trip
3. Sunglasses—especially important for alpine and snow travel, and in desert lands
4. Knife—for first aid and emergency fire-building (to make kindling)
5. Firestarter—a candle or chemical fuel for wet wood
6. First aid kit
7. Matches—in a weatherproof container

8. Flashlight—with extra bulb and batteries
9. Map—be sure it's the right one for the trip
10. Compass—be sure to know the declination, east or west

In Arizona's generally arid climate, an eleventh item of great importance should always command room in your pack—water! Experts say a gallon per person per day is a good rule of thumb.

When planning an overnight trip you cannot go wrong by investing in (or renting) good camping equipment. First, take a look at your shoes—with added weight on your back, it is important that your ankles are supported with higher boots. To carry that extra weight in the most comfortable manner possible, a good backpack is a must. Packs have become quite sophisticated, especially in harness systems. Be sure that you bring extra clothing, including a change of socks for each day. A good lightweight sleeping bag will be a friend for years to come if properly cared for. And a sleeping pad cannot be beat for added warmth and comfort.

Shelter is an important consideration. Some hapless hikers may assume that it is not going to rain, or that they can find natural shelter along the way. It is far beter, however, to pack along a good, lightweight tent to ensure your comfort and safety.

You may want to bring extra water, especially if none is available along the route. Checking beforehand with the managing agency on water availability is extremely important, as is carrying a good water filter. Plan your meals carefully so that you do not either go hungry or wind up carrying too much food.

You will need a cook kit, spoon, fork, cup, and lightweight stove for preparing meals. In this day and age, a stove is not only convenient but a real godsend for the environment. Let's face it: Campfires may be romantic, but they are messy eyesores once they are extinguished. If you really need something to curl up with at night, bring a good book.

A Note About Safety

Safety is an important concern in all outdoor activities. No guidebook can alert you to every hazard or anticipate the limitations of every reader. Therefore, the descriptions of roads, trails, routes, and natural features in this book are not representations that a particular place or excursion will be safe for your party. When you follow any of the routes described in this book, you assume responsibility for your own safety. Under normal conditions, such excursions require the usual attention to traffic, road and trail conditions, weather, terrain, the capabilities of your party, and other factors. Keeping informed on current conditions and exercising common sense are the keys to a safe, enjoyable outing.

The Mountaineers

1 BRIGHT ANGEL TRAIL

Distance: 19.2 miles round trip
Difficulty: strenuous
Hiking time: 2 days
Elevation: 6,840 to 2,400 feet
Management: Grand Canyon NP

Wilderness status: none
Season: year-round
USGS maps: Bright Angel,
 Grand Canyon, Phantom
 Ranch

In addition to offering the most convenient access to the bottom of the Grand Canyon, the Bright Angel Trail is also one of the most popular hiking routes in the park. Wide enough to allow safe passage for tourist-toting mules, this is a virtual highway among backcountry trails. Although the Bright Angel Trail ends at the Colorado River, this description continues on to the Silver Bridge and Phantom Ranch beyond.

The Bright Angel trailhead is located at the west end of the Grand Canyon Village, just past the Bright Angel Lodge. (To reach the Bright Angel Lodge from Flagstaff, drive north on US Highway 180 to the Grand Canyon Village.) From the start, the route wastes no time in snaking its way down Garden Creek as it drops 3,000 feet in the first 3.1 miles. Along this stretch are two rest shelters that offer emergency phones and drinking water from mid-May to October. Beyond the second rest house, the trail soon enters a relatively level stretch of canyon bottom.

At about 4.5 miles from its start, the Bright Angel Trail reaches Indian Gardens. A popular destination for day hikers, Indian Gardens features a campground and a reliable source of drinking water. Additionally, a 1.4-mile side trail leads from here to Plateau Point on the rim of the Inner Gorge. This verdant oasis within the canyon enjoys a rich past. The prehistoric Anasazi Indians raised crops here, as did the Havasupai during more recent times. Miners frequented Indian Gardens in the late 1800s. By the turn of the century, the area's potential

Riparian growth along the Bright Angel Trail

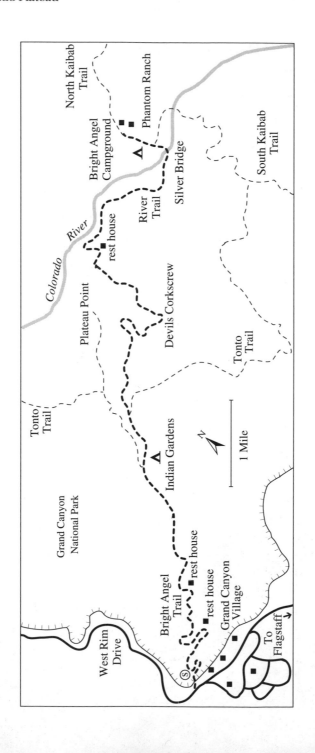

for tourism was being realized. In 1903 Ralph Cameron gained control of the Bright Angel Trail and turned it into a toll route.

Although it marks the halfway point of the hike in terms of distance, Indian Gardens is about two-thirds of the way down in elevation. By this point, the trail has encountered several layers of geologic history. First to be traversed is Kaibab Limestone. Light in color, this formation was deposited in a shallow sea about 250 million years ago. Next in line is the Toroweap Formation, a layer of tan-colored sandstones and limestones. It is followed by Coconino Sandstone, a heavily cross-bedded rock that consists of deposits by ancient sand dunes. Hermit Shale—a deposit that collected in swamps and lagoons—is next, followed by the Supai Group Formation. Near the Three-mile Resthouse is the top end of the imposing Redwall Limestone. Below that are layers of Temple Butte and Muav limestones. And forming the gently sloping Tonto Plateau below is the Bright Angel Shale Formation. Dating back about 540 million years, Bright Angel Shale originated from mud deposited in a shallow sea. Beyond Indian Gardens the Bright Angel Trail encounters two additional formations before reaching the Colorado River. First is a layer of Tapeats Sandstone and then comes the very impressive Vishnu Schist. Dropping into the Inner Gorge, this dark rock dates back some 1.7 billion years.

From Indian Gardens the Bright Angel Trail passes through the Tapeats Narrows before reaching the Devils Corkscrew—a lengthy set of switchbacks that cascades down the Vishnu Schist Formation. At the bottom the trail takes up Pipe Creek before finally reaching the river. At this point, 7.8 miles from the trailhead, the Bright Angel Trail ends and the River Trail begins. A rest house here is equipped with an emergency phone and a chemical toilet. For the next 1.4 miles the River Trail parallels the Colorado River to the Silver Bridge, across which lie a ranger station and the Bright Angel Campground.

Because of the Bright Angel Trail's popularity (some 100,000 people hike the trail each year), camping is restricted to the established Indian Gardens and Bright Angel campgrounds. Needless to say, reservations for sites at both facilities must be made well in advance. Similarly, an overnight stay at Phantom Ranch, in either dorms or private cabins, should be planned months ahead of time. Constructed in 1922, Phantom Ranch includes a snack bar and restaurant. There is even a pay phone.

No matter what time of the year you go, expect to see a lot of other hikers on the Bright Angel Trail. When encountering mules it is best to step off the trail and let them by. Water in Garden and Pipe creeks is not potable, but you can count on finding reliable sources at the upper rest houses between May and October, and at Indian Gardens and Bright Angel campgrounds year-round. Summer temperatures regularly climb above 100 degrees Fahrenheit in the Inner Canyon, so plan accordingly. Most important, keep in mind that the hike back out involves nearly a vertical mile of climbing. Many unprepared hikers have found themselves in a lot of trouble because they were fooled by the easy descent to the bottom. While the hike down to the river takes about 5 hours, the walk back out may take twice as long.

$\underline{2}$ TONTO TRAIL

Distance: 28.4 miles one way   Wilderness status: none
Difficulty: strenuous   Season: year-round
Hiking time: 4 days   USGS maps: Bright Angel, Cape
Elevation: 7,400 to 3,800 feet   Royal, Phantom Ranch,
Management: Grand Canyon NP   Grandview Point

Visitors to the South Rim get a wonderful bird's-eye view of the Grand Canyon, but a walk along part of the 92-mile Tonto Trail provides a very different, yet equally spectacular, look at this scenic wonder. There are several possible hikes to choose from on the Tonto; this description follows a 20-mile segment from the Grandview Trail west to the South Kaibab Trail.

Begin the hike at Grandview Point, which is 11 miles east of the Grand Canyon Village on the East Rim Drive. (To reach the East Rim Drive, drive north from Flagstaff on US Highway 180.) The trailhead is well marked and ample parking is provided.

Dropping convincingly, the Grandview Trail descends 2,600 feet in 3 miles to reach Horseshoe Mesa below. Within the first mile, the trail descends through a moderately steep series of switchbacks. After passing a small saddle it then begins dropping at a steeper rate along the upper reaches of the Cottonwood Creek drainage. Leveling out a bit after the second mile, the route traverses north toward Horseshoe Mesa. Although the trail is never hard to follow, because it features loose rocks in many sections, care should be taken.

Horseshoe Mesa, an aptly named tableland at an elevation of 4,800 feet, has long been a source of copper. It is believed that prehistoric Indians used the blue copper ore as an ingredient for paint. In 1892, Pete Berry, Niles Cameron, and Ralph Cameron began extracting high-grade ore from underground mines on the mesa. The operation ceased in 1907, but not before a handful of structures were built. The remains of one building, along with some antiquated mining machinery, are still visible today.

When securing a backcountry permit (required for overnight hikes in the canyon), keep in mind that the Horsehoe Mesa area is popular. Camping on Horseshoe Mesa is confined to a backcountry campground that fills up fast. Alternate sites exist along Cottonwood Creek, although staying there would make for a long first day of hiking. Water is sometimes available at an intermittent spring here, but it is advisable to check with the National Park Service's Backcountry Office about the availability of water all along the Tonto Trail before setting out.

To reach the Tonto Trail from Horseshoe Mesa, turn west onto a trail located in the vicinity of the old cabin foundation and head into the Cottonwood Creek drainage. Within a mile this route reaches the canyon bottom 800 feet below, and at about 1.5 miles from the turnoff it joins the Tonto Trail.

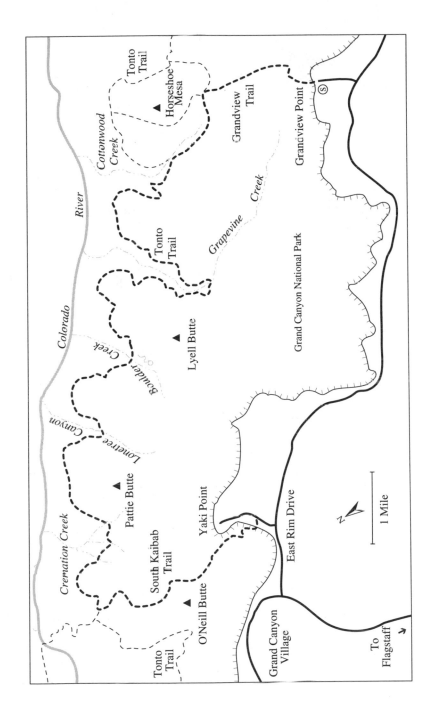

A backpacker sets up camp along the Tonto Trail.

The grade of the Tonto Trail changes surprisingly little as the route follows the relatively flat Tonto Plateau. Formed by the Bright Angel Shale Formation, the Tonto Plateau appears as a benchland from the rim above. Although easy enough to follow, the route does run dangerously close to the edge of the Inner Gorge in places. In addition, very little shade exists because plant life here includes blackbrush, saltbush, prickly pear cactus, century plants, and little else.

Continuing west from the Cottonwood Creek drainage, the Tonto Trail soon runs into the imposing Grapevine Creek. In a place like the Grand Canyon, even insignificant side drainages can prove impassable. Once it encounters Grapevine Creek, the trail must skirt several miles to the southwest before getting around to the other side. After rounding Lyell Butte, the route arrives at the smaller Boulder Creek drainage. Part-time springs and suitable camping spots are located along both Grapevine and Boulder creeks.

From Boulder Creek, the Tonto Trail continues on to Lonetree Canyon, the site of the last spring along the hike. Suitable camping is available here, as well as in Cremation Creek, the next drainage over. Fanning out between Pattie Butte and Skeleton Point, the Cremation Creek basin is comparatively broad as the trail crosses three tributaries. You may find evidence of prehistoric people in this desolate area of the canyon.

A mile beyond Cremation Creek is the South Kaibab Trail. From this junction it is a 4.4-mile, 3,000-foot climb up to the South Rim and the end of this hike. Because the South Kaibab is one of two major routes into the canyon, expect to see a lot of hikers along the way. Like the Bright Angel Trail, the South Kaibab Trail challenges hikers with its near-constant climb in elevation.

Because summer brings extremely high temperatures to the lower canyon, late fall, winter, and spring are the best times to hike the Tonto Trail. The availability of water can also be a factor in determining when to go. It is not advisable to hike the Tonto Trail alone because it is remote and rugged in places.

3 DRIPPING SPRINGS

Distance: 6 miles round trip
Difficulty: moderate
Hiking time: 4 hours
Elevation: 6,700 to 5,200 feet
Management: Grand Canyon NP

Wilderness status: none
Season: year-round
USGS maps: Bright Angel,
  Grand Canyon

For a moderately easy introduction to the world below the rim of the Grand Canyon, this 3-mile-long trail to Dripping Springs offers both spectacular views and a perennial source of cool water.

To reach the Grand Canyon Village, drive north on US Highway 180 from Flagstaff. This hike begins at Hermits Rest, which is located at the end of the West Rim Drive. Between the months of May and September, day hikers must park at the Grand Canyon Village and ride the free shuttle out. Buses run at 15-minute intervals from 7:30 A.M. to sunset. From Hermits Rest, walk west to the road's end (less than 0.25 mile) and find the start of the Hermit Trail, a popular route to the river below.

The Hermit Trail begins by making a moderately steep descent into Hermit Basin, a broad, gently sloping expanse covered by arid pinyon–juniper forests. The trail is rocky in many parts, although some stretches were riprapped with sandstone slabs in the early part of this century. The result is an unusual tread that is both easy to walk and visually interesting. A little more than a mile into the hike, the Hermit Trail connects with the Waldron Trail, a 2-mile route that climbs back up to the rim. Keep right at this junction. A short distance farther, approximately 1.5 miles from the trailhead, take the signed left-hand turn for Dripping Springs. From this junction, the Hermit Trail continues down Hermit Gorge, while the Dripping Springs Trail traverses west along the head of the gorge. Skirting along the top of the deep red Supai Group Formation, this segment of the hike opens up to awesome views of the canyon below.

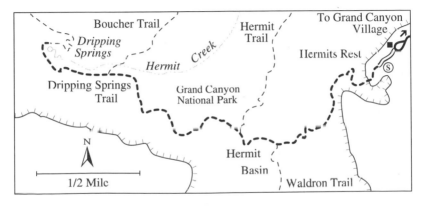

Hermit Gorge as seen from the Dripping Springs hike

Within a mile of the Dripping Springs–Hermit Trail junction is the start of the Boucher Trail, a route that eventually connects with the Tonto Trail. The Dripping Springs Trail stays left here and climbs a few hundred feet before reaching its namesake in another 0.5 mile. Nestled in a protective alcove at the base of the Toroweap Formation, Dripping Springs is a relatively small flow that drops from the rock wall above. The Park Service suggests treating the water before drinking it.

Louis Boucher, the hermit in Hermits Rest, maintained a camp at the springs around the turn of the century, and reportedly kept goldfish in a trough here. He also planted fruit trees along nearby Boucher Creek. Although this hike ends at the springs, a much-faded trail does climb steeply to gain the rim above.

Carry plenty of water along on this hike, even if you plan on filling up at the springs. Camping is prohibited in the vicinity of the springs due to the fragile nature of plant life in the area.

4   CLEAR CREEK

Distance: 32.6 miles round trip
Difficulty: strenuous
Hiking time: 4 days
Elevation: 7,200 to 2,400 feet
Management: Grand Canyon NP

Wilderness status: none
Season: year-round
USGS maps: Bright Angel,
   Phantom Ranch

Just as the Tonto Trail follows its namesake plateau below the South Rim, the Clear Creek Trail travels across the same landform on the north side of the river. Climbing east from Phantom Ranch, the Clear Creek Trail eventually winds up in a major drainage of the North Rim. Among the rewards of this lengthy hike are spectacular views of the Inner Gorge, a clear running creek, and access to the Colorado River.

Following Clear Creek down to the Colorado River

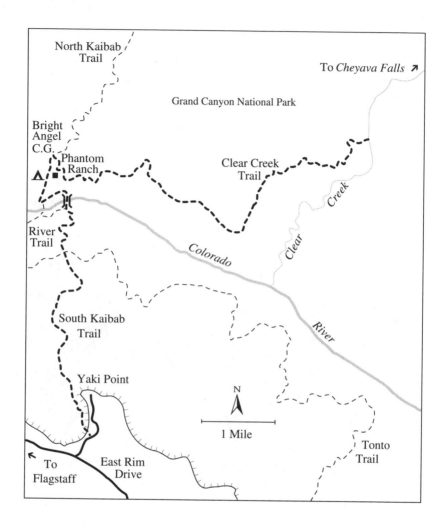

Although the Clear Creek Trail starts at Phantom Ranch, this description begins at Yaki Point and the South Kaibab trailhead. (From Flagstaff, Yaki Point is reached by driving north on US Highway 180 to the East Rim Drive. Turn right on the East Rim Drive and follow it for a little over 1 mile.) Providing the quickest access to Phantom Ranch, the South Kaibab Trail is a well-developed and heavily used corridor to the canyon bottom. The geology along the South Kaibab route is easily identifiable as it descends through layer upon layer of the Earth's history. Of particular interest are the rose-colored bands of Zoroaster Granite that slice through dark walls of Vishnu Schist in the

Inner Gorge. These were formed when molten rock intruded into cracks in the surrounding bedrock. In 6.4 miles the trail drops 4,780 feet to the Kaibab Suspension Bridge (itself a marvel of turn-of-the-century engineering) and the Colorado River. It reaches Phantom Ranch in about another mile.

Campsites are available at the Bright Angel Campground, adjacent to Phantom Ranch. If this facility is full, your only alternative is to climb out of Bright Angel Canyon and find a spot on the Tonto Plateau above. However, this would make for an extremely long day of hiking, and rangers report that many hikers in fact have trouble completing it. Make certain you have a permit, which means a reserved campsite.

From Phantom Ranch the Clear Creek Trail climbs rather steeply (1,500 feet in the first 2 miles) to the Tonto Plateau. From the rim of the plateau, it is a 6-mile traverse east to the lip of Clear Creek Canyon. Although this segment is mostly level, some grade changes are encountered as the route crosses smaller drainages. In the last mile to Clear Creek the trail drops about 500 feet to the drainage bottom below. Here, among scattered cottonwoods, are found several suitable camping spots. In all, Clear Creek is 9 miles from Phantom Ranch.

At Clear Creek, two exceptional side trips are possible, both of which take most of a day to complete. The first is an 8-mile hike (round trip) to Cheyava Falls, the highest falls in the canyon. To reach this spectacle, follow the main fork of Clear Creek upstream. The second side trip follows Clear Creek down to the Colorado River. Twisting and bending for about 5 miles, the creek drops through a narrow labyrinth of Vishnu Schist. At one point a 10-foot-high waterfall seems to block passage, but it is possible to scramble around to the right. Hikers with a fear of heights may want to bring a rope for this portion. Within 0.25 mile of the river, watch for schools of spawning trout. Once at the river, you may see a rafting party drifting by.

When considering this hike, keep in mind that water is available only at Phantom Ranch and Clear Creek; it is advisable to treat water from the latter. A backcountry permit is required for overnight stays. Be prepared for very hot temperatures in the summer.

5 NORTH KAIBAB TRAIL

Distance: 28.4 miles round trip
Difficulty: strenuous
Hiking time: 3 days
Elevation: 8,240 to 2,400 feet
Management: Grand Canyon NP

Wilderness status: none
Season: May to October
USGS maps: Bright Angel Point, Phantom Ranch

Although they are separated by only 10 air miles, the South Rim and the North Rim of the Grand Canyon are worlds apart. Only 10 percent of the millions of people who visit the park each year ever make it to

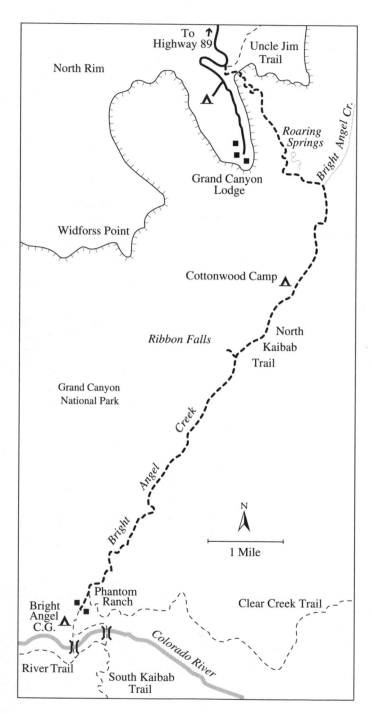

To Highway 89

Uncle Jim Trail

North Rim

Roaring Springs

Bright Angel Cr.

Grand Canyon Lodge

Widforss Point

Cottonwood Camp

North Kaibab Trail

Ribbon Falls

Grand Canyon National Park

Bright Angel Creek

N

1 Mile

Phantom Ranch

Clear Creek Trail

Bright Angel C.G.

Colorado River

River Trail

South Kaibab Trail

the remote North Rim. For hikers that means a less crowded alternative to the popular Bright Angel and South Kaibab trails. Beginning at the North Rim, the North Kaibab Trail provides a longer, but in many ways more interesting, avenue to the canyon bottom.

The North Kaibab trailhead is located about 3 miles north of the Grand Canyon Lodge on the North Rim. To reach the North Rim, follow US Highway 89 north from Flagstaff to Alternate US Highway 89. Turn west and drive 55 miles to Jacob Lake. Turn south on State Highway 67 and drive 45 miles to the North Rim. It is a 215-mile drive from rim to rim.

Starting out among tall stands of Douglas fir, Engelmann spruce, ponderosa pine, and aspen, the North Kaibab Trail begins descending almost immediately into the upper end of Roaring Springs Canyon. Within the first 0.5 mile a number of switchbacks are encountered as the route drops at a moderate to steep pace. In about another 0.5 mile the route reaches the usually dry bottom of upper Roaring Springs Canyon, where it again must switchback to maintain a suitable grade.

Ribbon Falls along the North Kaibab Trail

After crossing a bridge the trail takes up the southwest wall of the canyon and makes a long traverse high above the canyon floor. Sections of this corridor have been blasted into solid rock. Eventually, the trail drops through a few final switchbacks to reach the mouth of the canyon and a side trail that leads 0.25 mile to Roaring Springs. In the nearly 5 miles between the trailhead and this junction, the trail descends some 3,000 feet.

A popular destination for day hikers, Roaring Springs is quite a sight to behold. From caves at the base of the Redwall Limestone Formation, a massive discharge of water spews noisily out. A picnic area is located near the springs, and a shady mix of cottonwoods and other deciduous trees haunt this riparian environ.

Continuing on from the Roaring Springs turnoff, the North Kaibab Trail turns south to follow the perennial Bright Angel Creek. The trail crosses a bridge about 0.5 mile beyond the junction, then follows the creek downstream, mostly staying in the canyon bottom for the rest of the way. Grades beyond the creek crossing are easy to moderate in difficulty.

Nearly 7 miles from the trailhead (and 2.2 miles from Roaring Springs) is Cottonwood Camp. Featuring picnic tables, toilets, drinking water, shade trees, and a ranger station, Cottonwood Camp is the first designated camping spot along the North Kaibab Trail. The camp can be hot in the summer, but the fishing is reported to be good.

From Cottonwood Camp the route descends easily for 1.8 miles to a short side trail that leads to Ribbon Falls. Enclosed in a red rock grotto, this 100-foot-high waterfall cascades over a travertine formation below to break up into thin laces of water. Beyond Ribbon Falls, the North Kaibab Trail continues for another 5.5 miles to Phantom Ranch. Much of this stretch follows the bottom of an impressive narrows section formed by ever-deepening walls of Vishnu Schist. Bridges allow for easy crossing of Bright Angel Creek in several locations. A lone, non-native palm tree is found on one bend of the creek, and thickets of tamarisk and willows grow in several places. Among the surrounding cliffs and slopes, a scrubby collection of barrel cactus, agaves, and other plants typical of the lower Sonoran life zone stand in stark contrast to the lush forests at the hike's beginning.

Phantom Ranch has cabins for rent, but reservations are hard to come by. The Bright Angel Campground, which is 0.3 mile beyond Phantom Ranch, is the only other overnight option, but it too is usually booked up months in advance. Because camping along the North Kaibab Trail is restricted to the Cottonwood and Bright Angel camps, it is important to plan your trip well in advance.

Potable water is available at the North Rim, Cottonwood Camp, Phantom Ranch, and the Bright Angel Campground. All other sources should be treated first. Watch for mules along the North Kaibab Trail and take care along the many precipitous sections of the route. Because the North Rim is open only from mid-May through October, hikers are likely to encounter very hot temperatures in the canyon bottom. And keep in mind that the climb out is very long and steep—nearly 6,000 feet!

6 WIDFORSS TRAIL

Distance: 10 miles round trip	Management: Grand Canyon NP
Difficulty: easy	Wilderness status: none
Hiking time: 5 hours	Season: May to October
Elevation: 8,100 to 7,800 feet	USGS map: Bright Angel Point

Accessing a highly scenic point on the North Rim of the Grand Canyon, the Widforss Trail is one of the most appropriately named trails in the park. Named in honor of Gunnar Widforss, an artist who painted extensively here in the 1920s, this 5-mile route offers one of the most memorable vistas anywhere. It also features some interesting lessons concerning the natural history of the North Rim area.

Drive about 4 miles north of the Grand Canyon Lodge to a gravel road signed for the trail. Turn left and follow this road for almost a mile through Harvey Meadow to the trailhead and parking area. To reach the Grand Canyon Lodge from Flagstaff, drive north on US Highway 89 to Alternate US Highway 89. Turn west and drive 55 miles to Jacob Lake. From this junction continue south on State Highway 67 for 45 miles to the lodge. The distance from Flagstaff to the North Rim is 211 miles.

With the exception of a short climb at the start and a few shallow drainages later on, the Widforss Trail is very level. This, combined with the fact that the entire route is well maintained, makes for an easy hike. A guide pamphlet that corresponds to numbered sites along the first 2.5 miles of the walk is available at the trailhead.

Within the first 0.5 mile the Widforss Trail reveals much of its natural character as hikers encounter various types of timber. Typical of the higher North Rim, these forests include blue spruce, Engelmann spruce, white fir, Douglas fir, and quaking aspen, plus several nice stands of ponderosa pine growing in the more arid areas. Patches of

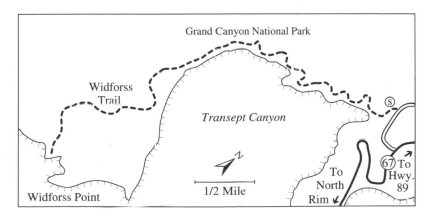

35

The view from Widforss Point

less impressive Gambel oak and maple are not uncommon. A variety of wildlife, including mule deer and elk, make their homes here.

Adding to the trail's allure are the many vistas that open up on the first half of the trail. At several places along this segment the route skirts the edge of Transept Canyon. While this abyss is only an insignificant side drainage of Bright Angel Creek, its size nevertheless hints at the true scale of the Grand Canyon. From some overlooks it is possible to see Bright Angel Point and the Grand Canyon Lodge on the far side of the drainage. On a clear day, you can even see the San Francisco Peaks, 70 miles to the south.

After 2.5 miles the Widforss Trail strays away from the canyon's edge and heads due south through the forest. Dropping ever so slightly, the route passes a couple of picnic tables before breaking out of the trees to reveal a grand panorama. The trail stops short of Widforss Point itself (it is located less than 0.5 mile to the southeast), but the vista at trail's end is nevertheless impressive. From this locale, the view looks into Haunted Canyon directly below and Phantom Creek just beyond. And it also takes in such landmarks as Osiris Temple, Tower of Set, Isis Temple, Cheops Pyramid, Buddha Temple, and Manu Temple.

Before setting out on the Widforss Trail, be sure to pack some water; none is found along the hike. Watch for lightning, especially during the thunderstorms that often build on summer afternoons. Although this hike takes 4 to 5 hours to complete, you may want to consider an overnight visit to enjoy the views during different times of the day. If so, be sure to obtain a backcountry permit.

7   UNCLE JIM TRAIL

Distance: 5 miles round trip
Difficulty: easy
Hiking time: 3 hours
Elevation: 8,200 to 8,400 feet

Management: Grand Canyon NP
Wilderness status: none
Season: May to October
USGS map: Bright Angel Point

The Uncle Jim Trail provides a short introduction to the forests and rim area of the North Rim. A somewhat dubious honor, the route was named for "Uncle Jim" Owens, a game warden who worked in the region in the early part of this century. Following accepted game management practice at the time, Owens reportedly killed more than 500 mountain lions in order to strengthen the deer population. The slaugh-

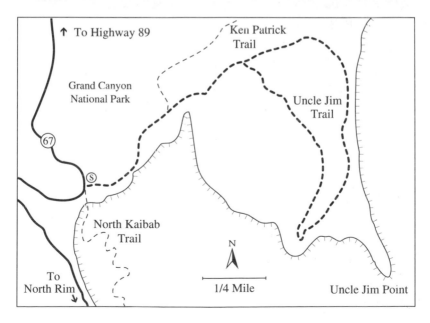

Uncle Jim Point on the North Rim

ter had just the opposite effect, however: the deer multiplied and reached numbers too great for the area to support. The resulting starvation of thousands of deer highlighted the importance of predators in maintaining nature's balance.

The Uncle Jim Trail shares a trailhead with the North Kaibab Trail. To find it, drive about 3 miles north from the Grand Canyon Lodge to the signed right turn. To reach the Grand Canyon Lodge from Flagstaff, drive north on US Highway 89 to Alternate US Highway 89. Turn west and drive 55 miles to Jacob Lake. Turn south onto State Highway 67 and continue for another 45 miles to the lodge. The distance from Flagstaff to the North Rim is 211 miles.

Like the Widforss Trail, this route leads through a variety of forests typical of the North Rim. Ponderosa pines grow in the dryer areas, while a lush mix of white fir, Douglas fir, Engelmann spruce, Colorado blue spruce, and quaking aspen is found in areas that hold more moisture. Many of these trees are quite mature and impressive, to say the least. Mule deer are a common sight along the trail, and signs of elk are everywhere.

From the trailhead, the Uncle Jim Trail follows the canyon rim for a short distance, offering views into Roaring Springs Canyon. In less than 0.5 mile, the trail reaches a junction. The Uncle Jim Trail keeps right, while the Ken Patrick Trail heads left. Shortly after, the route crosses a shallow drainage where the trail makes its only noticeable climb—less than 200 feet—out the other side. It then reaches a second trail junction, with a 1.5-mile loop. Either way is fine: both trails cut across mostly level terrain before reaching the vicinity of Uncle Jim Point. A hitching post at the trail's end and signs of heavy stock use along the route are evidence that Uncle Jim Point is a favorite destination for mule trains on the North Rim.

From land's end, you get a good view of both Roaring Springs Canyon and the sinuous North Kaibab Trail, which drops into its depths. It is also possible to peer into the upper end of the Bright Angel Creek drainage. Underfoot, note the variety of fossils embedded in the exposed Kaibab Limestone. This rock was deposited 250 million years ago at the bottom of a warm inland sea, and the accumulated remains of both plants and animals are great. The plants that haunt the rim area have a countenance that is strikingly different than that of the forests you just walked through. Because of the rim's southern exposure and steeper topography, it is both drier and warmer. This results in a floral community more typical of lower elevations, one where pinyon pine, juniper, Gambel oak, and manzanita are the dominant species.

No water is found along the Uncle Jim Trail, so pack your own. Watch for lightning during stormy periods.

8 LAVA FALLS

Distance: 3 miles round trip
Difficulty: strenuous
Hiking time: 7 hours
Elevation: 4,180 to 1,640 feet

Management: Grand Canyon NP
Wilderness status: none
Season: September to May
USGS map: Vulcans Throne

Considered the Grand Canyon's wildest ride, Lava Falls is situated deep within the canyon's remote western portion. Despite its isolated locale, however, a trail—more of a route, really—allows hikers to watch boaters run this most famous of western river rapids from shore. Although the route is only 1.5 miles long, hiking it is no easy task. This trail drops 2,500 feet, making for one of the roughest hikes in the state.

Because the Lava Falls Trail is located in the Tuweep section of Grand Canyon National Park, getting there is in itself an adventure. From Fredonia on the Arizona Strip, drive 8 miles west on State Road 389 to the turnoff for Toroweap Point (the largest sign at the junction points the way to Mount Trumbull). Turn left (south) and follow this well-maintained gravel road for 55 miles to the park boundary. A small ranger station is located here, should you have any questions.

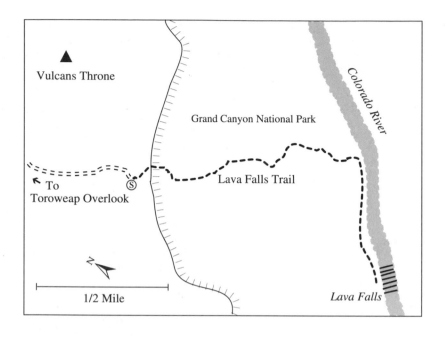

From the boundary, drive 4 more miles to a fork in the road. Turn right and follow the high-clearance 2WD road (almost a 4WD road) for 2.4 miles to its end. This road cuts to the west of the rounded Vulcans Throne, while the Toroweap Overlook is east of the mountain. On rare occasions Toroweap Lake, an abandoned stock pond, has water in it, making the drive to the Lava Falls trailhead impossible.

From the small parking area, the trail travels a short distance through a notch before dropping into a basin below. Within this basin the trail tread for the most part disappears and the route is instead marked by cairns. It is extremely important to watch for these cairns because you may otherwise wind up in an impassable area. This being a terrain of dark volcanic rock, the cairns are sometimes hard to find.

From the basin below the rim, the route drops down a small, rocky gulch beyond which are a few small precipices that hikers must scramble down. Next is a long, steady descent among dark volcanic boulders, barrel cactus, and century plants. A couple of different ways down this 30-degree slope are marked by cairns; both eventually lead to a small shelf area visible below. From here, the route continues to the left of some rock outcrops before dropping into an impassable-looking chute. Within this section you will encounter loose rocks that easily give way, plenty of unsteady scree gravel and sand, and some hand-and toehold scrambles. Extreme caution must be used to negotiate this section. Near the bottom (still a couple of hundred feet above the river), the route climbs out of the chute to avoid a pour-off. Watch for

Hiking the rugged Lava Falls Trail

cairns that mark the way to the right of the ravine. The rapids are located about 0.3 mile downstream, and, with luck, you will happen upon a raft party preparing to run them.

For all its difficulties, this route to the river is something of an anomaly in the Grand Canyon. Typically, the canyon consists of sheer cliffs. This area, however, has witnessed relatively recent volcanic activity. Beginning between 1 million and 2 million years ago, some sixty volcanic cones in the Tuweep area (Vulcans Throne being one) spewed molten lava into the canyon. These lava flows covered the normally perpendicular walls of the canyon, making the route down possible. From a boater's perspective, this geological activity resulted in the formation of the canyon's most challenging rapids. Lava Falls is all that is left of a 500-foot-high dam of lava that once impeded the river.

Because it is so rugged, do not attempt this hike alone. Wear sturdy hiking boots and carry at least a gallon of water per person—remember, the return trip is 2,500 feet nearly straight up. It is best to avoid the hike in the summer, when temperatures can easily top 110 degrees Fahrenheit in the canyon. Watch for rattlesnakes and scorpions, and be extra cautious about knocking rocks onto other hikers. Allow 2 hours for the hike in and 5 to 6 hours for coming out.

9 KANAB CREEK

Distance: 31 miles round trip
Difficulty: moderate
Hiking time: 4 days
Elevation: 3,800 to 3,200 feet
Management: BLM, Kaibab NF

Wilderness status: Kanab
  Creek WA
Season: year-round
USGS maps: Jumpup Canyon,
  Kanab Point, Grama Spring

Running some 60 miles from the town of Fredonia to the Colorado River, the lower corridor of Kanab Creek offers some of the finest canyon hiking anywhere. With its headwaters deep within Utah, this is the largest drainage system on the North Rim of the Grand Canyon. Within its last 30 miles, Kanab Creek has etched out a spectacular gorge among soaring red rock cliffs. This hike begins near Willow Spring in Hack Canyon and descends to the park boundary at the mouth of Jumpup Canyon.

One of two main access points for Kanab Creek, Hack Canyon is remote in comparison to most trailheads mentioned in this book. From Fredonia, drive 8 miles west on State Highway 389 to County Road 109, a well-maintained gravel road signed for Mount Trumbull. This is also the turnoff for Toroweap Point. Turn south and drive 23 miles to a sign for Hack Reservoir. Turn left onto a secondary dirt road and follow it 9.5 miles to the end. At one time improved to serve a uranium mine nearly 6 miles in, this road is sometimes in poor condition due to heavy rains and may require a 4WD vehicle. The 4 miles beyond the mine are characteristically rougher. The hike begins at a fence marking the Kanab Creek Wilderness boundary.

From the trailhead, the route follows the bottom of Hack Canyon to its confluence with Kanab Creek, 5 miles away. If you should happen to begin the hike on a hot afternoon, don't be discouraged by the desolate nature of the surrounding landscape. About 2.5 miles in, sandstone walls appear and eventually close ranks to give the canyon a more comfortable feel.

Dropping very little in 5 miles, Hack Canyon can be explored via the gently meandering but rocky wash bottom. You can also save time by picking out old cattle trails that cut across the meanders. Watch for shell fossils in the limestone rubble in the creek bed. Within the last mile of Hack Canyon, a fence dividing BLM and Forest Service lands is encountered.

When you reach Kanab Creek, turn downstream to follow the main canyon south. Here again, cow trails that cut across the meanders can save some time and wrangling among thick growths of tamarisk. Kanab Creek is intermittent at this point and the creek itself cannot be counted on as a source of water. About 2.5 miles downstream from the mouth of Hack Canyon is the first of several reliable springs along Kanab Creek. This one, located in a shady grotto in the canyon's east wall, is marked by a hanging garden of maidenhair fern and columbine. Here, steady drips will eventually fill water bottles.

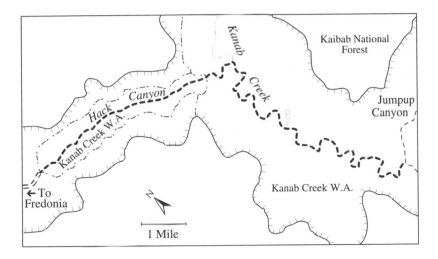

In addition to the canyon's prodigious colonies of tamarisk, some rather ancient cottonwood trees are also scattered along the creek bottom. Signifying the light use that the area receives, very few of these inviting trees are accompanied by the hiker-established campsites that plague the more popular canyons of the Colorado Plateau. As long as access remains difficult, Kanab Creek should stay this way.

Defined by cliffs of Supai sandstone, the hike along Kanab Creek is scenic, even in its early stages. Distant cliffs of Kaibab Limestone and the Toroweap Formation add depth and visual interest to the drainage. Beginning at the mouth of Jumpup Canyon, however, the canyon begins to descend through the massive layer of Redwall Limestone that gives the Grand Canyon much of its vertical latitude. From this point to the Colorado River, the route becomes considerably more rugged.

From Hack Canyon it is 10.5 miles to the mouth of Jumpup Canyon, the turnaround point for this hike. With a shuttle, you could continue hiking another 9 miles up Jumpup Canyon to the end of Forest Service Road 423. Because this road drops off from the Kaibab Plateau, it is not passable during the winter months. Several days of hiking may also be added by continuing downstream from Jumpup Canyon to the Colorado River, a one-way trip of 16 miles. Unlike the upper end of Kanab Creek, this route requires a bit of scrambling over boulders and across ledges, and perhaps even a swim or two. Because the national park boundary is crossed at Jumpup, a permit is required for overnight hiking beyond this point. Located about 5 miles downstream from Jumpup Canyon is Shower Bath Spring, an interesting discharge of water that was mentioned by John Wesley Powell. From the end of the road in Hack Canyon, it is a 63-mile round trip to the Colorado River.

Because Hack Canyon and the upper part of the Kanab Creek section of this hike are normally dry, be prepared to pack in two days' worth of water. Willow Spring lies within 0.25 mile of the trailhead,

Hiking along Kanab Creek

but it has been fouled by cattle. Summertime temperatures can be particularly high in this canyon system and it is not advisable to travel alone as this is one of the remotest sections of the state. Flash floods may pose a threat, especially in the summer months.

10   MOUNT TRUMBULL

Distance: 5.4 miles round trip
Difficulty: moderate
Hiking time: 3 hours
Elevation: 6,500 to 8,029 feet
Management: BLM

Wilderness status: Mount
   Trumbull WA
Season: April to November
USGS map: Mount Trumbull NW

Rising above the remote Tuweep region of the Arizona Strip, Mount Trumbull offers a wonderful walk through pine forests, plus some nice views.

Follow State Highway 389 west for 8 miles from Fredonia, and turn south onto County Road 109 at the BLM's Mount Trumbull sign. This long but good gravel road is also the way to Toroweap Point in Grand Canyon National Park. Follow it south for 47 miles to County Road 5, the turnoff for Mount Trumbull. Continue up this winding but maintained gravel road for 7 miles to a BLM administrative site. The signed trailhead is located just beyond on the right.

The hike begins by following an old road to the east, but it soon turns to a single-track trail. It also starts to climb at a moderate grade across the south face of Trumbull. Here, among mature stands of pinyon pine and sporadic patches of manzanita, much of the hike's 1,500-foot climb is achieved. Views to the south include Mount Logan, which, like Mount Trumbull, is an old basalt flow.

Taking in the view from Mount Trumbull

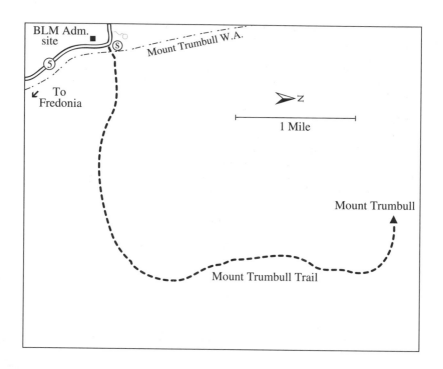

A forest of ponderosa pine dominates the southeastern face of the mountain, and scattered about are many stately old-growth trees, or yellow barks. Inhabitants of this timberland include mule deer and the tassel-eared Kaibab squirrel. Hiking among these tall trees is quite pleasurable.

At approximately 1.5 miles from the trailhead the actual trail disappears, but it is easy to bushwhack to the summit from this point. The forest understory is open save for a few thickets of Gambel oak, and while some may wish to use a compass and topo map, it is just as easy to follow an uphill grade in a northerly direction until you can climb no farther. In order to protect the pristine condition of the mountain's summit, the BLM has purposely forgone trail construction along this final leg of the hike. Hikers who are uncomfortable about traveling cross-country may want to avoid this route.

The summit is marked by geological survey markers, a pile of rocks, and the remains of an old weather station. A trail register dating back several years passes along the interesting experiences of previous hikers, and views to the north, south, and east are spectacular. Included in the panorama is the Toroweap section of the Grand Canyon and the wooded Kaibab Plateau.

Be sure to fill your canteen at the spring near the parking area; no water exists along the trail.

11   HAVASU CANYON

Distance: 20 miles round trip
Difficulty: moderate
Hiking time: 2 days
Elevation: 5,200 to 3,000 feet
Management: Havasupai Indian Tribe

Wilderness status: none
Season: year-round
USGS maps: Havasu Falls,
   Supai

Havasu is one of those places where a spectacular natural setting combines with the fascination of Native peoples to create a uniquely memorable backcountry excursion. Living for the past several centuries within this beautiful side canyon of the Grand Canyon, the Havasupai Indians are comfortably isolated from the maddening rush of the outside world. Adding to the Garden of Eden ambience of their home are the clear blue-green waters of Havasu Creek and the incredible waterfalls that are formed as the creek tumbles toward the Colorado River.

From Flagstaff, drive 74 miles west on Interstate 40 to the small town of Seligman. Turn onto State Highway 66 and follow it northwest for 28 miles to Tribal Road 18. Turn right and follow this paved road for 68 miles to Hualapai Hilltop at the road's end. The last services along this drive are in Seligman. Before leaving for this hike, you will need to reserve a permit with the Havasupai Tribe. The cost of the permit is $12 per person as of 1993. Because camping spaces are limited, it is advisable to make reservations well in advance. There is an additional fee for camping. Reservations may be made by calling (602) 448-2121 or writing the Havasupai Tourist Enterprise, Supai, AZ 86435.

With plenty of parking and stable facilities for the tribal horse packers, Hualapai Hilltop is the route's trailhead. For the first mile the trail descends through a series of moderately steep switchbacks. It then continues to drop at a moderate grade for another 0.5 mile before reaching the canyon bottom. For the rest of the way the trail is either

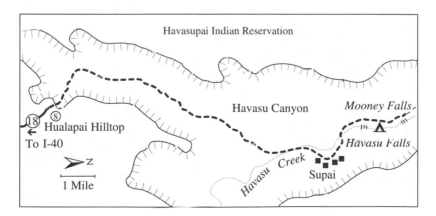

level or it descends along easy grade changes. Because the route is utilized by pack animals, it is well maintained and easy to follow.

For the first 6.5 miles from Hualapai Hilltop, the route follows a dry canyon. But 1.5 miles before reaching the village of Supai, it joins Havasu Canyon, in which flow the brilliant blue-green waters of Havasu Creek. Gaining its color from limestone deposits above, this permanent creek supports an inviting riparian ecosystem of cottonwoods, willows, and other water-loving trees, which provide welcome shade, especially on hot summer days.

Upon reaching Supai, 8 miles from the trailhead, the trail passes scattered homes and fields before arriving at the village center. You must stop at the Tourist Office to pick up your permit and pay your entry fee. A short distance beyond the Tourist Office is a restaurant that serves breakfast, lunch, and dinner. A store sells various food supplies, and a U.S. Post Office accepts outgoing mail. Because most supplies are brought to the town via horse or mule trains, everything is more expensive, but not unreasonably so.

After registering at the Tourist Office and stocking up on any extra supplies, continue through the village (signs point the way) and hike another 2 miles to Havasu Falls and the campground. The trail skirts the 100-foot-high Havasu Falls to the left, offering a good view of the spectacle. Navajo and Fiftyfoot falls, not visible from the trail, are passed on the way. Shortly beyond Havasu Falls you reach the campground, which is scattered along the next 0.5 mile of the creek. A campground host is usually on hand to check for your permit. Because ground fires are prohibited, you will need to bring a camp stove.

A short distance beyond the last campsite is the largest of the falls,

Havasu Falls

200-foot-high Mooney Falls. Good views can be had from the rim of the drop-off, but to really experience this natural wonder, make the climb down to the base. This is achieved by passing through two crude tunnels and then descending a steep (and frightening) series of ladders and steps built by miners around the turn of the century. This descent is an adventure in itself.

Beyond Mooney Falls, you can continue another 2 miles to smaller Beaver Falls and eventually to the Colorado River, 4 miles beyond. Because of recent flooding, however, the going is very slow beyond Mooney. Although flash floods are nothing new to Havasu Creek, an exceptionally violent one in February 1993 not only altered the creek bed all along the canyon, it also wiped out several natural pools at the base of Havasu Falls.

Be sure to plan your visit to Havasu Canyon well ahead by making reservations early. Temperatures in the canyon can be well above the century mark during summer afternoons. Be sure to bring plenty of water for the hike in (water is available at the village and campground), and pack along some sandals for wading and swimming in the creek.

12 PARIA RIVER CANYON

Distance: 37 miles one way
Difficulty: moderate
Hiking time: 4 days
Elevation: 4,300 to 3,200 feet
Management: BLM, Glen Canyon NRA

Wilderness status: Paria Canyon–Vermilion Cliffs WA
Season: April to November
USGS maps: Bridger Point, Wrather Arch, Water Pockets, Ferry Swale, Lees Ferry

Certainly one of the most impressive abysses of the Colorado Plateau, the Paria River Canyon makes for an exceptional 4- or 5-day hike. With sandstone walls soaring hundreds of feet above the wash bottom, this drainage offers an unforgettable introduction to the geology of northern Arizona's red rock country. So spectacular is this canyon that it has been highlighted in many national publications over the years. Unfortunately, this publicity has led to a hefty increase in visitation numbers—the end result of which has been the institution of a registration system and additional user regulations.

Before beginning the hike, be sure to register with the BLM at their Kanab Area Office in Kanab, Utah (801 644-2672) or in person at the Paria Ranger Station, which is located just off US Highway 89, 30 miles northwest of Page. A sign here posts updated weather information. In the event that flash flooding may occur, the canyon will be closed. This ranger station is normally staffed from 8:00 A.M. to 11:00 A.M., Thursday through Monday. It is possible to register without ranger assistance at the trailhead.

Although the canyon may be followed in either direction, it makes the most sense to begin upstream and travel down. Three trailheads

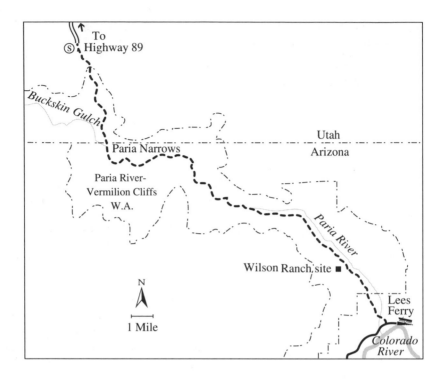

(all within Utah) allow access at the upper end of the canyon system—one on the main canyon and two on Buckskin Gulch. This description follows the Paria River Canyon route.

From the Paria Ranger Station, drive 2 miles south on a good gravel road to the White House trailhead. Begin the route by following the wash bottom downstream toward the south. Expect to make hundreds of stream crossings through ankle-deep water throughout the year. Upon passing beneath a power line 2.3 miles from the trailhead, the canyon enters the Paria Canyon–Vermilion Cliffs Wilderness Area.

Nearly 4 miles from the trailhead the river enters the Narrows. Prior to this point, the geologic landscape includes the colorful siltstones of the Carmel Formation. Upon entering the Narrows, however, the scene is dominated by soaring walls of Navajo Sandstone. In places these walls rise hundreds of feet straight up and are only a couple of dozen feet apart.

Because of this restricted canyon bottom, the Narrows is no place to be during a flash flood. Typically, a heavy rain upstream can send a wall of water up to 20 feet high gushing through the canyon, and a lack of high places in the Narrows precludes escape from this danger. For that reason, do not plan on camping within the Narrows. Suitable campsites are found both at the start of the Narrows and 4 miles farther downstream—about 8 miles from the trailhead. To avoid the threat of flooding, keep in mind that the flash flood season includes the

Hiking in Paria River Canyon

months of July, August, and early September (flash floods have also been known to occur at other times of the year) and that these summer cloudbursts often occur in the afternoon.

Partway through the Narrows, 7.1 miles from the trailhead, the Paria River reaches Buckskin Gulch. Even narrower than the main canyon, the walls of this abyss are only a few feet apart in places, obstructing the sky and sunshine completely. Rock- and logjams, along with stagnant pools of water, must be negotiated along the way, but this stunning slot canyon is well worth the adventure. From the Paria River it is 13.5 miles up Buckskin Gulch to the Wire Pass trailhead and 16.3 miles to the Buckskin trailhead.

A short distance beyond the mouth of Buckskin Gulch, the Paria River enters Arizona. The route still follows the canyon bottom at this point. About 12 miles from the trailhead (5.2 miles below Buckskin Gulch) is the first reliable spring. Although it flows throughout the year, stream water in this area should not be consumed, even after treating, because it may be tainted with pesticides. Its discoloration is due to bentonite. A second spring is located 22 miles from the trailhead, while a third is found 25.4 miles in. Although these are springs, you should treat the water anyway.

Throughout the hike you may come across evidence of prehistoric inhabitants of this part of the Colorado Plateau. Petroglyphs, and other artifacts, indicate the area's onetime occupation by the Anasazi Indians. Archaeologists believe that they utilized the Paria River Canyon as a travel route and for hunting and gathering. Use of the canyon during historic times is also evident. At 17.6 miles, at the mouth of Judd Hollow, are the remains of a pumping station installed by ranchers in the 1940s. The ambitious plan was to irrigate grazing lands hundreds of feet above. Nearly 33 miles from the trailhead is the old Wilson ranch site. And at trail's end, the antiquated John D. Lee homestead welcomes hikers back to civilization. Sent to this spot on the Colorado River to establish a ferry crossing in 1871, Lee and three others drove Lee's cattle downstream from the Mormon town of Pahreah, making them the first white men to traverse the entire length of the canyon.

After following the canyon bottom for 28 miles, the route follows a trail that leaves the wash to skirt around a boulder slide. Accessing a low benchland to the right of the river, this trail provides the most sensible route for the remainder of the hike. One other consideration when traversing the lower portion of the canyon is the fact that because the terrain opens up considerably, heat exposure can be a problem. Be sure to carry plenty of water through this last stretch.

Campfires are prohibited in the Paria River Canyon, and group size is restricted to ten or fewer. Drinking water is at a premium, as is shade in many parts of the canyon. Flash floods occur with considerable frequency, especially during the summer months. Peak visitation months include April, May, June, September, and October, and crowds are especially heavy during university spring breaks and on holiday weekends. The BLM can provide information on commercial shuttle services, as well as a detailed map and guide to the canyon for a nominal fee. This one-way hike takes 4 days or longer to complete and requires a shuttle back to the upper trailhead.

13 SPENCER TRAIL

Distance: 3 miles round trip
Difficulty: strenuous
Hiking time: 3 hours
Elevation: 3,180 to 4,740 feet

Management: Glen Canyon NRA
Wilderness status: none
Season: year-round
USGS map: Lees Ferry

Although a short hike distance-wise, the historic Spencer Trail climbs 1,500 feet in only 1.5 miles. This effort is not without its rewards, however: the top offers spectacular views of the Colorado River and the surrounding red rock desert.

The trailhead is located at Lees Ferry—the put-in for rafters headed down the Grand Canyon. To reach Lees Ferry, turn north from Alternate US Highway 89 at Marble Canyon and drive 5.9 miles to the end of the paved road at the boat ramp. Park here and walk upstream past a scattered collection of old stone structures.

The trail actually begins at the far end of the Lees Ferry Historic District. Sent to this spot in 1871 by the Mormon Church, John D. Lee established a ferry to transport travelers across the Colorado River. This is also the place where the Spanish explorer Silvestre Vélez de Escalante and his men crossed, in 1776. Because the Grand Canyon runs downstream from this point and Glen Canyon stretches upstream, this is the only suitable crossing for many, many miles. Among the antiquities still found today is the Lees Ferry Fort, built in the 1870s, a post office constructed in 1913, and an old boiler dating back to the early part of this century. The boiler recalls Charles Spencer's time spent at Lees Ferry. Convinced that there was gold in the local Chinle Shale, Spencer imported a lot of machinery to extract the precious metal. To supply the fuel needed to keep his equipment running, he built the Spencer Trail in 1910 so that mules could pack coal in from Warm Creek 28 miles to the north.

Just beyond the boiler, the Spencer Trail takes off up the rocky slope at trail marker 6. Not regularly maintained, the route is somewhat faint at this point, so be sure to follow it carefully. Very shortly, the trail begins a steep, 1,500-foot climb to the top of the cliffs directly in front. Conditions along the way include lots of loose rocks, a heavily

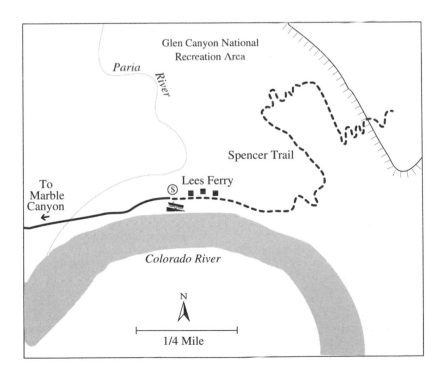

eroded tread, and exposure to severe drop-offs. The trail also climbs through several switchbacks. The up side to these difficult hiking conditions is twofold, however. First is the fact that the route receives little use; second is the nonstop scenery afforded along the way. Almost immediately, the view of the river flowing through the Lees Ferry area opens up into a sweeping panorama. The Echo Cliffs rise along the river's left bank, and the Vermilion Cliffs march southward to the right.

Also of interest along the Spencer Trail is the local geology. The Spencer Trail begins by climbing up the dark brown rock of the Moenkopi Formation. This is followed by the lighter brown Shinarump Formation and then the bluish shale of the Chinle Formation. Above it are the more vertical cliffs of the Moenave and Kayenta formations, and finally the impressive rimrock of Navajo Sandstone.

At trail's end you will find yourself on top of a narrow plateau that separates two meanders in the Colorado River. In addition to the previously mentioned landforms that lie south of Lees Ferry, this high point also affords views of Lake Powell, Navajo Mountain, and the Navajo Power Plant near Page to the north. In addition, you will get a feel for just how sinuous the Colorado River can be.

Upon the return hike you may notice the hull of a boat lurking in the shallow water near the bank directly below. This is the remains of the *Charles H. Spencer,* a 92-foot-long steamboat. Upon completing his trail, Spencer learned that mules could not haul enough coal to run his mining operation. Determined as ever, he brought in a boat, piece by piece, from San Francisco on which to float the coal down the river. After making five trips, however, he realized that the boat required all of the coal it could carry just to complete the trip. In the end, tests concluded that there was not even enough gold in these sedimentary rocks to turn a profit anyway.

Because the trail is steep and rugged, watch your footing. No water exists along the route, so be sure to bring plenty. And, because temperatures can easily top 100 degrees Fahrenheit from late spring to early fall, you may want to save this hike for cooler seasons.

14   SOAP CREEK

Distance: 9 miles round trip
Difficulty: strenuous
Hiking time: 6 hours
Elevation: 4,200 to 3,000 feet
Management: BLM, Grand Canyon NP

Wilderness status: none
Season: year-round
USGS maps: Emmett Wash,
  Bitter Springs

Providing an appropriate prelude for boaters heading down the Grand Canyon, Marble Canyon is itself a spectacular abyss worthy of investigation. For those on foot, one of the most interesting approaches is to hike down Soap Creek, which drains into the Colorado River a few miles downstream from the Marble Canyon Bridge.

This hike begins at a developed trailhead on BLM land. Drive about 8 miles southwest of Marble Canyon on Alternate US Highway 89 to the Cliff Dwellers Lodge. Drive another 1.1 miles past the lodge to a good dirt road that takes off to the left. A small sign is located near a gate (be sure to close it behind you) in the highway fence. At an old corral and cow camp the road veers left to reach the trailhead, which is 0.4 mile from the highway.

Generally speaking, the hiking route follows the canyon bottom downstream, but there are some variables along the way. From the parking area, a faded trail heads east into a wash. Follow this small side drainage for a way to see how this canyon develops as it drops in elevation. The canyon walls become more pronounced, and pour-offs that are at first insignificant eventually become more difficult to pass. At about 0.7 mile from the trailhead the route reaches the South Fork of Soap Creek. Keep left here and continue downstream.

After reaching the South Fork of Soap Creek, the hike becomes more interesting. At one point the canyon is blocked by a massive rockslide, part of which came down quite recently. To get through, simply pick whichever way looks best—there is no one route. Within 0.5 mile of this boulder choke a more ominous obstacle looms as an enormous pour-off drops 100 feet or so to the canyon bottom. Marked by cairns, a precarious trail climbs up and around to the right of the pour-off. Caution should be taken in this stretch because dangerous heights are encountered. The bypass ends by dropping down a stable boulder fall. Upon reaching the canyon bottom, the route continues through house-size rocks that require some basic bouldering skills to get through. Beyond this difficulty the hike becomes relatively tame, with only minor obstacles.

About 2 miles from the trailhead, the South Fork reaches a major canyon junction at which the route continues downstream to the right. A left turn accesses the North Fork of Soap Creek, which is impassable without ropes. Beyond here, Soap Creek Canyon continues due east for another 2.5 miles to the Colorado River, the turnaround for this hike. A popular camp spot for boaters, the mouth of Soap Creek is also the site of Soap Creek Rapids. Although a mere ripple compared to the big drops of the Grand Canyon, it is still exciting to watch rafters and kayakers run through. This is also a good place to take note of the local geology. The vertical walls of Marble Canyon, like those of Soap Creek

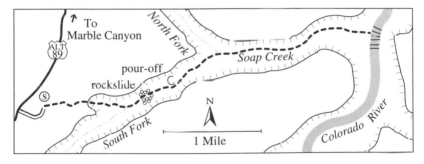

Soap Creek

Canyon, consist mostly of Coconino Sandstone, but there are exposed faces of Hermit Shale as well.

Because most of this hike lies within Grand Canyon National Park, you will need to obtain a backcountry permit for any overnight trips. Where water is concerned, it is either feast or famine in Soap Creek Canyon. Normally the canyon is dry, so be sure to pack a few quarts for drinking. On occasion, however, this drainage witnesses some horrendous flash floods. When planning a visit this should be taken into account. Typically, summer thunderstorms pose the biggest threat, but early fall and spring rain showers may also produce dangerous levels of runoff. Because summers can be unbearably hot, the best seasons for hiking down Soap Creek are spring and fall.

15　ONYX BRIDGE

Distance: 4 miles round trip
Difficulty: easy
Hiking time: 3 hours
Elevation: 5,800 to 5,500 feet
Management: Petrified Forest NP

**Wilderness status: Petrified
　Forest WA**
Season: year-round
USGS map: Kachina Point

Situated in the starkly beautiful Painted Desert region of Petrified Forest National Park, the Onyx Bridge is one of many petrified logs strewn across this desolate reach of Arizona. It earned its name because it spans a small wash. Certainly as interesting are the countless other pieces of fossilized wood found along the hike. Most of this hike falls within an established wilderness area, and the hike mostly cuts across open terrain rather than following an actual trail.

From the park's north entrance off Interstate 40, drive 2.4 miles to the Southwest-style Painted Desert Inn at Kachina Point. Built in 1924, this structure was rebuilt by the Civilian Conservation Corps (CCC) in the 1930s. It is now a National Historic Landmark. The hike begins behind the inn. Before you start, be sure to check with the ranger inside for complete directions. He or she can point out the location of the bridge in the distance and offer directions.

Dropping down the mesa from Kachina Point, a well-established trail accesses the flats below but fades after 0.5 mile, leaving you to follow small streambeds for the next 0.5 mile north to Lithodendron Wash. Because no trail exists beyond the 0.5-mile mark, it is important to keep a close eye on the landscape at all times. Upon crossing the wash bottom, the unmarked route cuts across a broad meander before reconnecting with the usually dry waterway. Follow the wash for another 0.25 mile to where it begins bending to the right, or east. A small side canyon or arroyo cut into a hillside on the left comes into view near there. Follow this arroyo upstream a short distance to where it splits. Keep to the right and follow the main channel past a scattered pile of petrified logs. Less than 100 yards beyond, a 15-foot-high pour-off is reached. Climb the steep bank to the left to find the bridge just above.

Like the countless other mineralized logs in the park, Onyx Bridge was washed to this former flood plain during the Triassic Period—about 225 million years ago. After being covered by mud, volcanic ash, and silt, the original wood fiber was slowly petrified by silicon-enriched groundwater. It is interesting to keep in mind that these trees, now jettisoned in a parched and desolate desert, are a product of an era when dinosaurs roamed lush forests. Just as fascinating, though, is the fact that the entire region was subsequently inundated by a freshwater sea, and that enough time has since passed to allow erosion to expose this geologic story.

Although finding the bridge may prove difficult, you are not likely to get lost, because the Painted Desert Inn at Kachina Point is plainly visible at all times. Because water is not available along the hike it is

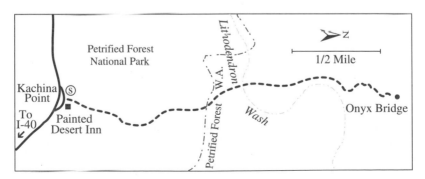

important to bring plenty, especially in the summer, when temperatures can top 100 degrees Fahrenheit. A hat and plenty of sunscreen are also advisable. Watch for lightning during afternoon showers in the summer months and flash floods after heavy rain showers. Also keep an eye out for the rattlesnakes that inhabit the area.

You don't need a permit for day hiking, but one is required for overnight stays. The park typically closes around sunset, though budget constraints may shorten the hours. If you want to witness the Painted Desert at dusk, plan on backpacking in. Of course, removing pieces of petrified wood or any other natural material is strictly prohibited. Prehistoric artifacts are protected by law, as well.

Onyx Bridge is actually a petrified tree trunk

16 KEET SEEL

Distance: 16 miles round trip
Difficulty: moderate
Hiking time: 2 days
Elevation: 7,000 to 6,300 feet
Management: Navajo NM

Wilderness status: none
Season: May to September
USGS maps: Betatakin Ruin,
   Keet Seel Ruin, Marsh Pass

Often billed as the largest cliff dwelling in the state, Keet Seel offers one of Arizona's best-preserved glimpses into the prehistoric past. Tucked inside a beautiful alcove in a remote canyon of the Navajo Indian Nation, the ruins provide the perfect reward for a long day's hike. The stunning red rock scenery found throughout the journey is equally rewarding.

Although it lies within the Navajo Indian Nation, Keet Seel is part of Navajo National Monument and is administered by the National Park Service. Before you begin the hike, you must first obtain a permit. Because the Park Service limits the number of visitors to Keet Seel to twenty people per day, it is a good idea to get the permit well in advance. The cliff dwelling is only open between Memorial Day and Labor Day weekends.

Drive 20 miles southwest from Kayenta on US Highway 160. Turn left on State Highway 564 at the sign for Navajo National Monument. Follow this road for 10 miles to the end of the pavement and the monument's headquarters.

Upon picking up your permit, be sure to obtain complete directions to Keet Seel from the park staff. The hike begins by following the same route that accesses the Betatakin Cliff Dwelling. Because the 5-mile round-trip hike to Betatakin is ranger-guided, it can be very informative. After paralleling an old dirt road for 1.5 miles, the route reaches Tsegi Point. From Tsegi Point the trail drops 700 feet through a series of switchbacks. The route to Betatakin heads to the right up a side

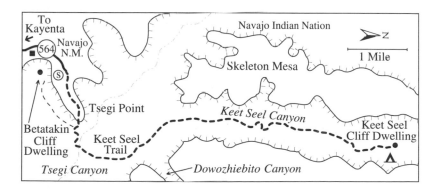

Detail of Keet Seel, the largest cliff dwelling in Arizona

canyon, while the Keet Seel Trail breaks off to the left toward Keet Seel Canyon. From this point, the hike is almost entirely along sandy wash bottoms, so the walking is easy, save for occasional soft ground. Numbered trail markers every 0.5 mile correspond to a trail guide published by the Southwest Parks & Monuments Association.

After entering Keet Seel Canyon, the route comes to a junction of two canyons. To the right is Dowozhiebito and to the left Keet Seel. Just upstream in Keet Seel Canyon is a small waterfall formed by a resistant layer of Wingate Sandstone. Formed some 200 million years ago, the Wingate Formation resulted from giant sand dunes. The canyon walls above this layer consist of the Kayenta and Navajo sandstones. Like the Wingate, the Navajo Formation once consisted of sand dunes. Shortly ahead, Battleship Rock rises to the right; beyond that a pinnacle known as Kachina Mother marks the halfway point of the hike. Between here and the ruins, three additional falls are encountered. All three are easily negotiated.

In different segments of the hike, you may notice old hogans or wooden corrals in the distance. A few Navajo families occupy these isolated homes at different times of the year. Unrelated to the prehistoric Anasazi Indians, the Navajo are thought to be Athabascan in origin; they migrated to the Colorado Plateau soon after the Anasazi left, perhaps during the fifteenth century. Traditionally nomadic, the Navajos acquired sheep from the Spanish hundreds of years ago and made them an integral part of their lives. Even today, many Navajos make a living raising sheep for wool in remote areas such as the Tsegi canyon system. Because these camps are home to Navajo people, it is imperative to observe them only from a distance.

Prior to the arrival of the Navajos, this region was occupied by the Anasazi. Keet Seel, as one of the best-preserved ruins in the Southwest, offers an exquisite view of this past. With 160 rooms, this well-protected cliff dwelling was built between A.D. 1250 and 1286. Some walls are of masonry construction, while others are wattle and daub, or vertical sticks with mud packed around them. Due to the fragile nature of Keet Seel, visitors to the ruin must be accompanied by a ranger. Stationed in quarters nearby, rangers conduct regular tours, but each group is limited to five people. A primitive campground is located nearby for anyone who wants to stay overnight at Keet Seel. A backcountry permit is required, however. Water is not available (other than the nearby stream water, which is not potable) and wood cutting is prohibited, so bring your own water and a stove. Because this is Navajo tribal land, exploring beyond the designated route to Keet Seel is strictly prohibited.

Temperatures in the canyon bottoms can approach 100 degrees Fahrenheit on summer afternoons, so carry plenty of water. Watch for flash floods during the rainy months of July and August. In addition, the Park Service warns of falling rocks near cliff bottoms. Disturbing or removing any artifacts is strictly prohibited. The best rule is look but don't touch. Although it is possible to complete this hike in a long day, an overnight stay would make the trip more pleasurable.

17 WHITE HOUSE RUIN

Distance: 2.5 miles round trip
Difficulty: moderate
Hiking time: 2 hours
Elevation: 6,000 to 5,500 feet
Management: Canyon de Chelly NM

Wilderness status: none
Season: year-round
USGS map: Del Muerto

Like Navajo National Monument, Canyon de Chelly National Monument includes some well-preserved Anasazi cliff dwellings found within the Navajo Indian Nation. Because of the fragile nature of the ruins, and to protect the privacy of the Navajo families who live here, hiking in Canyon de Chelly is permitted only when accompanied by a ranger or authorized Navajo guide. An exception to this rule is the short and pleasant hike to White House Ruin.

From US Highway 191, drive 2.7 miles east on State Highway 64 through the town of Chinle to reach the headquarters of Canyon de Chelly National Monument. From the White House Overlook, 6.4 miles from the monument's headquarters on the South Rim Drive, the route follows the canyon rim to the right for a short distance before passing through a tunnel. From here the trail switchbacks about 600 vertical feet down to the canyon bottom, where it enters a second tunnel. A

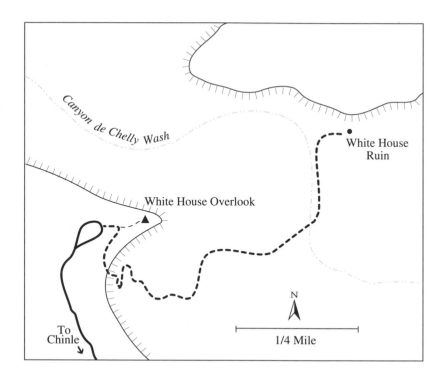

picturesque Navajo farm nearby is strictly off-limits to hikers. The ruins are located across the canyon, on the canyon floor and in an alcove just above. Some wading may be required. Don't be surprised if you meet up with large 4WD vehicles packed with tourists; this is how many visitors see the canyon—on guided tours that motor along the stream bottom.

A fence surrounds the actual ruins to protect them from the impact of visitors. Named for a section of white-plastered wall, White House Ruin was begun in A.D. 1040 and occupied until the late thirteenth century. Much like the Navajos today, the Anasazi grew corn and other crops on the canyon bottoms. For reasons not fully understood by archaeologists, the Anasazi abandoned this and other reaches of their homeland for areas to the south and east. Hypotheses include a prolonged drought, harassment by warring neighbors, and environmental degradation that resulted from overpopulation.

As for the species of plants encountered along the way, pinyon pine and juniper, along with prickly pear and cholla cactus, are common as the trail drops into the canyon. On the canyon bottom, watch for large cottonwoods, willows, Russian olives, and tamarisk. Like the Russian olive, tamarisk is not native to the Southwest. It was introduced as an erosion control agent by the U.S. Department of Agriculture in the

White House Ruin in Canyon de Chelly

early part of this century. Unfortunately, it has spread so rapidly that it now chokes canyon bottoms throughout the Southwest.

Bring plenty of drinking water; the stream is not safe for consumption. Summer ushers in bright sun and high temperatures in the canyon, so plan accordingly. And take care along the precipitous canyon edge.

18 MOUNT ELDEN LOOKOUT

Distance: 6 miles round trip
Difficulty: strenuous
Hiking time: 5 hours
Elevation: 6,900 to 9,295 feet

Management: Coconino NF
Wilderness status: none
Season: May to October
USGS map: Flagstaff East

Climbing some 2,400 feet above the east end of Flagstaff, the Elden Lookout Trail rewards hikers in more ways than one. Not only does the summit afford a great bird's-eye view of the city and the surrounding Coconino Plateau, it also provides insight into how nature mends itself after a large forest fire.

The Mount Elden trailhead is located just north of the Coconino National Forest office on US Highway 89—not far from the Flagstaff Mall. Ample parking is provided for this locally popular trail.

The first 0.5 mile of the trail follows an easy grade through stands of pinyon pine, juniper, and ponderosa pine. Signs in this lower section point out the 1.8-mile Fatman's Loop and the 2.8-mile Pipeline Trail, which circles south along the base of Mount Elden. Watch for mountain bicyclists on these lower trails.

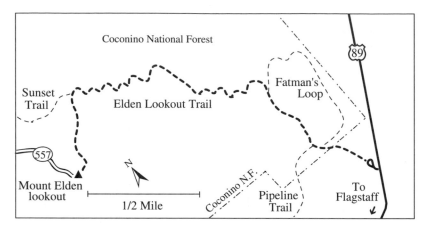

Upon reaching the toe of the mountain, the trail begins climbing at a moderate to steep pace. Several switchbacks are included in this section, and areas of loose rock can be expected. As the trail climbs the east face of Mount Elden, it encounters some features of the local geology. Volcanic in origin, Mount Elden is characterized in places by interesting rock formations that resulted from the cooling and shrinking of lava flows. Growing in this rocky terrain are alligator juniper, mountain mahogany, Gambel oak, cliff rose, and ponderosa pine, with Douglas fir higher up.

From the ridge top, 2.8 miles from the trailhead, an entirely different perspective on the area's natural history opens up. Devastated by the expansive Radio Fire in 1977, most of the timberland in the upper reaches of the mountain now stands as a skeleton forest of blackened tree trunks. But growing back with vigor are young thickets of aspen. Eventually, these aspens will mature into a forest of tall trees, which

Hiking through a burn area on the trail to Mount Elden

will then provide shade for evergreen saplings. These will in turn crowd out the aspens and return the area to its original mixed conifer forest. From a signed trail junction on the ridge, a left turn leads 0.2 mile to the lookout and a right turn starts you down the 4-mile-long Sunset Trail, which leads to Schultz Pass.

Although it is surrounded by radio towers, the lookout is still high enough to afford a spectacular 360-degree view. To the north are the San Francisco Peaks and spreading out just below is the city of Flagstaff. Oak Creek Canyon and Mingus Mountain are visible to the southwest. The heavily forested Mogollon Rim country spreads south to a low horizon and dark cinder hills dot the landscape to the east.

Bring water; none is found along the way. Leave early in the morning during the summer months to avoid lightning.

19 HUMPHREYS PEAK

Distance: 9 miles round trip
Difficulty: strenuous
Hiking time: 6 hours
Elevation: 8,800 to 12,633 feet
Management: Coconino NF

Wilderness status: Kachina
  Peaks WA
Season: June to September
USGS map: Humphreys Peak

As the highest summit in the state, Humphreys Peak (12,633 feet) is more reminiscent of Colorado than Arizona. Reaching above timberline, it features the only true alpine environment in Arizona. Needless to say, the views from the top are awesome. Because it stands virtually

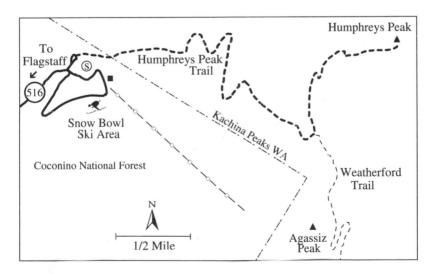

Stopping for a rest while en route to Humphreys Peak

alone (nearby Agassiz and Fremont peaks excepted), Humphreys' summit offers hikers a real "top of the world" feeling.

The Humphreys Peak Trail begins in the lower parking lot of Snow Bowl, Flagstaff's local ski area. Drive north on US Highway 180 for 7 miles to Forest Road 516. Turn north and follow this paved route for 7.4 miles to the first parking lot on the left. The trailhead is located at the far end.

The route begins by traversing a large meadow that is filled with wildflowers in the summer. Ski lifts hang empty overhead, and Agassiz Peak towers above to the east. Shortly, the route crosses into the Kachina Peaks Wilderness Area and enters a thick forest cover that typifies much of the hike to the top. Species of trees here include Engelmann spruce, cork-bark fir, and an occasional aspen. Well maintained and easy to follow, the trail climbs along a moderate grade to a saddle that connects Humphreys and Agassiz peaks. Here, the tall timber is replaced by a stunted forest of bristlecone pine.

Situated at 11,800 feet, the saddle is a fine place to take in views that were for the most part blocked out by the forest cover below. Timberline is not far beyond this point. Because of the fragility of the alpine environment, camping is not permitted in the vicinity. More specifically, because a very rare plant known as *Senecio franciscanus* grows here and nowhere else in the world, hikers are restricted to the established trail. From the saddle, the trail roughly parallels a rocky ridge that runs north for another mile to the summit of Humphreys Peak. Climbing steeply in some sections and often quite rocky, this segment of the hike is strenuous.

From the summit, incredible views stretch out in all directions. The

Grand Canyon, Painted Desert, Oak Creek Canyon, Mogollon Rim, Mingus Mountain, Bill Williams Mountain, and Kendrick Mountain are but a few of the landmarks that are visible. Equally memorable is the surrounding mountain terrain. Agassiz (12,356 feet) and Fremont (11,969 feet) peaks rise along the ridgeline running south and southeast, while the Inner Basin drops immediately away to the south and east. Collectively, these peaks were once part of a large volcano and the Inner Basin was its crater.

Because no water is available along the Humphreys Peak Trail, be sure to bring plenty. Be prepared for rapidly deteriorating weather conditions even in the summer months and watch for lightning. Thunderstorms of dangerous intensity often develop with very short notice.

20   KACHINA TRAIL

Distance: 7.5 miles one way
Difficulty: easy
Hiking time: 4 hours
Elevation: 9,200 to 8,000 feet
Management: Coconino NF

Wilderness status: Kachina
   Peaks WA
Season: June to October
USGS: Humphreys Peak

A relatively new hiking route, the Kachina Trail forgoes the high alpine terrain of the San Francisco Peaks in favor of old-growth forests that inhabit the range's lower elevations. A gentle walk that traverses the southern slope of the peaks, the Kachina Trail is ideal for hikers of all abilities.

The Kachina Trail runs from the Snow Bowl Ski Area to Schultz Pass. To take advantage of its gradual drop in elevation, this description begins at Snow Bowl—the route's upper end. From Flagstaff, drive north on US Highway 180 for 7 miles to Forest Road 516, the road into Snow Bowl. Follow this paved route north for 7.4 miles to the first parking lot on the right. The Kachina Trail begins at a signed trailhead at the lot's far end.

For the first 2 miles the Kachina Trail passes among mature aspen groves that are interspersed with small openings thick with ferns and

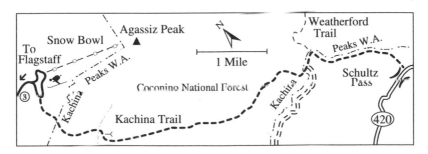

Ferns grow thick along the Kachina Trail.

other lush undergrowth. Stands of old-growth Douglas fir—some with diameters of 5 feet or more—add to the forest's allure, as does the possibility of spotting mule deer or elk. Only two annoyances detract from the beauty and tranquillity of this end of the trail: it parallels the road (a source of traffic noise) for the first 0.5 mile and it crosses under a power line about 1 mile in. Because the Kachina Trail enters the Kachina Peaks Wilderness Area just beyond the power line, however, hikers are assured of eventually finding peace and solitude.

After 1.5 miles the Kachina Trail drops into a small drainage where it then skirts past small cliffs and scattered house-size boulders. A trailside cave offers protection in the event of rain. Beyond this drainage the trail slowly winds its way around to the south-facing slopes of Agassiz and Fremont peaks. As it does it is easy to see how important slope aspect is in determining forest composition. While aspens still grow in great numbers along these drier slopes, the firs have mostly been replaced by ponderosa pines. Additionally, meadow areas that were previously waist-high with ferns now include lupine, Indian paintbrush, and a number of grasses. Adding variety to the hike is the fact that these aspen-ringed meadows are now broad enough to allow beautiful views of the peaks above.

Because the Kachina Trail is new, its southeastern end has yet to be well defined. The route officially ends 6.3 miles from Snow Bowl trailhead on a closed primitive road well short of Schultz Pass. The trail's terminus is marked by a sign, but nothing else. To reach Schultz Pass from this point, turn left on the road and follow it about 0.25 mile uphill to where it connects with the Weatherford Trail. This unmarked intersection is just downhill from where the Weatherford Trail enters the Kachina Peaks Wilderness (the boundary is marked by two brown wilderness signs). Turn right onto the Weatherford Trail and follow it 2 miles downhill to the Schultz Tank trailhead.

No water is found along this hike, so you will need to pack a couple of quarts. Although not a constant threat, lightning is a possibility, especially in exposed areas near the southern end of the trail. Arrange a shuttle for this trip. If that's not possible, you may want to walk the Kachina Trail from one end or the other as far as time allows.

21 AUBINEAU–BEAR JAW LOOP

Distance: 6 miles round trip
Difficulty: moderate
Hiking time: 4 hours
Elevation: 8,500 to 10,400 feet
Management: Coconino NF

Wilderness status: Kachina
  Peaks WA
Season: June to September
USGS maps: Humphreys Peak,
  White Horse Hills

Because it receives relatively little use compared to other parts of the San Francisco Peaks, the north side of the range offers some fine hiking without the crowds. The premier route in this area follows the Aubineau and Bear Jaw trails to create a nice loop through pristine conifer and aspen forests.

Drive 14 miles north on US Highway 89 from Flagstaff. About 1.5 miles past the turnoff for Sunset Crater, turn left onto Forest Road 418 and drive 8.9 miles west to the signed turnoff at Forest Road 9123J. The newly constructed trailhead is located at road's end, 0.6 mile from Forest Road 418.

Ponderosa pines along the Bear Jaw Trail

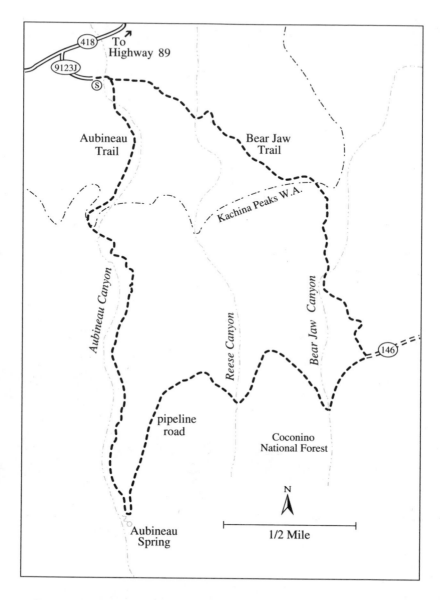

From the trailhead the route travels 0.3 mile before reaching the first junction. A left turn leads to the Bear Jaw Trail, while the route to the right begins climbing up Aubineau Canyon. Although either way is suitable, following the Aubineau Trail first gets the hike's climb over with sooner.

Beginning at this trail junction, the Aubineau Trail climbs moderately among a forest mix of ponderosa pine and aspen. Eventually, though, the ponderosa is replaced by Douglas fir, some of which are quite large. After 1 mile, the trail steepens somewhat and the tread becomes considerably rockier. The Aubineau Trail stays mostly in the bottom of Aubineau Canyon (more of a drainage than a canyon), although for the last 0.5 mile it breaks out into an area cleared of trees by avalanches. After climbing 1.8 miles the Aubineau Trail tops out on an old road that serves a pipeline. Conducting water from Aubineau Spring to the Inner Basin, the pipeline is part of Flagstaff's municipal water system. Although both the Aubineau and Bear Jaw trails fall within the Kachina Peaks Wilderness, this road has been excluded so that service trucks can access facilities. While motor vehicles are rare, mountain bicyclists do occasionally pedal this route.

The junction of the Aubineau Trail and the pipeline road is situated in an open meadow area on the north slope of Humphreys Peak. Avalanche paths allow for a nice view of the summit above and low-lying areas to the north. This is the best place on the hike for views because the rest of hike is mostly in the trees. From the junction, follow the road east for 2 miles to the signed turnoff for the Bear Jaw Trail, 0.25 mile past the Bear Jaw drainage. This last leg of the hike travels 2 miles back to the trailhead. Dropping at varying grades, the route accesses some abandoned sheep camps, complete with old carvings on aspen trunks. Eventually crossing the Bear Jaw drainage, the trail then breaks out into open stands of yellow-bark ponderosa pine. Within the last 0.75 mile, the Bear Jaw Trail divides. A right turn leads to the old trailhead, while staying to the left brings you back to the lower end of the Aubineau Trail. Follow the sign for the latter.

Although most of this hike crosses forested lower slopes, lightning can be a hazard, especially along the pipeline road. Water is not available on this trail, so pack a couple of quarts.

22 INNER BASIN

Distance: 4 miles round trip
Difficulty: moderate
Hiking time: 3 hours
Elevation: 8,600 to 10,000 feet
Management: Coconino NF

Wilderness status: none
Season: June to October
USGS maps: Humphreys Peak,
** Sunset Crater West**

As its name suggests, the Inner Basin is a sheltered area surrounded by the impressive San Francisco Peaks. In geologic terms, however, it is much more than a beautiful montane landscape. The Inner Basin is actually the inside of an ancient volcano, one that came to a fiery end millions of years ago—much in the same way that Mount St. Helens did in 1980.

Drive about 12 miles north from Flagstaff on US Highway 89. Upon passing the turnoff for Sunset Crater, drive an additional 0.8 mile to an unmarked left turn best identified by a large pile of black cinder

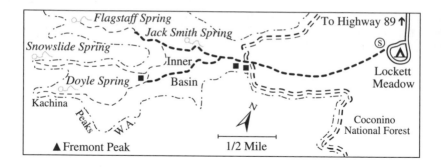

stored for road use. Drive 1.2 miles and then turn right at the sign for Lockett Meadow. Follow this road 3.3 miles to where it ends at a campground. The road is steep and narrow, but is usually passable to passenger cars. A developed trailhead marks the start of the Inner Basin Trail.

Because the Inner Basin provides the city of Flagstaff with water, overnight camping in the basin is prohibited. In addition, the Inner Basin trail system actually follows a network of service roads. This means you may occasionally encounter a city truck, as well as mountain bicyclists. The springs in the basin and some wells have also been developed. Despite these man-made intrusions, however, this hike is still rewarding.

From the Lockett Meadow trailhead, the route climbs steadily up a moderate grade for 1.5 miles to a trail junction. Surrounded mostly by mature aspen stands, this section of the walk is especially colorful in late September. At the junction, service roads branch off to follow various pipelines. One traverses around the north face of the San Francisco Peaks to springs in the Aubineau Creek area, another travels around to the south end of the peaks and to Flagstaff beyond, and still another continues on into the Inner Basin, where it branches again to access several springs. A cluster of buildings (one of which serves as lodging for backcountry rangers) also marks this junction.

Follow the middle road at the junction; a left turn shortly beyond leads 0.5 mile to the Inner Basin. Here, forests of aspen, spruce, and fir have receded enough to make way for large open meadows that are filled with orange sneezeweed, Indian paintbrush, and other wildflowers in the summer. A well and pumphouse are located in the center of the first meadow, but the outstanding scenery negates this sometimes noisy intrusion. Encircling the Inner Basin are the 12,000-foot summits of Humphreys and Agassiz peaks, and the slightly lower Fremont and Doyle peaks. Indeed, it is easy to envision the fact that you are standing inside a long-extinct volcano.

Two miles from the trailhead, the Inner Basin is the turnaround point for most hikers, but the walk can be extended another mile or more to one of the springs situated at the foot of the peaks. Reach Doyle Spring by continuing southwest, or turn right at the pumphouse

Wildflowers are plentiful in the Inner Basin.

and follow separate spur trails to visit Snowslide and Flagstaff springs. Because these springs are enclosed and tapped for municipal use, do not expect to find water flowing from them.

It is best to bring your own drinking water—there are no reliable sources along this hike.

23 WALNUT CANYON

Distance: 4 miles round trip
Difficulty: easy
Hiking time: 3 hours
Elevation: 6,950 to 6,800 feet

Management: Coconino NF
Wilderness status: none
Season: April to November
USGS map: Flagstaff East

Most people know Walnut Canyon for the small national monument located just east of Flagstaff. Tucked away in this end of the canyon are several Sinagua cliff dwellings dating back 700 years. But Walnut Canyon stretches for several miles across the Coconino Plateau, and a hike into a section upstream from the monument reveals the beauty of this small but interesting canyon without the crowds.

Follow the Lake Mary Road 5.5 miles southeast from where it turns off US Highway 89. Just past the second cattle guard, turn left and drive to the far end of a small campground. This hike utilizes the 1-mile-long Sandy's Canyon Trail to access the canyon bottom.

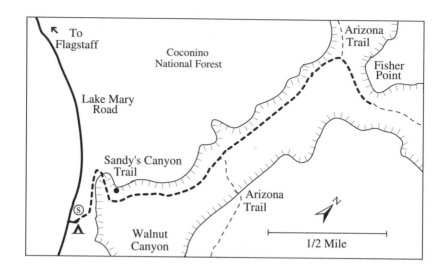

From the trailhead the Sandy's Canyon Trail traverses north across flat terrain to the canyon's edge, 0.25 mile away. The rim offers a fine view into shallow but well-defined Walnut Canyon. Capped by the dark lava bed that covers the entire Coconino Plateau is a layer of Coconino Sandstone, the same rock found in the upper walls of the Grand Canyon. At about 0.5 mile, the trail reaches a short side canyon (Sandy's Canyon) through which it gains access to the main canyon's bottom. Within the protected environment of Sandy's Canyon grow several yellow-bark ponderosa as well as a few aspens and lesser shrubs.

Detail of Fisher Point in Walnut Canyon

From the mouth of Sandy's Canyon, the trail continues north along the level bottom of Walnut Canyon to where it soon reaches the Arizona Trail. The hike then takes up this new trans-state route for another mile, to where the canyon bends to the east. The Arizona Trail climbs up a side canyon at this point and heads toward Flagstaff. To the right soars Fisher Point, an impressive rise of Coconino Sandstone. Note the crossbedding in this former desert sand dune.

The end of the established trail and the turnaround point for this hike is Fisher Point, although an unofficial trail does continue downstream. To protect the riparian plants (box elder, oak, walnut, ash, and poison ivy, among other species) the Forest Service is considering closing off this bootleg route.

Water is not available along the route, so pack a quart or two. Be prepared to encounter mountain bicyclists, especially along the Arizona Trail segment.

24   RED MOUNTAIN

Distance: 2.5 miles round trip
Difficulty: easy
Hiking time: 2 hours
Elevation: 6,800 to 7,200 feet

Management: Coconino NF
Wilderness status: none
Season: April to November
USGS map: Ebert Mountain SE

Despite the exceptionally easy nature of this hike, it provides one of the most fascinating looks at Arizona geology to be found anywhere.

Drive 33 miles north of Flagstaff on US Highway 180. At mile marker 247, turn left onto a good dirt road and drive about 0.4 mile to a fence. Although there are no signs, this is the trailhead.

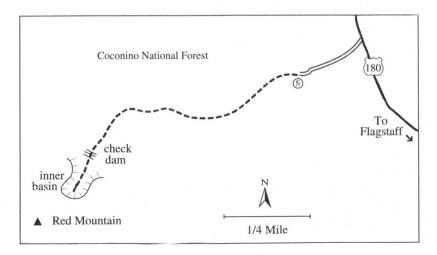

The trail winds for a pleasant 1.25 miles through pinyon pine and junipers toward a broken rise of cinder and red rock easily visible to the west. Marked by small white triangles, the route is easy to find, even when it takes up a wash for the last 0.5 mile. Originating inside Red Mountain, this wash is home to scattered ponderosa pines, which often grow on barren black cinder slopes. A 6-foot-high stone check dam that must be climbed (it is also possible to scramble up and over the cinder hill to the right) marks the entrance into the mountain's interior.

Eroded away over time, this small inner basin features a fascinating collection of rock pinnacles and pillars. It is actually the interior of an ancient volcano, and the soft tuff has been sculpted into a variety of well-rounded shapes. Red in color, this geological montage is a great place to spend hours exploring various nooks and crannies. You can access the mountain's 7,965-foot summit by following an old road along the south ridgeline and then picking your way through the ponderosa forest on top. A hardened lava flow is located southwest of the summit.

Water is not available on this hike, so bring a quart if you plan to stay for any length of time. Care should be taken when climbing around in the rock formations.

Looking inside Red Mountain's inner basin

25 SLATE MOUNTAIN

Distance: 4.8 miles round trip
Difficulty: easy
Hiking time: 3 hours
Elevation: 7,362 to 8,215 feet

Management: Coconino NF
Wilderness status: none
Season: April to November
USGS map: Kendrick Peak

Although seemingly uneventful at the start, the hike up Slate Mountain offers a wonderful reward in its 360-degree panorama of the surrounding countryside.

Drive about 30 miles north of Flagstaff on US Highway 180 to Forest Road 191. Turn left (there is a sign on the highway for Slate Mountain) and drive 2 miles on good gravel road to the marked trailhead.

Following an old road that is now closed to vehicles, the Slate Mountain Trail climbs easily along the south face of the mountain before looping east around a shoulder of the peak. It then crosses the north-facing slope before returning to the south side of the mountain again. Near the top it actually corkscrews around the summit, providing the greatest scenic variety possible. All along the route interpretive signs identify area plant life. Included are pinyon and ponderosa pine, alligator juniper, mountain mahogany, Douglas fir, cliff rose, currant, and Fremont hollygrape among others. Not specified in any of the signs, however, is the origin of the mountain's name. Early settlers mistook the peak's light gray rhyolite (a volcanic rock) for slate.

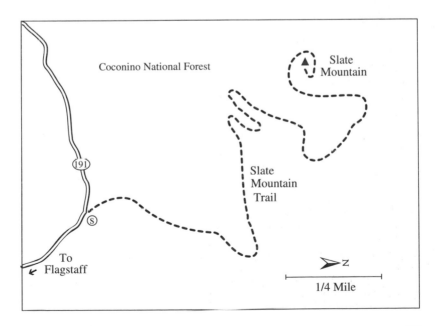

The views from Slate Mountain are far-reaching.

Although vistas in various directions open up at different parts of the hike, the all-inclusive panorama from the top takes in such spectacles as the San Francisco Peaks, the Painted Desert, the North Rim of the Grand Canyon, nearby Kendrick Mountain and Red Mountain, and the forested Coconino Plateau.

Water is unavailable on this hike, so pack at least a quart. Watch for lightning during afternoon showers in the summertime.

26 KENDRICK MOUNTAIN

Distance: 7 miles round trip
Difficulty: moderate
Hiking time: 5 hours
Elevation: 7,980 to 10,418 feet
Management: Kaibab NF

Wilderness status: Kendrick
  Mountain WA
Season: May to September
USGS map: Kendrick Peak

Capping its small namesake wilderness area, Kendrick Mountain (also known as Kendrick Peak) offers some of the finest views in the northern portion of the state. Of the three different routes that access the summit, the Kendrick Mountain Trail is the most direct and easiest to follow.

Drive 15 miles north from Flagstaff via US Highway 180 to mile marker 230. Turn left onto Forest Road 245 and follow this maintained gravel road for 3.1 miles to the junction with Forest Road 171. Turn

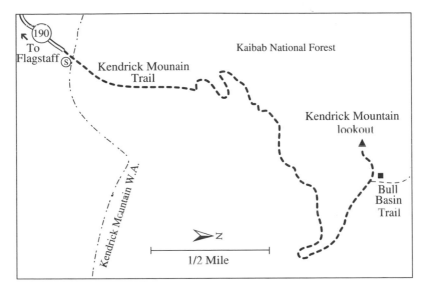

right and drive 3.2 miles, then turn right onto Forest Road 190 and follow it for 0.4 mile to the developed trailhead. Some older descriptions of the hiking route show the trail beginning on Forest Road 171A, but the trail has since been rerouted and the trailhead facilities improved.

For the first 0.5 mile the route follows a newly constructed foot trail up a moderately steep grade. This in turn is followed by 1 mile of old

Looking toward the San Francisco Peaks from Kendrick Mountain

roadbed, which is succeeded by a well-constructed trail that switchbacks the rest of the way up the south face of the mountain. Problems with the cutting of switchbacks in the past have led to erosion, so it is imperative to stay on the established trail. Note changes in vegetation along the climb to the summit. Ponderosa pines eventually give way to mixed forests of Douglas fir, white fir, cork-bark fir, and Engelmann spruce. Glades of white-barked aspen are also encountered, along with sloping meadows of ferns. This is ideal habitat for mule deer and elk.

Within 0.25 mile of the summit, the trail reaches a saddle where an old cabin, complete with two cots, provides shelter for overnight hikers. This small structure was built around 1912 and occupied by fire lookouts until the 1930s, when the current tower was constructed on the summit. It is now listed on the National Register of Historic Places. The Bull Basin Trail, which climbs the north face of the mountain, connects with the Kendrick Mountain Trail at this saddle.

Situated on the summit, a lookout that is still in use provides some spectacular views of the surrounding country, but be sure to ask permission of those persons stationed there before climbing up. To the north, the Grand Canyon and Vermilion Cliffs are plainly visible. Oak Creek Canyon and Mingus Mountain can be spotted to the south. The San Francisco Peaks loom to the east, while Bill Williams and Sitgreaves mountains rise to the west. Poking above the ubiquitous ponderosa forests that stretch out in all directions from Kendrick Mountain are several small, symmetrically shaped cinder cones. These small volcanoes, like Kendrick Mountain itself, reveal the fiery past of the Coconino Plateau.

Water is not available along the route, so bring two or more quarts. Watch out for lightning during the rainy summer season.

27 BILL WILLIAMS MOUNTAIN

Distance: 7 miles round trip
Difficulty: moderate
Hiking time: 4 hours
Elevation: 7,000 to 9,256 feet

Management: Kaibab NF
Wilderness status: none
Season: May to September
USGS map: Williams South

A smaller version of Kendrick Mountain to the northeast, Bill Williams Mountain is a wonderful summit to hike, partly for the view from the top, and partly because of the lush forest encountered near the top. Closing in on this trail are towering aspen and fir, along with a riotous growth of underbrush.

The Bill Williams Mountain Trail (formerly called the Clover Trail) begins at the Williams Ranger District Office, 1 mile west of Williams. From Interstate 40 take Exit 161 and follow the signs.

Originally built as a toll trail in 1902, this route accesses the summit via the mountain's north face. Climbing a bit within the first mile, the route levels a bit for most of the second mile. About 0.75 mile in, a

View from the top of Bill Williams Mountain

short side trail takes off to Clover Spring. Keep right at this junction to head for the summit.

The lower elevations of the hike support a mostly low-profile forest of alligator juniper, pinyon pine, and Gambel oak, occasionally spiked by taller ponderosa pines. Eventually, though, the trail encounters stands of monstrous Douglas firs and mature aspens. This change in forest becomes especially evident when the trail takes up the bottom of a shady ravine. An undergrowth of ferns, Oregon grape, and Arizona wild rose add to the allure of this section.

After mile marker 2 the trail steepens as it begins to climb toward the summit in earnest. About 3 miles from the trailhead the route

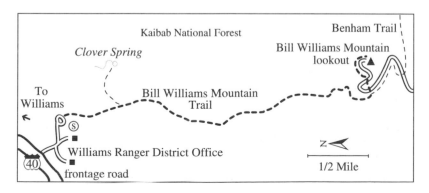

crosses a gravel road that accesses a fire lookout tower and accompanying radio towers on the summit. The first real view of the hike comes just before you reach the gravel road, from a rock outcrop just to the right of the trail. Looking west, you can see Interstate 40 dropping off toward the town of Ash Fork.

After crossing the road, the trail cuts up to the next switchback in the road, which it then follows for the remaining 0.5 mile to the top. Built in 1937, the fire lookout on top replaced the original wooden structure, which in turn replaced an even earlier "lookout tree." The 360-degree view from the tower is impressive, although a plethora of radio towers intrudes on all sides.

Water is unavailable on this hike, so bring plenty. You could arrange for a shuttle to pick you up or drop you off on top thereby cutting the walk in half. Or you could descend the Benham Trail, which drops down the east face of the mountain, and have a shuttle pick you up at the Benham trailhead at the eastern foot of the mountain.

28   SYCAMORE RIM

Distance: 11 miles round trip
Difficulty: easy
Hiking time: 7 hours
Elevation: 6,700 to 7,287 feet
Management: Kaibab NF

Wilderness status: Sycamore
  Canyon WA
Season: April to November
USGS maps: Davenport Hill,
  Garland Prairie

A little-known hiking route that runs along the rim of Sycamore Canyon, the Sycamore Rim Trail (also known as the Sycamore Trail) offers a wonderful look at the unique ecosystems along the Mogollon Rim.

Exit Interstate 40 at Garland Prairie Road (Exit 167) and drive 9 miles southeast on Forest Road 141. Turn right on Forest Road 56, signed for the "Rim Trail," and drive 1.9 miles to the trailhead. Because this description follows the trail clockwise, begin by hiking southeast across the meadow.

Established in 1979, the Sycamore Rim Trail was originally marked by frequently placed rock cairns. In 1992, however, tread construction was completed along the entire 11-mile loop. With the exception of a couple of short stretches, the Sycamore Rim Trail is level and the terrain is open. In addition, several other trailheads offer convenient access throughout the loop.

After traversing a meadow, the route enters an open ponderosa pine forest. Ponderosa pine is the predominant plant for much of the hike. About 0.5 mile from the start, the trail reaches the rim of a small canyon, which it then follows for the next mile or so. Scattered timbers and an interpretive sign mark the site of an old sawmill dating back to about 1910. After passing beneath a high-tension power line, the trail accesses views of wonderful pools of water in an ever-deepening canyon below.

Approximately 3 miles from the trailhead, the Sycamore Rim Trail

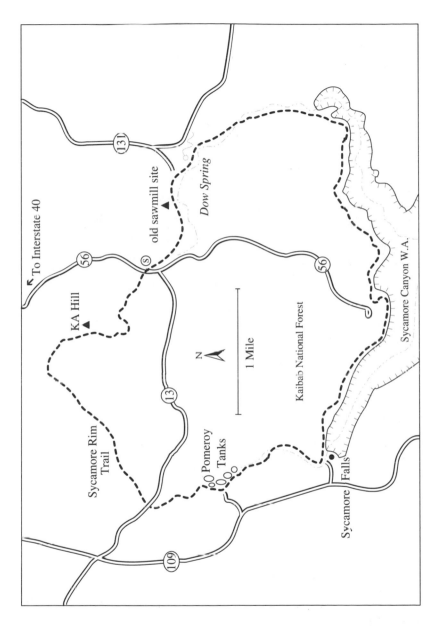

reaches the rim of Sycamore Canyon. For the next several miles this rimrock marks the boundary of the Sycamore Canyon Wilderness Area. The views along this section are of volcanic cliffs and the verdant canyon bottom. Because the canyon is so wild in its upper reaches, only very rough routes access the bottom.

The Pomeroy Tanks along the Sycamore Rim Trail

Although ponderosa pines of all sizes are found along most of the Sycamore Rim Trail, some other interesting ecosystems are also present. A few sunny sections of mesa top harbor small clusters of agaves or century plants. Some opportunistic aspen trees grow in a narrow stretch of canyon near the normally dry Sycamore Falls, about 6 miles from the trailhead. And a little more than 7 miles from the start are the Pomeroy Tanks. These perennial pools of clear water support a population of small fish and provide an important source of water for terrestrial fauna.

Within the last 2 miles of the hike, the Sycamore Rim Trail climbs some 500 feet to the top of KA Hill (7,287 feet). Although the climb is not particularly hard, this change in topography is enough to allow for the addition of alligator junipers and Gambel oaks to the nearly ubiquitous ponderosa pine forests. From the top of KA Hill you get a nice view of nearby Garland Prairie and the San Francisco Peaks beyond.

Although water is present along the trail, it should be treated, so you may want to bring your own. Lightning can be a hazard, especially along the open rimrock. Because four other trailheads (one at Sycamore Falls, one at Pomeroy Tanks, one at the end of Forest Road 56 near the canyon rim, and one at Dow Spring near the first power line crossing) are situated along the route, you can make the walk shorter by setting up a shuttle or by returning to your car along the same stretch of trail.

29 WEST FORK OAK CREEK

Distance: 8 miles round trip
Difficulty: easy
Hiking time: 4 hours
Elevation: 5,400 to 5,600 feet
Season: March to November

Management: Coconino NF
Wilderness status: Red Rocks–
   Secret Mountain WA
USGS maps: Wilson Mountain,
   Munds Park, Dutton Hill

With colorful walls rising hundreds of feet straight up, a picturesque stream, and an interesting collection of flora and fauna, the West Fork of Oak Creek is one of the most spectacular canyon systems in the state. What makes this hike especially wonderful is that it all begins within a few minutes of the trailhead. Although such a combination can make for some crowded hiking—as many as 300 visitors a day—the West Fork is too good to miss.

The hike starts 10.5 miles north of Sedona, near mile marker 385 on Alternate US Highway 89. Park on the west side of the road.

The West Fork Trail is as level and easy to follow as any trail around. Several crossings of the shallow stream are necessary, but with normal runoff these may be completed via stepping stones. Such conditions make it easy for hikers of all ages to enjoy the natural history and beauty of the area.

Besides being included within the Red Rocks–Secret Mountain Wilderness, much of West Fork Canyon falls within the Oak Creek Research Natural Area. This designation came about because of the diverse plant life found here. In addition to the monstrous ponderosa pines and Douglas firs that shade the canyon bottom, the area also supports box elder, cottonwood, velvet ash, Arizona walnut, bigtooth maple, and Gambel oak. Willows, columbine, Arizona rose, sumac, wild grape, Virginia creeper, asters, lupine, and poison ivy grow here, as

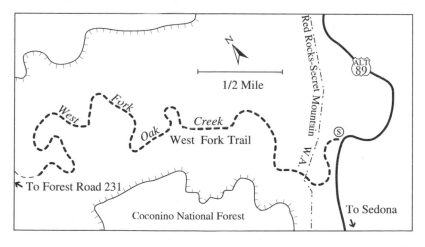

The West Fork of Oak Creek near Sedona

well. Included among the canyon's wildlife are Abert's, red, and Arizona gray squirrels; mule deer; and the narrow-headed garter snake.

Encasing this diverse biological community are soaring walls of Coconino Sandstone. Heavily crossbedded, these impressive cliffs were once wind-drifted sand dunes. At the creek level are deep red facades of the Supai Formation. Seeps of water, the same agent responsible for cutting this deep abyss, are found in various places along the canyon walls.

For the first 2 miles the hiking remains very easy, but shortly after that the trail becomes overgrown and even climbs out of the canyon bottom at one point. These inconveniences tend to thin out the crowds, but the going is still relatively easy. Eventually, any trace of a trail disappears as the route simply follows the creek bottom.

At about the 4-mile mark, a thigh-deep, wall-to-wall pool of water marks the hike's turnaround point. It is possible, however, to continue up the canyon the rest of the way to Forest Road 231—a 14-mile hike in all. The upper portion of the West Fork requires additional wading, some swimming, and lots of boulder hopping, but the hike is well worth the effort. Should you be interested in an overnight hike, keep in mind that camping is prohibited in the lower 6 miles of the canyon to prevent damage to this unique riparian environment.

Plan on taking 4 hours to complete the first 4-mile leg of this canyon, a couple of days if you want to go all the way. The stream water should be treated if you plan to drink it. Watch for poison ivy and be mindful of flash flooding, especially in the summer months.

30 EAST POCKET

Distance: 4.8 miles round trip
Difficulty: strenuous
Hiking time: 4 hours
Elevation: 5,200 to 7,196 feet
Management: Coconino NF

Wilderness status: Red Rocks–
Secret Mountain WA
Season: March to November
USGS maps: Wilson Mountain,
Munds Park

Following the A. B. Young Trail, the hike to the East Pocket Lookout Tower climbs up the steep west side of Oak Creek Canyon. First constructed in the late 1880s, this route was rebuilt by the CCC under the supervision of A. B. Young. Steep and sinuous for most of the way, this hike is worth it simply for the views.

Drive 8.5 miles north from Sedona on Alternate US Highway 89 to

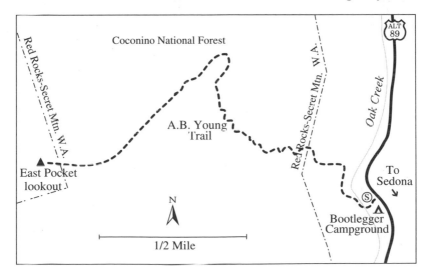

Looking into Oak Creek Canyon from East Pocket

the Bootlegger Campground. Parking is not available in the facility, but a few spaces may be found along the east shoulder of the highway. Watch for traffic. Cross the road and find a set of stairs leading down to the creek at the south end of the campground. Boulder hop across the creek and climb the far bank to an old road and power line. Watch for poison ivy along the creek bottom. Follow this roadbed north, or upstream, a short distance to where the trail (marked by a sign) takes off up the hillside.

Climbing 1,600 feet to the west rim of the canyon in only 1.6 miles, the A. B. Young Trail is a real grunt of a walk. En route it makes nearly three dozen switchbacks, seldom relinquishing its moderate to strenuous gradient as it climbs. Little shade exists along the way as the trail climbs through thickets of shrub live oak, manzanita, alligator juniper, and mountain mahogany. Watch for blooming century plants in early summer.

Upon reaching the rim, the trail continues for another 0.8 mile through mixed stands of ponderosa pine and Douglas fir. In addition to being relatively shady and cool, this segment of the trail also allows for easy access to the shelf of Kaibab Limestone that rims the canyon. Vistas from this precipitous edge are spectacular, to say the least. The final 0.25 mile of the route up to the lookout becomes somewhat indistinct as it follows widely spaced rock cairns. A wooden structure, the fire lookout provides views of the San Francisco Peaks, Mingus Mountain, and a lengthy stretch of the Mogollon Rim. Located just outside the wilderness boundary, it is accessed by a dirt road.

Be sure to bring plenty of water and a hat for protection from the sun on summer days, and watch for lightning.

31 WILSON MOUNTAIN

Distance: 11.2 miles round trip
Difficulty: strenuous
Hiking time: 6 hours
Elevation: 4,600 to 6,960 feet
Management: Coconino NF

Wilderness status: Red Rocks–
**   Secret Mountain WA**
Season: March to November
USGS maps: Wilson Mountain,
**   Munds Park**

Wilson Mountain, like other high points in the Sedona area, offers a wonderful vantage point from which to enjoy the surrounding red rock terrain. The Wilson Mountain Trail runs mostly in the Red Rock–Secret Mountain Wilderness and was designated as a National Recreation Trail in 1979.

Drive north from Sedona on Alternate US Highway 89 for about 1.5 miles. Immediately after crossing the Midgley Bridge, turn left into a parking area. Don't be alarmed if a lot of cars are parked here. Most belong to people stopping to look at the bridge. Be sure not to block the locked gate at the far end of the lot.

For the first 0.25 mile or so, the trail climbs quickly to gain a ridge just east of Wilson Canyon. This is followed by a mile of easier grades as the route continues north and approaches the base of the mountain. The terrain along this stretch is dry, open desert. Scattered pinyon pine, juniper, manzanita, agave, yucca, and bear grass are common, but shade is not.

After 1.25 miles, the trail begins switchbacking up a considerably steeper grade as it heads for what appears to be a saddle. This is the First Bench of Wilson Mountain. Along this ascent the trail is steep and rocky in places, and occasionally overgrown with shrub live oak. Although this climb is long, the views of the Midgley Bridge and Sedona far below are spectacular.

Once on top of First Bench, a 0.5-mile stretch of nearly level trail traverses open grassland. This is a good place to take in the ever-changing scenery. The area's century plants bloom in early summer, as do many perennial flowers. The Mogollon Rim is visible to the east

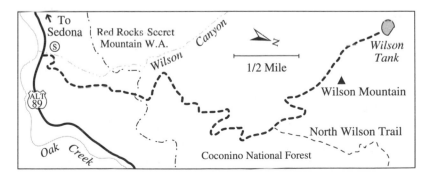

across Oak Creek Canyon. And the Wilson Mountain Trail connects here with the upper end of the North Wilson Trail—a 2-mile alternate route that begins at the Encinoso Picnic Area in the bottom of Oak Creek Canyon.

From First Bench the Wilson Mountain Trail begins to make its final ascent to the mountain's summit above. Not as steep or nearly as long as the climb below, this pitch is also less difficult because of the shade afforded by the ponderosa pines and Gambel oaks that grow most of the way up. Near the top, note where the trail encounters the mountain's rim of volcanic rock. This cap of dark basalt typifies much of the expansive Mogollon Rim.

The actual summit of mostly flat-topped Wilson Mountain lies a short distance southeast of where the trail tops out. The established route, however, continues north for about 1.25 miles to Wilson Tank on the far end of the mountain. To follow this last stretch of trail, watch for cairns and tree blazes where the actual tread fades or is nonexistent. Also keep an eye out for mule deer and elk among the ponderosa forests and open meadows along the way. For the best views you will need to travel a short distance (perhaps 0.25 mile) off the trail to get to the mountaintop's edge. Although Wilson Tank is little more than a glorified mud hole, a search for tracks along its banks may reveal signs of some of the nocturnal creatures that inhabit the area.

During the summer months you may want to leave early to avoid the heat of the day. Lightning may also pose a problem in July and August. No potable water is found along the way, so bring plenty of your own, especially in the summer.

The views are spectacular along the Wilson Mountain Trail.

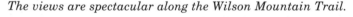

32   VULTEE ARCH

Distance: 3.4 miles round trip
Difficulty: easy
Hiking time: 3 hours
Elevation: 4,800 to 5,200 feet
Management: Coconino NF

Wilderness status: Red Rocks–
  Secret Mountain WA
Season: year-round
USGS map: Wilson Mountain

This short hike allows easy access to a well-known geologic feature of the Sedona area, plus it reveals some of the vegetation that is typical of this red rock country. A favorite among locals, this route sees a lot activity, especially on weekends.

Drive west from downtown Sedona on Alternate US Highway 89 to the Dry Creek Road. Turn north and drive another 2 miles to the turnoff for the Vultee Arch Road (Forest Road 152.) Follow this dirt road 4.3 miles to its end. Although rough in spots, this road is passable to cars during dry weather. The Vultee Arch Trail heads east from the right side of the parking area.

Entering the Red Rock–Secret Mountain Wilderness Area almost immediately, the trail follows the gentle bottom of Sterling Canyon. The route is well marked the entire way, and shade is provided by thick stands of alligator juniper, Gambel oak, and Arizona cypress, or by tall ponderosa pines. White-barked sycamore trees also grow along the normally dry wash bottom.

Within the last 0.25 mile the Sterling Pass Trail branches off to the right. Keep left, however, and climb a short distance farther to a brass plaque commemorating aviation pioneer Gerard Vultee and his wife, Sylvia. The two died in a plane crash about a mile north of this spot in January 1938. The natural arch that shares their name is located high above on the canyon's north wall, protected by thick brush. It would be very difficult to reach the arch.

From the plaque you get a good view of the canyon below. It is easy

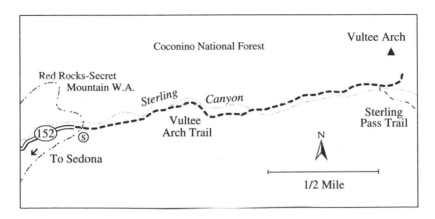

The Vultee Arch spans a small side drainage of Sterling Canyon.

to see how slope aspect plays an important role in this rugged terrain. Because the canyon's north side faces south, it is more arid. Consequently, it supports thickets of manzanita, shrub live oak, and other desert plants. The shadier south side of the canyon supports tall stands of Douglas fir and ponderosa pine.

Although this is a short excursion, it is advisable to bring drinking water, especially in the hot summer months.

33 SECRET CANYON

Distance: 8 miles round trip
Difficulty: easy
Hiking time: 4 hours
Elevation: 4,700 to 5,300 feet
Management: Coconino NF

Wilderness status: Red Rocks–
   Secret Mountain WA
Season: year-round
USGS map: Wilson Mountain

Like many other trails in the west Sedona area, the Secret Canyon Trail is an easy-to-follow route that explores the depths of a beautiful box canyon. As the name intimates, however, Secret Canyon is not as well known as some of the others.

Drive west from Sedona on Alternate US Highway 89. Turn north onto the Dry Creek Road and follow it for 2 miles to the signs for

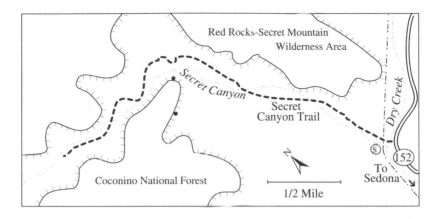

Vultee Arch. Turn onto Vultee Arch Road (Forest Road 152). This dirt road is rough in places, but is passable to cars in dry weather. The trail begins 3.4 miles up the road, on the left side.

From the parking area, the Secret Canyon Trail immediately crosses Dry Creek before taking up a broad sandy pathway along the bottom of Secret Canyon. Because the first mile traverses an area thick with alligator juniper, pinyon pine, and manzanita, little shade is available. Additionally, the canyon walls at this point are too distant to add much visual excitement to the scenery. Eventually, however, a fortress of red rock to the north and another to the southwest do break up the skyline.

Along the Secret Canyon hike

In about 1.25 miles, the trail climbs out of the canyon bottom and continues along the east side of the canyon. For the next 0.75 mile the trail remains shadeless (this section can be quite hot in the summer). After crossing two shallow side washes, the trail bends south to drop back into the canyon bottom. At this point, cliff faces of Coconino Sandstone and Kaibab Limestone quickly close ranks to make for some rather dramatic scenery. Protected by sheer walls, the canyon bottom is shaded by some beautiful ponderosa pines, Douglas firs, Gambel oaks, and sycamores. The trail mostly follows the wash bottom for the next 2 miles before eventually petering out all together. The hike's turnaround point is wherever you please.

Be sure to carry plenty of drinking water—none is available along this hike. Plan on encountering some hot temperatures and little relief from the sun for the first 2 miles. Watch for poison ivy, especially in shady areas. Flash floods are a possibility in the narrow confines of the upper canyon.

34 BOYNTON CANYON

Distance: 5 miles round trip
Difficulty: easy
Hiking time: 3 hours
Elevation: 4,600 to 5,100 feet
Management: Coconino NF

Wilderness status: Red Rocks–
  Secret Mountain WA
Season: year-round
USGS maps: Wilson Mountain,
  Loy Butte

Located within minutes of Sedona, Boynton Canyon is a popular hike for locals and visitors alike. Entering a highly scenic canyon boxed in by large red rock buttes and cliffs, this trail accesses some truly outstanding scenery. Wildlife is plentiful and the flora is fascinating.

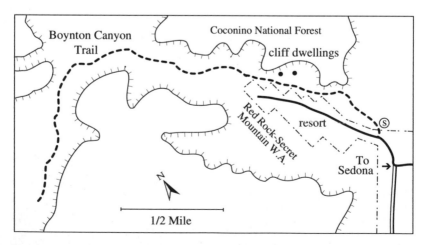

Drive west from Sedona on Alternate US Highway 89 to the Dry Creek Road. Turn north and drive 3 miles to the Boynton Pass Road. Turn left at this junction and continue 2 miles to the Boynton Canyon trailhead. A small parking area is located on the right side of the road.

The route begins by skirting to the east of a luxury resort that sprawls across the mouth of the canyon. For this first mile the trail traverses dry foothills before dropping back into the canyon bottom. Some minor grade changes can be expected in this first section, but once the canyon bottom is reached, upstream from the resort, the hike is mostly level. Along the way be sure to scan the rock walls immediately above for small cliff dwellings. These were constructed by the Sinagua around A.D. 1200.

Upon reaching the canyon bottom, the trail is well marked and easy to follow. Although normally dry, this drainage supports a surprisingly thick forest of evergreen trees. Ponderosa pine and Douglas fir make up the larger species of trees, while manzanita, Arizona cypress, and a variety of oaks constitute the thick understory. Species of wildlife that reside here include Coues white-tailed deer, javelina, and Arizona gray squirrel. Mountain lions no doubt frequent the canyon's rugged upper reaches, while badgers, coyotes, and ringtail cats reside throughout.

As the trail nears the canyon's abrupt end, it becomes somewhat overgrown, but it is still easy to follow. Here, where the magnificent canyon walls draw closer, you can really appreciate the amazing scale of Sedona's red rock country. Soaring some 800 feet above are colorful faces of Coconino Sandstone and Kaibab Limestone. Adding a metaphysical complexion to the geology of the area is the reported presence of a vortex, or concentration of electromagnetic energy within the earth below, near the mouth of Boynton Canyon. The location of four such vortices in the Sedona area have made it a mecca for New Age followers.

Because water is nonexistent along this trail, be sure to bring along a quart or two. Don't be surprised to see a lot of cars crammed into the small trailhead parking area, especially on weekends.

Boynton Canyon offers some interesting views.

35 SECRET MOUNTAIN

Distance: 16 miles round trip
Difficulty: moderate
Hiking time: 9 hours
Elevation: 4,720 to 6,600 feet
Management: Coconino NF

Wilderness status: Red Rock–
Secret Mountain WA
Season: April to November
USGS maps: Loy Butte, Wilson
Mountain

Soaring high above the red rock country west of Sedona, Secret Mountain offers a unique perspective on the surrounding landscape. To the north of the flat-topped summit is Secret Canyon, while stretching southward is the expansive Verde Valley. This hike begins by following the length of Loy Canyon to a small saddle at its head. From there it is a pleasurable walk through pine forests to the mountain's scenic southern edge.

Drive 10 miles west of Sedona on Alternate US Highway 89 to the Red Canyon Road (Forest Road 525). Turn north and continue 3.4 miles on this maintained gravel road to a fork. Stay right and continue on Forest Road 525 for another 6.8 miles to the trailhead, following the signs for Loy Butte. The trail takes off to the right just before a cattle guard. The parking area is on the left.

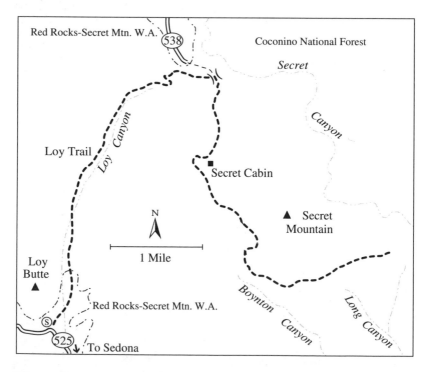

The views are stunning from Secret Mountain.

For the first 4 miles, the hike to Secret Mountain follows the bottom of very scenic Loy Canyon. Maintaining a mostly easy grade, this segment is in itself a pleasurable hike. Rising to the left is Loy Butte, the site of several Sinagua cliff dwellings. Defining the skyline to the right is Secret Mountain, and straight ahead is the Mogollon Rim. Vegetation along this lower section of the hike includes pinyon pine, juniper, manzanita, shrub live oak, and an occasional ponderosa pine growing along the wash bottom. Wildlife in this arid terrain includes javelina, coyote, Coues white-tailed deer, and jackrabbits.

Completing approximately half of its 1,700-foot climb in the first 4 miles, the Loy Trail climbs considerably in its last mile. This steep and narrow stretch of trail ends at a saddle that connects Secret Mountain with the Mogollon Rim. A left turn at the saddle leads 0.25 mile to the end of Forest Road 538, while the route to the right accesses Secret Mountain via an easy 200-foot climb.

Secret Mountain's terrain is mostly level and quite shady. You may have noted stands of Douglas fir growing in the protected areas to the right of the saddle. Growing all across the mountain's summit, however, is a drier forest of ponderosa pine with an occasional Gambel oak or alligator juniper mixed in. Mule deer are plentiful in this high terrain and elk occasionally migrate to the mountain from the nearby Mogollon Rim.

From where it tops out 0.25 mile past the saddle, the trail continues south through the pines for nearly 1 mile before reaching Secret Cabin. Although the history of this antiquated log structure is sketchy at best, one story claims that horse thieves hid out here while another claims it was home to a group of Mormon polygamists. Just beyond the cabin is the first of several viewpoints. Looking down into Loy Canyon, this vista also takes in the Sycamore Pass area, Mingus Mountain, and the Verde Valley. Continuing on from this point, the trail cuts through the forest for less than a mile before again finding the mountain's edge. The views here are still of the Loy Canyon drainage, but continue another mile and you can peer into the head of Boynton Canyon. The trail continues a bit farther before ending at the mountain's easternmost point. This neck of land is bounded by Long Canyon to the south and Secret Canyon to the north.

Although some small springs are found on Secret Mountain, they are not always reliable, so it is best to bring all the water you will need. Watch for lightning on the rim areas, especially during summer thunderstorms. If you want to visit all of the overlooks, you might want to spend the night. Several nice camping areas are available.

36 JACKS CANYON

Distance: 13 miles round trip
Difficulty: moderate
Hiking time: 6 hours
Elevation: 4,360 to 6,320 feet
Management: Coconino NF

Wilderness status: Munds Mountain WA
Season: March to November
USGS map: Munds Mountain

At 18,150 acres, the Munds Mountain Wilderness encompasses some interesting terrain southeast of Sedona. The primary landmark here is the area's 6,825-foot namesake summit, but a number of scenic canyons also highlight the wilderness. Running the length of one of these is the Jacks Canyon Trail. The drainage got its name from Jack Woods, a railroad engineer from Winslow, Arizona, who grazed sheep here in the latter part of the nineteenth century.

From Sedona, drive about 6 miles south on State Highway 179 to the Oak Creek Village center. Turn left on Jacks Canyon Road and drive 0.9 mile to where the road turns right. Continue for another 1.7 miles

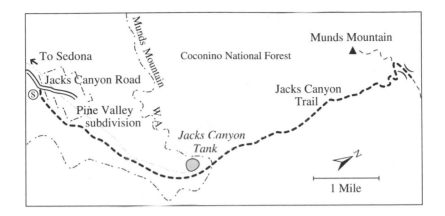

on this good gravel road to the entrance of the Pine Valley subdivision. Currently, the trailhead and a small parking area are located just to the right of the gate. Plans are in the offing, however, to move the trailhead 0.5 mile west of the subdivision entrance.

Except for a 0.3-mile section that climbs around the upper end of the housing development, the first 1.5 miles of the Jacks Canyon Trail follows an abandoned road up the gently ascending canyon bottom. Plant life along this first stretch include mostly pinyon pine, juniper, and

The Sedona area as seen from the top of the Jacks Canyon Trail

shrub live oak. At the 1.5-mile mark the road reaches the Jacks Canyon Tank, where the road ends and the route becomes a single-track trail for the rest of the way. Although it usually contains water, this stock pond is not fit for consumption.

From Jacks Canyon Tank, the trail continues to the dry wash bottom, which it then closely parallels for the next 4 miles. At the many streambed crossings along the way the trail is marked with cairns on either side to avoid confusion. Otherwise, the route is well established as it passes among beautiful stands of Arizona cypress that are intermixed with an occasional alligator juniper or patch of manzanita.

Climbing along an easy grade for the first several miles, the Jacks Canyon Trail becomes considerably steeper in the last 1.5 miles. Completing nearly half of the route's 2,000-foot climb in this final segment, much of the grade is moderate in difficulty, although a few stretches can be considered strenuous. In addition, parts of the trail are badly eroded and the footing is occasionally loose. Along this upper end, Gambel oaks and ponderosa pines become more common.

Near the trail's end, a saddle is reached that marks the head of Jacks Canyon. Be sure to note the Douglas fir forest growing on the protected north side of the ridge. At the saddle, this hike turns right to access the Mogollon Rim a short distance to the east. A secondary trail turns left, however, and climbs another 500 feet to the top of Munds Mountain. After staying right, continue for another 0.25 mile to reach the rim and its spectacular views. The Schnebly Hill Road lies directly below, while Oak Creek Canyon opens up to the north. Wilson and Secret mountains rise to the west and, looking back down the Jacks Canyon drainage, you can see part of the Verde Valley far to the south.

No potable water is found along the Jacks Canyon Trail, so be sure to bring plenty; the summer months can be hot.

37   TAYLOR CABIN

Distance: 17 miles round trip
Difficulty: moderate
Hiking time: 2 days
Elevation: 4,900 to 4,200 feet
Management: Coconino NF,
   Prescott NF

Wilderness Status: Sycamore
   Canyon WA
Season: year-round
USGS maps: Loy Butte, Sy-
   camore Point

To visualize Sycamore Canyon, imagine Oak Creek Canyon without the highway and homes, without its resorts and lodges, its campgrounds, and the crowds. What you have left is a wilderness canyon that cuts deeply into the Mogollon Rim. Like Oak Creek Canyon, Sycamore Canyon (not to be confused with the other Sycamore Canyon listed in this book) features impressive cliffs of Coconino and Supai sandstone, verdant riparian plant life, and beautiful desert terrain. Ringtail cats far outnumber tourists in this 55,937-acre wilderness,

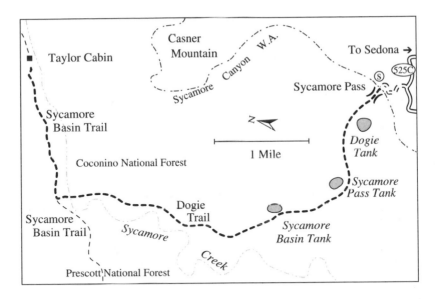

and the only "developments" you will find are antiquated cow camps and backcountry trails. The hike to Taylor Cabin from Sycamore Pass provides a great introduction to Sycamore Canyon.

Drive 10 miles west of Sedona on Alternate US Highway 89 to the Red Canyon Road (Forest Road 525). Turn north and drive 3.4 miles on this good gravel road to where Forest Road 525C branches off. Turn left here and continue for another 9.1 miles to Sycamore Pass. All but the last 0.5 mile of this road is passable to cars. This last section is a very rough 4WD road that is far easier to walk than drive.

From Sycamore Pass, the hike follows the Dogie Trail west into the canyon below. Broad and open, this section of Sycamore Canyon includes gently sloping basins with pinyon pine and juniper forests. Nearly impassable thickets of shrub live oak are common, as are manzanita bushes and various species of cacti. This upland desert community is occasionally interrupted by small islands of cottonwoods and other deciduous trees that encircle stock ponds. A short distance from the pass, the trail encounters the first of these watering holes, Dogie Tank. Sycamore Pass Tank is about 1 mile from the trailhead, and Sycamore Basin Tank is 1 mile farther. While not fit for human consumption, these ponds are important sources of water for the canyon's deer, javelina, mountain lion, black bear, fox, coyote, rabbit, ringtail cat, skunk, and squirrel populations.

During the first 2 miles to the Sycamore Basin Tank, the route descends easily from an elevation of 4,900 feet at the pass to around 4,400 feet. Beyond this point the trail angles north to parallel Sycamore Creek for 3 additional miles. Although it dips in and out of small drainages along the way, the trail has dropped only a few hundred feet overall by the time it reaches the canyon bottom. Although easy to follow, this section is rocky in places.

Approximately 5 miles from the trailhead, the route reaches Sycamore Creek. Although this drainage is usually dry, pools of water may linger after rainstorms or periods of snowmelt. In spite of this, the canyon bottom is able to support a nice riparian community of Arizona walnut, cottonwood, willow, and, of course, sycamore.

Upon crossing the creek bed, the Dogie Trail continues for another 0.5 mile to where it connects with the Sycamore Basin Trail. Lands west of Sycamore Creek are included in the Prescott National Forest, while those to the east fall under the jurisdiction of the Coconino National Forest. Turning left at the Sycamore Basin Trail junction leads you several miles south toward the mouth of the canyon. Turning right at this junction, however, leads you upstream along the west side of Sycamore Creek for 3 miles to Taylor Cabin. A national historic site, Taylor Cabin was built in the early 1930s as a line camp for cowboys grazing cattle in the canyon. The brands of the various ranches that have utilized the structure are carved into the front wall, while the preexisting sandstone cliff constitutes its back wall.

Although this hike turns around at Taylor Cabin, it is possible to extend the trip by several miles. Approximately 2 miles beyond Taylor Cabin, a trail junction provides a couple of options. Turn left and you will soon climb out of the canyon on the Winter Cabin Trail. This route eventually tops out on a remote part of the Mogollon Rim some 40 miles from Flagstaff. A right turn at the junction follows the Taylor Cabin Trail, which climbs 1,800 feet in 2 miles up Buck Ridge to the east. From here it is possible to return to Sycamore Pass by following a rugged power line road for 7 miles over Casner Mountain. Or, you could pick up the Mooney Trail, which follows Mooney Canyon south to Forest Road 525C.

Because finding water in the creek bed is not always a sure bet, it is best to pack in all you will need. The summer months can be hot, while the dead of winter may prove to be uncomfortably cold in Sycamore Canyon. Watch for rattlesnakes in this remote wilderness. While the hike to Taylor Cabin and back can be completed in 2 days, an added day will allow for further exploration of this beautiful wilderness area.

A canyon vista along the trail to Taylor Cabin

38 PARSONS SPRING

Distance: 7.4 miles round trip
Difficulty: easy
Hiking time: 4 hours
Elevation: 3,600 to 3,800 feet
Management: Coconino NF,
Prescott NF

Wilderness status: Sycamore
Canyon WA
Season: year-round
USGS maps: Sycamore Basin,
Clarkdale

At 55,937 acres, the Sycamore Canyon Wilderness Area can be a daunting place to explore. That is because many of its finer areas can be reached only after hiking long distances, usually with overnight gear in tow. But heading upstream from the canyon's mouth for nearly 4 miles is the Parsons Trail. Accessing one of the finest riparian areas in the state, this route offers day hikers a golden opportunity to get to know Sycamore Canyon.

Drive Alternate US Highway 89 north from Cottonwood to the turn-off for Tuzigoot National Monument. Turn right toward the monument and take the first left past the bridge. Following the east bank of the Verde River, this good gravel road becomes Forest Road 131 at the Coconino National Forest boundary, 4 miles from the bridge. Continue on this route for another 6.5 miles to the developed trailhead.

Dropping 200 feet in the first 0.1 mile, the Parsons Trail levels off once it reaches the creek bed below. It then remains level as it follows the canyon bottom for the rest of the way. Featuring a perennial flow of water, the first 4 miles of the canyon includes a wonderful collection of deciduous trees: sycamores, cottonwoods, and Arizona walnuts, to name a few. Wild grape and poison ivy add to this junglelike environment. Fed by several springs, the creek forms pools all along the way, providing dazzling reflections of the verdant canopy above and

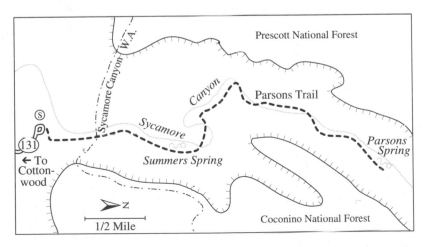

suitable habitat for great blue herons and river otters.

After 1.1 miles, the Parsons Trail reaches Summers Spring, the first of two signed trailside seeps. Although this steady flow of groundwater comes from under the rocks on the right bank of the stream, it should be treated if you plan to drink it because of the proximity of the trail. Shortly past Summers Spring, the trail makes the first of several crossings over Sycamore Creek. A second crossing follows in less than 0.2 mile. Marked by cairns on either bank, these crossings are easy during normal runoff.

Beyond the second crossing, the route becomes less distinct thanks to severe flooding in 1980. A trail of sorts follows close to the right canyon wall for a little over a mile before crossing to the west bank of the creek. After a short while, the route crosses back to the right and continues for another 0.75 mile or so to Parsons Spring. Although grade changes are nonexistent along the canyon bottom, this route does require some boulder-hopping and route-finding skills.

Identified by an old sign, Parsons Spring is an unimpressive pool of still water that marks the end of the trail and the turnaround point for this hike. It is possible to continue beyond the spring, but the perennial stream ends a short way beyond. In addition, the going can be rough thanks to thick growth and many large boulders. In order to protect this fragile riparian environment, camping is prohibited below Parsons Spring. Suitable sites can be found a short way upstream, however.

All water along the Parsons Spring Trail should be treated before drinking. Be aware that flash flooding can occur during the summer months.

Reflections along the hike to Parsons Spring

39 WET BEAVER CREEK

Distance: 6 miles
Difficulty: easy
Hiking time: 3 hours
Elevation: 3,820 to 4,100 feet
Management: Coconino NF

Wilderness status: Wet Beaver
Creek WA
Season: year-round
USGS map: Casner Butte

Slicing deep into the Mogollon Rim, Wet Beaver Creek is a welcome reprieve in this otherwise arid desert terrain. With deep pools of clear water and lush riparian growth, the canyon's oasislike ambience is a real treat for hikers.

This hike enters the mouth of Wet Beaver Creek Canyon via the Bell Trail. To find the trailhead, turn off Interstate 17 at the Sedona exit and drive 2 miles southeast on Forest Road 618. Turn left on Forest Road 618A (follow the sign for the trailhead) and continue another 0.25 mile to the parking area.

For the first 2 miles the Bell Trail follows an old road that is closed to most motorized traffic (government maintenance crews do occasionally drive the road) but open to mountain bicycles. It crosses arid terrain that is characterized by juniper, prickly pear cactus, and sparse grasses. These sections may be quite hot in the summer months.

About 1.5 miles from the trailhead, the White Mesa Trail branches off to the north. In another 0.25 mile, the Apache Maid Trail also heads north to climb a mesa. Keep right at both of these junctions. The road ends soon at the wilderness boundary, where a trail register and a bicycle rack are provided. Here a third trail junction is encountered. The right-hand route is the Wier Trail, which parallels the creek upstream for another 0.5 mile. To stay on the Bell Trail, keep left.

From this point, the Bell Trail climbs for a short distance to gain a narrow bench that runs along the canyon's north wall. From here it is

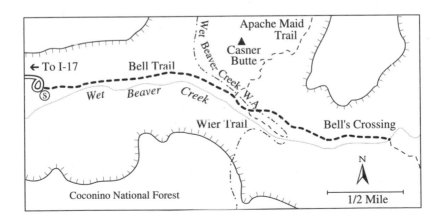

Along Wet Beaver Creek near Bell Crossing

easy to see why the trail was located above the thick tangle of cotton-wood, alder, ash, and sycamore that grow in the canyon bottom below. This vantage point also provides a good look at the geology of the canyon. Topping cliffs of the Supai Formation, Kaibab Limestone, Toro-weap Sandstone, and Coconino Sandstone is a layer of dark volcanic rock. Characterizing much of the Mogollon Rim, this basalt was deposited more than a million years ago during volcanic eruptions to the north. The canyon reaches a depth of about 1,000 feet in this lower end.

Approximately 3 miles from the trailhead, the Bell Trail drops back down to the canyon bottom where it fords the creek at Bell's Crossing. The trail and stream crossing are named after Charles Bell, a local rancher who constructed the route in 1932. From the crossing the Bell Trail climbs for 1.5 miles to the south rim, where it then continues for another 6.5 miles to Forest Road 214.

Because the canyon bottom is pleasant and shady, this hike turns around at Bell's Crossing, but be sure to venture less than 0.25 mile upstream to a series of fine swimming holes. With deep, crystal-clear pools and several rock ledges from which to dive, this destination offers a great way to cool off after trekking through the desert below. Although it is possible to continue upstream from this point, the going is very slow thanks to thick growth, boulder chokes, and pools that require swimming.

Because water is not readily available until you reach Bell's Crossing, it is a good idea to bring your own. The creek water should be treated before drinking. Watch for rattlesnakes along the entire hike and poison ivy in the canyon bottom. Keep in mind that it can be quite hot—above 100 degrees Fahrenheit—in the summer months.

40 WEST CLEAR CREEK

Distance: 11 miles round trip
Difficulty: easy
Hiking time: 6 hours
Elevation: 3,700 to 4,100 feet
Management: Coconino NF

Wilderness status: West Clear
Creek WA
Season: year-round
USGS maps: Walker Mountain,
Buckhorn Mountain

Extending east for 30 sinuous miles from the Camp Verde area, West Clear Creek is the longest drainage on the Mogollon Rim. Nearly 2,000 feet deep in places, this canyon system is a real delight to explore, for it features not only rugged beauty but also an interesting ar-

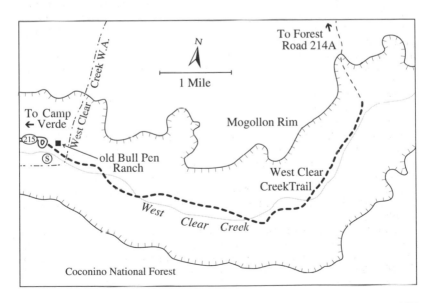

ray of flora and fauna. A good introduction to this spectacular drainage is the West Clear Creek Trail, which extends upstream from the canyon's mouth.

From Camp Verde, drive 6 miles southeast on the General Crook Trail (a good paved road) to the turnoff for Forest Road 618. Turn north and drive 2.2 miles to the signed turnoff for the Bull Pen area. Turn right onto Forest Road 215 and continue 3.2 miles to its end. Forest Road 215 is rough in places, but it is passable to carefully driven cars when dry. Do not attempt the drive after a rain. The West Clear Creek Trail begins at the Bull Pen dispersed camping area, on the eastern side of the Verde Valley.

Until recently, the West Clear Creek Trail began by traversing nearly 2 miles across desert foothills well north of the creek. This detour was necessary to avoid private land below. Fortunately, the Forest Service has since acquired the ranch and the trail now follows the level canyon bottom along an old road. An interesting rock cabin with cactus growing on the roof is passed along the way. Shaving nearly a mile off the hike, this approach allows for quicker access to the more interesting parts of the canyon.

After reaching the far end of the old Bull Pen Ranch, the trail follows the left stream bank rather closely to provide a fine introduction to the lush forest that grows along this perennial creek. Sycamore enjoy the greatest numbers, but cottonwood, Arizona walnut, and ash trees are also prevalent. The first of many deep pools is reached in a short time. Ideal for swimming on a hot summer's day, these pools also provide habitat for a thriving trout population.

About 1.25 miles from the trailhead, the West Clear Creek Trail makes the first of four stream crossings. Cairns mark either side of each crossing to make route finding easier. Under normal runoff conditions these crossings should not be a problem, and they may even be completed without getting your feet wet if you are good at boulder hopping. During times of snowmelt or after heavy rains, however, they may be dangerous, if not impossible.

A second crossing not far from the first returns the trail to the north bank. From here the route gains a slightly elevated bench where it distances itself from the creek by a few hundred yards. Although still within earshot of the creek, the trail now passes through a plant community that is remarkably different from the leafy growth found along the creek bed. A true desert environment of scattered juniper and mesquite brush typifies this arid topography. Prickly pear cactus are plentiful, as are a number of grasses. Because of the canyon's great diversity, a wide variety of wildlife is found here. Javelinas, ringtail cats, coyotes, mountain lions, deer, black bears, and elk are included in this lengthy list, as are bald eagles, red-tailed hawks, and a variety of songbirds.

From this open desert terrain it is possible to get a good look at the geology of the lower West Clear Creek Canyon. For the most part, these canyon slopes consist of the same volcanic rock that caps much of the Mogollon Rim, although this deposit of dark basaltic rock is much thicker here than in other areas. In addition, a face of the vermilion-

Ocotillo growing along the West Clear Creek Trail

tinted Supai Formation is exposed near the first two stream crossings.

About 2 miles from the trailhead, the West Clear Creek Trail makes its third stream crossing. It then follows along the south bank for another 2.5 miles before reaching the last ford. From this point the trail continues for another mile before turning up a side canyon that extends north from the creek. Although this hike turns around here, the West Clear Creek Trail does continue up the draw to climb nearly 1,800 feet in 2 miles. Gaining the Mogollon Rim above, the route ends at a trailhead on Forest Road 214A. It is then possible to return to the Bull Pen trailhead by hiking this road for 1.3 miles to the upper end of the 2.5-mile Blodgett Basin Trail.

Another option is to continue upstream from where the West Clear Creek Trail turns north. Although no established trail exists beyond this point, it is possible to follow the canyon bottom for several miles with a lot of boulder hopping and wading or swimming many deep pools. A portable raft or inner tube is needed to float your pack across these pools, and the trip would have to be made during the warmer months of the year. A shuttle would be necessary, as well. The rewards of such an adventure, though, are many. As the canyon climbs toward its headwaters, ponderosa pine and Douglas fir grow among the canyon's upper reaches and sheer walls of Coconino Sandstone become much more prevalent as the drainage narrows.

Cool, clear water is available all along this hike, but it should be treated first. Watch for flash floods during the rainy months of July and August. To complete the hike from Bull Pen to where the West Clear Creek Trail climbs north, plan on a minimum of 3 hours. If you continue upstream be prepared spend up to several days longer.

41 FOSSIL SPRINGS

Distance: 7.5 miles round trip
Difficulty: easy
Hiking time: 4 hours
Elevation: 3,800 to 4,240 feet
Management: Coconino NF

Wilderness status: Fossil
   Springs WA
Season: year-round
USGS map: Strawberry

Given both its geology and human history, the Fossil Springs Wilderness is one of the more interesting places along the Mogollon Rim. Thanks to the wilderness area's namesake—a series of natural gushers—the Fossil Creek drainage includes a wonderful riparian plant community and a turn-of-the-century flume, an engineering marvel that is still in use today. Three trails access Fossil Springs; this hike follows the Flume Road Trail because of its historical features.

The start of the Flume Road Trail is best reached from the small town of Strawberry, which is just below the Mogollon Rim on State Highway 87. Turn west at the community's only intersection and drive 9.7 miles on Forest Road 708. A good gravel road, this route switchbacks down a steep incline for the last few miles. The signed trailhead is on the right just before the Irving Power Plant.

From the trailhead the route immediately crosses Fossil Creek, then passes through a gate in a fence that parallels the creek a short distance above. If you have difficulty locating the trail on the north side of the creek, scramble up a dry cascade of brown mineral-encrusted rocks for a short way to the fence.

Beyond the fence the trail begins a very steep, 0.25-mile ascent up the north side of the canyon. Climbing some 400 feet, this first segment may raise questions about the "easy" rating of this hike. Once you reach the Flume Road, however, the rest of the way to Fossil Springs follows a mostly level grade. Paralleling within a few feet of

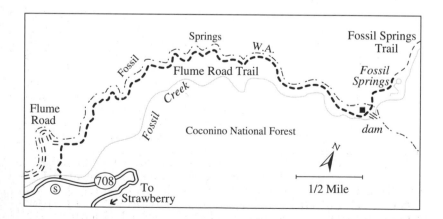

the old flume in most places, this hike offers an up-close look at this unique structure. Built in 1916, the flume is now listed on the National Register of Historic Places. Despite its historic status, however, it still channels water to the Irving Power Plant. The flume is covered for its entire length and signs periodically warn hikers to keep off for safety and maintenance concerns.

While the flume itself is a source of interest, so too are the many views afforded along the high route that it takes. Looking downstream, Fossil Creek Canyon frames the rugged Verde River Canyon to the west. Precipitous Deadman Mesa rises to the south. Following the creek directly below is a verdant ribbon of deciduous trees. And growing among the hillsides immediately above and below the trail are pinyon pine, juniper, and various species of oak. An occasional century plant and plenty of prickly pear cactus are found here as well.

Upon reaching the old concrete dam that feeds water into the flume, the trail passes to the right of a small building before continuing upstream to the springs. Just beyond the structure the route enters the Fossil Springs Wilderness, the boundary of which parallels the north side of the flume. Within 0.25 mile of entering the wilderness the trail reaches the springs.

Actually a series of several springs that surface along the left bank of the creek, Fossil Springs produces over a million gallons of heavily mineralized water per hour. Because the water is a constant 72 degrees Fahrenheit, the area immediately downstream is incredibly rich in flora and fauna. Some thirty different species of trees and shrubs

A historic flume runs the length of the Flume Road Trail.

have been identified here, including sycamore, cottonwood, Arizona walnut, and alder. Undergrowth includes wild blackberries, columbines, and a signed patch of highly poisonous hemlock. Among the species of fish found in the deep, wide pools directly below Fossil Springs is the round-tailed chub. A hundred different species of birds have been spotted in the area. Wildlife found throughout the wilderness area includes both white-tailed and mule deer, javelina, mountain lion, coyote, badger, ringtail cat, and black bear. Although there are fossils in a nearby face of Redwall Limestone—the same Redwall Limestone that is found in the Grand Canyon—Fossil Springs got its name from the way minerals in the water are deposited on rocks in the streambed.

Upstream from the springs, Fossil Creek is little more than a trickle during times of normal runoff. Although this hike turns back at the springs, the Fossil Springs Trail continues a short distance upstream to a crossing. From there it climbs out of the canyon to a trailhead on the south rim, 5 miles west of Strawberry on Forest Road 708. Dropping into the canyon from the north rim is the 3.1-mile Mail Trail. Following part of the old mail route between Camp Verde and Payson, this trail is reached from the paved General Crook Trail.

While water is available at Fossil Springs, it is best to bring your own because of the mineral content. Plan on 4 hours to complete this hike, longer if you extend your explorations beyond the springs.

WOODCHUTE MOUNTAIN

Distance: 6 miles round trip
Difficulty: easy
Hiking time: 3 hours
Elevation: 7,100 to 7,700 feet
Management: Prescott NF

Wilderness status: Woodchute WA
Season: April to November
USGS maps: Hickey Mountain, Munds Draw

Small and often overlooked, the Woodchute Wilderness offers uncrowded hiking along with some spectacular vistas. Reaching the top of

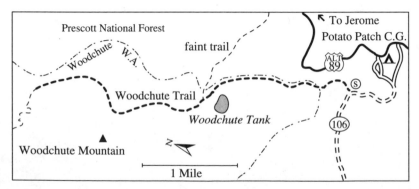

The views are far-reaching from Woodchute Mountain.

Woodchute Mountain, the easy Woodchute Trail provides the best access to the area.

Drive 8 miles south from Jerome on Alternate US Highway 89. Upon topping the mountain, turn right at the sign for the Potato Patch Campground and continue 0.3 mile to Forest Road 106, the first left. Follow this route for 1 mile to the signed trailhead. This road is passable only to 4WD and high-clearance 2WD vehicles. A new trailhead was recently constructed a short distance up Forest Road 106. Although the Prescott National Forest has plans to extend the Woodchute Trail to this point, users of this new facility should simply follow the road to the old trailhead.

Within the first 0.25 mile the trail climbs gently through a ponderosa pine forest before breaking out onto a ridge that runs north toward Woodchute Mountain. For the next mile, this mostly level stretch provides spectacular views of the Verde Valley, Sedona area, Mogollon Rim, and San Francisco Peaks to the right, and the Prescott area to the left. Vegetation consists mostly of ponderosa and pinyon pine, alligator juniper, and shrub live oak.

After 1.25 miles the route drops moderately before reaching a broad saddle directly south of Woodchute Mountain. A faint trail approaches from the right, but the main trail continues left before reaching Woodchute Tank a short distance farther. Surrounded by an open grassy meadow, this area is a good place to spot both deer and elk. From the tank the trail begins a 400-foot climb to the south rim of Woodchute Mountain. Making this ascent in 0.5 mile, the grade is easy to moderate in difficulty.

Upon reaching the mostly level mountaintop the trail continues for a mile before reaching the north end of Woodchute Mountain. The last 0.3 mile crosses a beautiful meadow area. At the north rim of the mountain an awesome view opens up beyond. Again, the San Francisco Peaks, Mogollon Rim, and Sedona's red rock country are visible. But so too are the upper Verde River, Sycamore Canyon, Bill Williams Mountain, and the more distant Kendrick Mountain. This hike turns around here, but beyond this point the Woodchute Trail continues for another 3 miles as it drops to a forest road that runs along the wilderness boundary.

Potable water is not available along the Woodchute Trail, so bring a quart or two. Watch for lightning during summer showers.

43 GRANITE MOUNTAIN

Distance: 7.6 miles round trip
Difficulty: moderate
Hiking time: 5 hours
Elevation: 5,600 to 7,185 feet
Management: Prescott NF

Wilderness status: Granite
**   Mountain WA**
Season: April to November
USGS maps: Iron Springs,
**   Jerome Canyon**

Among the more interesting geological features of the Prescott area are the exposed boulders and buttresses of Precambrian granite. Well rounded by erosion, this pinkish rock is often rendered all the more colorful by lichen. While most visitors to Prescott may enjoy the unusual formations of the Granite Dells area just north of town, hikers will find

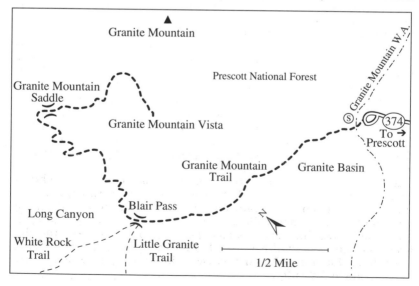

An old alligator juniper along the Granite Mountain Trail

a whole mountain of this fascinating rock in the Granite Mountain Wilderness to the northwest. The premier hike in this wilderness follows the Granite Mountain Trail up its namesake peak.

Drive 3 miles west from Prescott on the Iron Springs Road. At a sign for the Granite Basin area, turn north onto Forest Road 374 and drive 4 miles to the end of this partially paved road. Signs for the trailhead indicate the way at two intersections within the last mile of the drive. The Granite Mountain Trail begins near Granite Basin Lake at the foot of the mountain.

From the trailhead it is easy to see why Granite Mountain is popular among rock climbers. Soaring cliffs fortify much of the mountain's south face. These sheer walls are also ideal nesting grounds for peregrine falcons. While the Forest Service closes off the cliff areas from February to July, these restrictions do not apply to trail use.

Following a shallow drainage bottom for the first mile, the Granite Mountain Trail ascends along an easy grade among pinyon pine, alligator juniper, manzanita, a variety of oaks, and scattered ponderosa pine. The edge of a large burn area is also encountered. The trail climbs about 400 feet in 1.25 miles to reach Blair Pass, a low saddle that lies between Granite Basin and Long Canyon to the north. From the pass two other trails take off in different directions: the Little Granite Trail heads south toward Little Granite Mountain, while the White Rock Trail crosses over into Long Canyon. The Granite Mountain Trail, however, turns right to climb northeast toward Granite Mountain Saddle.

In the next 1.3 miles from Blair Pass to Granite Mountain Saddle, the route climbs a mostly moderate grade through several switchbacks. Trail conditions include loose rocks in places. Be sure to note a change in vegetation along this stretch of the hike. The pinyon pine and juniper that grow below have thinned out to make way for a tangled mix of manzanita, mountain mahogany, and shrub live oak. This plant community reflects the drier conditions found along this sunny, south-facing terrain. Partway up the mountain, you get an up-close look at the granite of Granite Mountain. Nearly 2 billion years old, these boulders have weathered into beautiful shapes and textures.

Upon reaching the Granite Mountain Saddle, the trail turns right and climbs a bit farther among nice stands of ponderosa pines. The route then levels off and begins winding toward the mountain's southern edge. Approximately 1.5 miles long, this last stretch of the trail dips in and out of shallow washes before reaching the Granite Mountain Vista. Several nice campsites are passed and the actual summit (elevation 7,626 feet) of Granite Mountain is visible to the east. Situated on a high point above the trailhead area, the vista takes in not only Granite Basin Lake directly below, but also the Granite Dells, Prescott, and the Bradshaw Mountains beyond. Interestingly, a few scraggly aspen grow among boulders near the vista.

No drinking water is found along the Granite Mountain Trail. Watch for lightning in the higher, exposed terrain.

44 GROOM CREEK LOOP

Distance: 9 miles round trip
Difficulty: moderate
Hiking time: 5 hours
Elevation: 6,400 to 7,693 feet

Management: Prescott NF
Wilderness status: none
Season: May to October
USGS map: Groom Creek

Circling through the gently rising mountains south of Prescott, the Groom Creek Loop Trail offers both a memorable hike among beautiful stands of timber and the promise of expansive views from the top of Spruce Mountain.

Drive a few blocks east on Gurley Street from downtown Prescott to South Mount Vernon Street. Turn right and follow the road 6.7 miles to the developed trailhead on the left. Upon leaving Prescott, Mount Vernon Street becomes Forest Road 52, locally known as the Senator Highway.

Following the loop clockwise, the hike begins by turning left at the trailhead. It then parallels Forest Road 52 for about 0.25 mile. Upon crossing a secondary road, the trail turns east to begin the 1,200-foot climb up Spruce Mountain. Following a gentle ridge to the top, this 3-mile ascent is mostly easy, although a few stretches are moderately difficult. Because the route is popular among mountain bicyclists and equestrians alike, it is well maintained and easy to follow. Additionally, it sticks mostly to shaded forest areas. For the first couple of

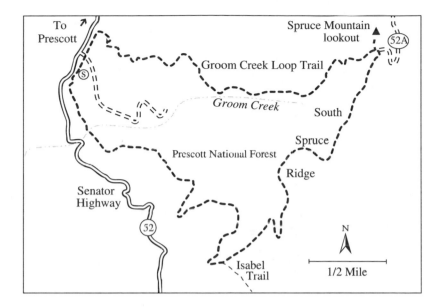

miles this timberland features ponderosa pine with some oaks and alligator juniper mixed in. As the trail nears the upper reaches of Spruce Mountain, however, fir become more common. In fact, the "spruce" of Spruce Mountain are actually white fir; the misnomer was common among early settlers throughout the West. Along the climb to Spruce Mountain two intersecting routes are encountered, but the Groom Creek Loop is clearly signed.

On top of 7,693-foot Spruce Mountain you will find a dirt road (Forest Road 52A) that also climbs the peak. A few picnic tables are scattered about under the trees and a small fire lookout sits atop a knoll that is the actual summit. From this high point the view to the north takes in Prescott, Granite Mountain, Mingus Mountain, the Mogollon Rim, and the San Francisco Peaks. Toward the east is the Verde Valley, and the forested ridges marching southward eventually give way to the more rugged Bradshaw Mountains.

At the summit the Groom Creek Loop continues to the right to follow South Spruce Ridge. Descending easily among a mix of ponderosa pine and fir, the route eventually intersects the Isabel Trail, which drops for 1 mile to the old mining area of Potato Patch and Forest Road 197. Shortly after this trail junction, the Groom Creek Loop begins dropping a bit more steeply. As the route winds around to south-facing slopes, it enters more arid stands of ponderosa pine and Gambel oak.

After crossing a small ravine, the trail keeps left and for the most part levels off for the rest of the way. Within this last 1.5 miles, several old mining roads and trails are crossed. While the Groom Creek Loop is marked with small signs (TRAIL 307) at most of these intersections, a few may not be signed. At these junctions look for blaze marks on the trees. For the last 0.25 mile the Groom Creek Loop again parallels

The fire lookout on top of Spruce Mountain

Forest Road 52 as it heads north to the trailhead.

Although water is sometimes available at the lookout during the fire season, it is best to bring all that you will need. Lightning may pose a threat on top of Spruce Mountain, especially in the summertime.

45   PINE MOUNTAIN

Distance: 9.6 miles round trip
Difficulty: moderate
Hiking time: 7 hours
Elevation: 5,100 to 6,814 feet
Management: Prescott NF

Wilderness status: Pine Moun-
**   tain WA**
Season: year-round
USGS map: Tule Mesa

As one of Arizona's lesser-known wilderness areas, the Pine Mountain Wilderness offers fine hiking without the crowds. A nice loop hike through the heart of this parcel takes in a section of the Verde Rim as well as Pine Mountain itself. As one might expect, the views are superb along many sections of this hike. And nice stands of the mountain's namesake, the ponderosa pine, are featured all along the way.

Drive 5 miles north of Cordes Junction on Interstate 17 to the Dugas exit. Turn east and follow the Dugas Road (Forest Road 68) 19 miles to the road's end. The last 8 miles of the drive may require a high-clearance 2WD vehicle. Parking is available in the Salt Flat dispersed camping area.

From the Salt Flat trailhead, this route follows the Nelson Trail up the usually dry Sycamore Creek drainage. Within 0.5 mile of the start the trail reaches Nelson Place, an abandoned homestead that includes some dilapidated stone walls. Shortly beyond, the Nelson Trail passes the mouth of Beehouse Canyon, which branches to the south. The very faint Pine Flat Trail turns right here to climb steeply up this side drainage. Continue following the main canyon upstream, however, to the vicinity of Willow Spring, 2.7 miles from the trailhead. Just before the springs, the Willow Spring Trail continues straight while the Nelson Trail turns south to climb out of the drainage. Stay right and continue up the Nelson Trail. Whereas the first part of this hike ascends easily along the drainage bottom, this section follows a more moderate grade.

About 0.5 mile from Willow Spring, the Nelson Trail reaches the lower end of the Pine Mountain Trail at what is called the Cloverleaf Junction. Turn left at this intersection and follow the Pine Mountain Trail for 1.2 miles to where it connects with the Verde Rim Trail. Climbing moderate to occasionally steep grades, this trail gains about 700 feet in all. Some views of Pine Mountain open up along this trail and a large burn area that resulted from a 1989 fire is encountered. Caution should be used in the burn area due to falling snags.

Upon reaching the Verde Rim Trail, turn left and follow this route north for 0.9 mile. Near the midpoint of this section of the hike a short but steep side trail leads to 6,814-foot Pine Mountain, the high point of the wilderness. Views from the summit, as well as from most of the Verde Rim, take in the rugged Verde River Canyon and the Mazatzal Mountains farther to the east. While the river itself is hidden from

A sign greets hikers to the Pine Mountain Wilderness.

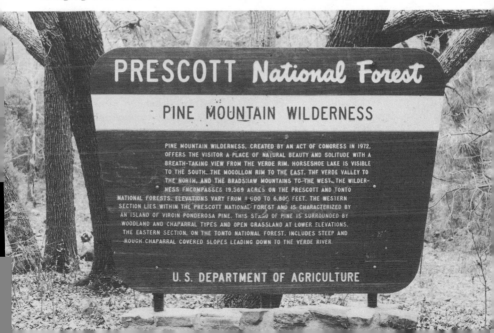

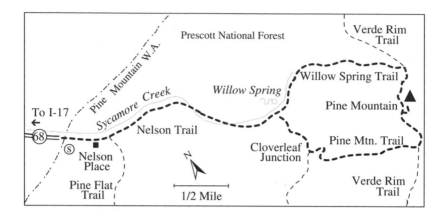

view, you can look far to the south to see Horseshoe Lake north of Phoenix. Vegetation along this section of the hike includes a variety of oaks, alligator juniper, and mountain mahogany.

Within the 0.5 mile following the Pine Mountain turnoff, the Verde Rim Trail descends some steep switchbacks before reaching a saddle at the head of Sycamore Creek. Here a left turn onto the Willow Spring Trail leads 1.6 miles to Willow Spring and the Nelson Trail. The trailhead is another 2.7 miles farther.

Because springs along this hike cannot always be counted on, it is best to bring all the water you will need. Summer days may be too hot for comfortable hiking, while winter rains may make trailhead access difficult. Watch for lightning along the higher portions of this hike.

46 HORTON CREEK

Distance: 9.4 miles round trip
Difficulty: strenuous
Hiking time: 7 hours
Elevation: 5,360 to 6,700 feet

Management: Tonto NF
Wilderness status: none
Season: May to November
USGS map: Promontory Butte

Over 50 miles long, the Highline Trail offers a lengthy route for those interested in exploring the Mogollon Rim. Running just below the rim itself, this national recreation trail accesses some of Arizona's most scenic backcountry. For a memorable day hike along this route, take a loop that follows the Horton Creek Trail to Horton Springs, continues south on the Highline for a few miles, and then returns to the trailhead via the Derrick Trail.

Drive 37 miles west from Heber (or 17 miles east from Payson) on State Highway 260. Turn north onto the Tonto Creek Road (Forest Road 289) and drive 1 mile to the Upper Tonto Creek Campground.

Although the trailhead is located in the campground, the only parking available is in the Horton Creek Picnic Site just across the bridge.

Historically speaking, the Highline Trail was established in the late nineteenth century as a connecting route between several homesteads below the Mogollon Rim. One homestead was the property of L. J. Horton, who moved to this part of Arizona in 1881 and soon settled in the drainage that borrowed his name. Building a small cattle business, Horton was running some 200 head on his ranch by 1888. Upon returning from a trip, however, he found that rustlers had stolen the entire herd, forcing him to give up ranching for good.

Today, the 4-mile-long Horton Creek Trail climbs a little over 1,000 feet along an easy to moderate grade. At the start, Horton Creek itself looks to be a dry wash, but this perennial stream actually runs beneath the ground through limestone caverns. Surfacing after the first 0.5 mile, the creek carries enough volume to support a promising population of trout. Forested along the entire route, the Horton Creek Trail

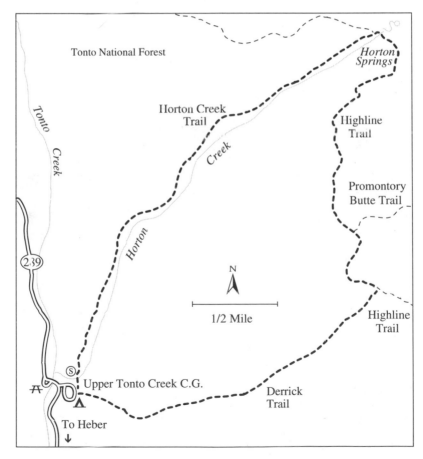

passes beneath stands of ponderosa pine and Douglas fir, and among understories of oak, alligator juniper, and maple.

Upon reaching Horton Springs, be sure to take a moment to enjoy the spring itself. Enclosed by a fence to keep livestock out, Horton Springs gushes from the hillside amid a verdant and pristine community of horsetails, mosses, maples, and giant Douglas fir.

From the springs the route turns right onto the Highline Trail and climbs steeply for a short distance to gain a ridge directly south. The trail then drops into the next drainage before climbing again for about a mile. Steep in places, this stretch has many loose rocks and is less distinct than the Horton Creek Trail. After 2.2 miles the Highline Trail reaches the start of the Promontory Butte Trail—a very challenging 0.75-mile route that climbs to the mesa top above. Less then 0.5 mile beyond this junction is the top end of the Derrick Trail, the return leg of the hike. Dropping 1,300 feet in 2.5 miles, this trail descends a moderate grade through a sunny forest of alligator juniper, manzanita, and small ponderosa pine. Watch for loose rocks here as well.

Water is plentiful along Horton Creek (surface water should be treated) and at Horton Springs. Beyond the springs there is none, however. Although the Horton Creek and Derrick trails are moderate in difficulty, parts of the Highline Trail are rugged and should be considered strenuous.

Water gushes from Horton Springs.

47 INDIAN SPRINGS

Distance: 7.5 miles round trip
Difficulty: easy
Hiking time: 4 hours
Elevation: 9,100 to 8,800 feet
Management: Apache–Sitgreaves NF

Wilderness status: none
Season: May to October
USGS map: Big Lake

Newly constructed, the Indian Springs Trail loops through the beautifully forested highlands that surround Big Lake. Because the route is designated for mountain bicyclists as well as hikers, most of the trail is graveled. This, combined with the trail's slight grade change, makes for an easy half day hike.

Drive west on State Highway 260 from Eagar to State Highway 273.

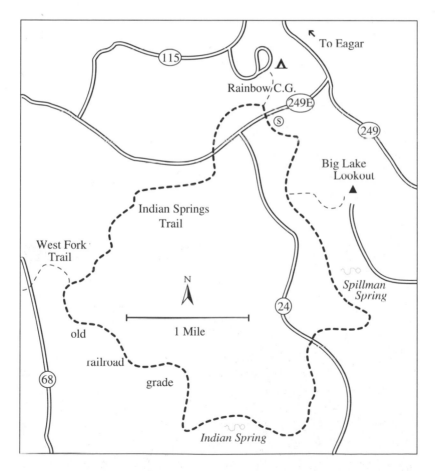

Turn south and drive 18 miles to the end of the pavement. At this point keep left and continue another 2.5 miles to Forest Road 249E. Turn right and drive 0.5 mile south to the signed trailhead.

Following the Indian Springs Trail clockwise, this hike begins by heading south into a mixed forest of ponderosa pine, Douglas fir, Engelmann spruce, Colorado blue spruce, and quaking aspen. Small meadows that occasionally break up these timbered areas add variety to the scene. About 0.5 mile from the start, the trail reaches a short side trail (0.5 mile long) to the Big Lake Lookout. This route climbs a few hundred feet, but the view from the tower is worth it. At the 1-mile mark is Spillman Spring, where old, hollowed-out logs serve as rustic troughs.

Within the next 2 miles the Indian Springs Trail crosses Forest Road 24 before reaching its namesake watering hole. Unlike Spillman Spring, Indian Springs is little more than a stock pond and it is not a suitable source of drinking water. In the vicinity of Indian Springs the trail follows a beautiful grassy meadow in which deer and elk might be spotted in the early morning hours.

About 0.5 mile past Indian Springs the trail takes up the grade of the Old Apache Railroad. Laid in the 1940s to service the area's once-booming logging industry, the tracks were pulled out during the 1970s. At the 5-mile mark is the signed turnoff for the West Fork Trail. After following the railroad grade for 2.5 miles, the Indian Springs Trail bears right onto a foot trail that ducks into the timber. In another mile the trail crosses Forest Road 249E and then climbs a bit before reaching a side trail to the Rainbow Campground. After keeping right at this junction, the route crosses Forest Road 249E again just before returning to the trailhead.

Although water is available at Spillman Spring, it is best to bring your own since livestock in the area can foul the spring. Be sure to watch for mountain bicyclists, especially on weekends.

Old troughs channel water from Spillman Spring.

48   WEST FORK BLACK RIVER

Distance: 6 miles round trip
Difficulty: easy
Hiking time: 3 hours
Elevation: 8,900 to 8,550 feet
Management: Apache–Sitgreaves NF

Wilderness status: none
Season: May to October
USGS map: Big Lake

Rising in the White Mountains, the Black River flows west across the Fort Apache and San Carlos Indian reservations before emptying into the Salt River. A remote stretch of the river is currently under consideration for Wild and Scenic River status, but an upper tributary of the drainage is easily accessed by following the West Fork Trail.

Although the Indian Springs and West Fork trails are connected, the West Fork does have its own trailhead. To reach it, drive west from Eagar on State Highway 260 to the turnoff for State Highway 273. Turn south, drive 18 miles to the end of the pavement, and then keep left. Continue for another 2.5 miles to Forest Road 249E. Turn right and drive 2.2 miles to where Forest Road 68 turns off. Follow this road for 1.3 miles to the developed trailhead.

Like the Indian Springs Trail, the West Fork Trail is graveled for much of the way to accommodate mountain bikes. With the exception of a short segment at the end, it follows a mostly level grade through mixed conifer stands. These forests include ponderosa and white pine, Engelmann and Colorado blue spruce, Douglas fir, and an occasional quaking aspen. Two natural meadows are encountered, both of which are ideal places to spot mule deer and elk in the hours around dawn and dusk. Other wildlife living in this forestland includes black bear, coyote, and an occasional mountain lion.

In approximately 2 miles the trail reaches the edge of the canyon through which the West Fork of the Black River flows. Although no more than a few hundred feet deep at this point, the canyon is picturesque

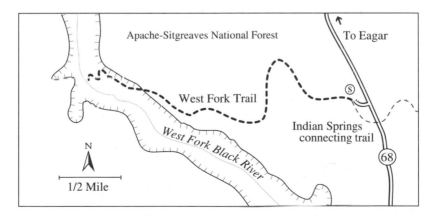

The canyon of the West Fork of the Black River

thanks to the volcanic cliffs that form the rim. After the 2.5-mile mark the trail begins to descend easily as it breaks over the canyon's rim. Only within the last 0.25 mile does it drop through a moderately steep switchback to reach the river below.

Small enough for you to hop across on rocks without getting your feet wet, the West Fork provides a good example of a montane riparian community. Although it does not contrast as much with the surrounding upland forests as lower-elevation riparian areas do to desert environments, this streamside community does include thickets of willow and alder, as well as open meadow areas. The West Fork also supports a healthy population of trout, and if you venture a short distance up the tributary opposite from the trail you will see the work of nature's most prolific engineer, the beaver.

Water from the West Fork should be treated before drinking. Watch for mountain bikes on this route.

49   MOUNT BALDY

Distance: 13.5 miles round trip
Difficulty: moderate
Hiking time: 8 hours
Elevation: 9,200 to 11,350 feet
Management: Apache–Sitgreaves NF

Wilderness status: Mount Baldy
   WA
Season: June to October
USGS map: Mount Baldy

Reaching an elevation of 11,403 feet, the summit area of Mount Baldy features a subalpine environment not typically associated with Arizona. Gnarled krummholz trees grow here, as do a variety of alpine grasses. Of course, the scenery is nice from this highest of the peaks in the White Mountains, but if your only intent is to "bag" the actual summit, you may be in for a disappointment. Because it is located just outside of the national forest on the Fort Apache Indian Reservation, access to the top is cut short by less than 0.25 mile.

Two maintained trails approach the summit; this description follows the West Fork of the Little Colorado River from the Sheep Crossing trailhead. To reach the trailhead, drive west on State Highway 260 for 3 miles from Eagar, which is just south of Springerville. Turn south on State Highway 273 and drive 18 miles to the end of the pavement. Continue west for another 7.2 miles on the graveled Highway 273. Upon crossing the West Fork of the Little Colorado River, turn left and continue 0.5 mile to the road's end. Because the Sheep Crossing trailhead was once a campground, most old maps and trail narratives list it as such. Today, however, camping is prohibited in the area.

The first 2 miles of this well-maintained trail are quite scenic, thanks in part to the Little Colorado River, which flows nearby. Benefiting from the construction of single-log dams that have created small pools, this stretch of the river is today a blue-ribbon trout stream. Adding to the natural beauty of the surrounding terrain are large grassy meadows. Ringed by Colorado blue spruce, these openings are good places to spot mule deer, elk, coyote, and other species of wildlife in the early morning hours. Grades along this segment are mostly level.

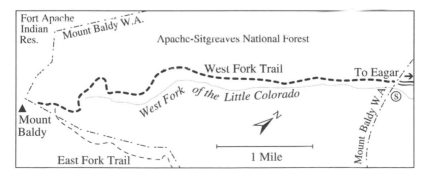

Expansive meadows along the hike to Mount Baldy

After the 2-mile mark the trail enters an old-growth forest of Engelmann spruce, cork-bark fir, and Douglas fir. By this point the route has drifted out of earshot of the river, but it does cross a couple of smaller side streams. Save for a few small meadows still to come, the trail will not break out of the timber until the final approach to the top. About 3 miles from the trailhead the route begins to climbs easily for a short distance before reaching steeper terrain. Completing nearly half of the hike's 2,100-foot climb in the next mile, this section of the trail follows a mostly moderate grade to gain a ridge to the west. Once on top of this ridge, the grade levels off some as it passes through a nearly pure stand of Engelmann spruce.

Following this high ridgeline southwest toward the summit, the route leaves the tall timber where it intersects with the top end of the East Fork Trail. A little more than 6 miles from the trailhead at this point, the route continues for another 0.5 mile before reaching the reservation boundary and the turnaround for this hike. With only a small yellow sign and a metal USGS marker denoting the boundary, it is tempting to continue up the final 0.25 mile to the top. Trespassers have had their packs confiscated, however, and it is important to respect the sovereignty of Native American lands. Although Mount Baldy is sacred to the Apache, the tribe has issued permits to allow access to the top in the past.

While the summit may be off-limits, views from the mostly open ridge just below are spectacular. Spreading west across the Fort Apache Reservation are thickly forested ridges and mountains. Mount Warren is situated just north of Baldy. Escudilla Mountain is visible to the east, while the western horizon includes the rugged Mazatzal Range. Also of note are the stunted krummholz trees that grow in this subalpine environment.

Water is plentiful along the first half of the hike but nonexistent up high. Be sure to treat all surface water before drinking. Watch for lightning in open terrain. Day hikers can expect to complete this hike in 8 hours, but it would also make for a nice overnight trip.

50 ESCUDILLA MOUNTAIN

Distance: 6 miles round trip
Difficulty: moderate
Hiking time: 4 hours
Elevation: 9,560 to 10,876 feet
Management: Apache–Sitgreaves NF

Wilderness status: Escudilla WA
Season: May to October
USGS map: Escudilla

Reaching an elevation of nearly 11,000 feet, Escudilla Mountain maintains a real presence on the skyline of the White Mountains. To early Spanish explorers Escudilla's broad top resembled a bowl, hence the name. Centuries later, the mountain greatly impressed noted naturalist Aldo Leopold during his tenure with the Forest Service in the White Mountains. In his book, *A Sand County Almanac*, Leopold states, "Life in Arizona was bounded under foot by grama grass, overhead by sky, and on the horizon by Escudilla." He goes on to elegantly describe the taking of Arizona's last grizzly on the mountain. Today Escudilla Mountain is the centerpiece of the 5,200-acre Escudilla Wilderness Area, and the main trail to the top is a National Recreation Trail.

The trailhead for the Escudilla Trail is located south of the mountain in the vicinity of Terry Flat. From Alpine drive 5.5 miles north on US Highway 191 (formerly 180/666). Turn right onto Forest Service Road 56 and continue on this good gravel road for another 4.6 miles to a junction. Keep left and drive another 0.5 mile to the developed trailhead.

Following an old road that once served the fire lookout on top, the hike up Escudilla Mountain is easy to follow the entire way. For the first mile this route climbs gently through dog-hair stands of aspen. Among these thickets you may see the charred stumps of giant Douglas firs. This area was scorched by a 23,000-acre fire in 1951. In the years since then, the natural process of succession has spurred prodigious

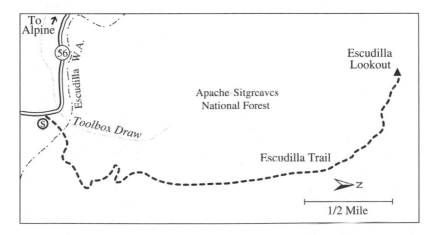

new growth of aspen. Conifers that take root in the shade of the aspen, however, will eventually crowd the deciduous trees out.

After a mile, the trail begins to steepen somewhat as it enters a large meadow that slopes across Toolbox Draw to the left. In itself quite impressive—especially in the summer when wildflowers are blooming—this expansive break in the forest allows spectacular views to the south and west. Less than 0.5 mile farther, the trail tops forested Profanity Ridge, then drops slightly through stands of Engelmann spruce and fir. In a second natural meadow a sign marks the location of the now-defunct Government Trail, which climbs up the west slope of the mountain. No longer maintained, this trail is very difficult if not impossible to follow.

Continuing north across this meadow, the Escudilla Trail soon reenters the forest and continues for another mile before reaching the Escudilla Lookout. Although it is located on a point a few feet lower than the actual summit, the lookout provides a commanding view in all

The Escudilla Lookout is Arizona's highest fire tower.

directions. To the southeast you can see into New Mexico's Gila Wilderness. Southward the panorama takes in the Blue Range and Mount Graham. Westward is Mount Baldy, and on clear days the San Francisco Peaks near Flagstaff come into view. Constructed at an elevation of 10,876 feet, this is Arizona's highest fire tower.

Because water is generally not available on this hike, be sure to bring your own. Overnight camping is permitted on all of Escudilla Mountain except for Bead Springs Meadow just north of the lookout. This is because an important water source for deer, elk, and other wildlife is located there.

51 MOONSHINE PARK

Distance: 10.3 miles round trip
Difficulty: strenuous
Hiking time: 8 hours
Elevation: 8,400 to 7,100 feet
Management: Apache–Sitgreaves NF

Wilderness status: Blue Range PA
Season: May to October
USGS maps: Hannagan Meadow, Blue, Strayhorse, Bear Mountain

Encompassing 173,000 acres of rugged terrain along the Arizona–New Mexico border, the Blue Range Primitive Area ranges from 5,000 to 9,000 feet in elevation. Within this span a variety of vegetation zones are represented. Exploring the highest reaches along the primitive area's west side is the hike to Paradise and Moonshine parks.

This hike begins at an obscure trailhead 2.9 miles north of Hannagan Meadows (or 19.6 miles south of Alpine) on US Highway 191 (formerly 180/666). From a gravel parking area on the east side of the highway, the trail crosses a small ditch before heading into the forest beyond. A trail sign for P BAR LAKE is bolted to a tree not far from the parking area.

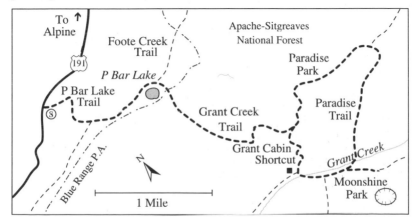

A selection of antlers at Moonshine Park

For the first 0.5 mile this hike follows the P Bar Lake Trail, which climbs up a moderate grade to gain the ridge running east of the road. After this ascent of 500 feet the route levels off before connecting with the Foote Creek Trail. Turning left at this junction the route continues for another 0.5 mile to P Bar Lake. Although little more than a glorified stock pond, this permanent watering hole is surrounded by an interesting meadow complete with old stock corrals. Look for mule deer and elk tracks in the lake's muddy edge.

At the far end of the P Bar Lake meadow, the route keeps right at a second trail junction. This is the start of the Grant Creek Trail. Continuing through a mixed forest of Engelmann spruce, Douglas fir, ponderosa pine, and quaking aspen, the route soon begins to descend—at first gently but then more severely—into more arid timberlands below. Over the span of 1 mile the Grant Creek Trail drops about 1,000 feet in all. Although it is an easy descent, keep in mind that this will make for a strenuous climb on the return trip. As the trail drops, some spectacular views of the Blue River drainage are afforded.

After keeping left at a trail junction at the bottom of this descent (about 1.25 miles from P Bar Lake), the Grant Creek Trail turns east and levels off before entering Paradise Park. Unlike most natural parks, Paradise Park features not a meadow but rather a nearly pure stand of ponderosa pine. Interestingly, the area does have the open feel of a park as the forest floor is free of undergrowth.

About 1 mile past the last trail junction (and 2.7 miles from P Bar Lake), the hike turns off the Grant Creek Trail to take up the Paradise Trail. For the next 1.7 miles this route drops gently westward toward Grant Creek along south-facing slopes. Growing here are a variety of oaks—shrub live oak, silverleaf oak, and Arizona white oak—as well as other arid-terrain trees common to the Blue Range's lower elevations. Additionally, some memorable views are afforded from various points along this segment.

Growing along Grant Creek is a leafy community of Arizona alder, box elder, and other deciduous trees. Upon crossing this small trout stream, the route reaches another trail junction, where a left turn leads to Moonshine Park. Contouring out of the creek bottom, this trail breaks out into an open ponderosa pine forest 0.5 mile past the creek crossing. The park itself is located a couple of hundred yards to the right, and because no trail leads the way, you will have to venture through the forest on your own to find it. About 10 acres in size, Moonshine Park is an inviting grassy opening surrounded by tall ponderosa pines. Suitable campsites are found at the forest edge surrounding the park. Deer and elk antlers scattered about attest to the popularity that this break in the forest enjoys with wildlife.

Upon returning to the Grant Creek crossing from Moonshine Park, follow the Upper Grant Creek Trail along the left bank of the stream for 0.4 mile to a junction just before the remains of an old ranch cabin and corral. Turn right on the Grant Cabin Shortcut and continue for 0.9 mile up several steep switchbacks to the junction with the Grant Creek Trail. Beyond this intersection the hike returns to the trailhead on the same route that it followed earlier. From the hike's low point at the Grant Creek crossing to its high point at P Bar Lake, it is a strenuous climb of 1,800 feet.

Water is always available in Grant Creek, but it should be treated before drinking. With nice camping spots in Paradise and Moonshine parks and along Grant Creek, this hike makes a nice overnight trip.

BEAR MOUNTAIN

Distance: 18.5 miles round trip
Difficulty: strenuous
Hiking time: 2 days
Elevation: 5,600 to 8,550 feet
Management: Apache–Sitgreaves NF

Wilderness status: Blue Range PA
Season: May to November
USGS maps: Blue, Bear Mountain

Although it is one of Arizona's largest tracts of unspoiled wilderness, the Blue Range Primitive Area is familiar to only a handful of hikers. This is in part due to its isolated locale in the east-central part of the state, but it may also be attributed to the fact that official wilderness designation has eluded the area for more than sixty years. The Blue, as it is often called, is the last primitive area on national forest land. Despite their official status, these highly scenic mountains offer some of Arizona's best opportunities for finding solitude. A good backpacking trip in the Blue Range Primitive Area follows Lanphier Canyon, the Mogollon Rim, and Largo Creek, accessing the Bear Mountain Lookout in the process.

Drive south from Alpine on US Highway 191 (formerly 180/666) for 14 miles. Turn left onto Forest Road 567 and continue for 12.1 miles to the Blue River and Forest Road 281. Turn right just beyond the river crossing, which may be impassable during high water, and drive 3.5 miles to Blue Camp. The signed trailhead and parking area are located on the left side of the road. Although Forest Roads 567 and 281 are maintained, these winding gravel routes may be washboarded in places.

From the trailhead the route follows an old road for a short distance as it cuts behind private land to a river crossing. Although the crossing can normally be completed by hopping across stepping stones, high water may make it difficult if not impossible. Beyond the river, the trail heads past an old corral and into the mouth of Lanphier Canyon. Shortly, it climbs out of the canyon bottom and crosses the dry east slope of the drainage. Vegetation here includes Mexican pinyon pine, alligator juniper, and various species of oaks.

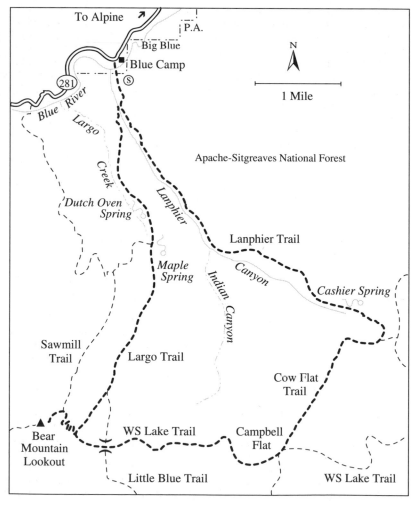

Tangled riparian growth along Lanphier Canyon

In a little more than 0.5 mile from the trailhead the route drops back to the creek where the Largo Trail comes in. As this is the return route for the hike, keep left on the Lanphier Trail. For the next 3 miles the trail remains in the canyon bottom, where an interesting riparian community of Douglas fir, Arizona walnut, box elder, bigtooth maple, ash, and wild grape is found. After 2.7 miles the Lanphier Trail encounters the mouth of Indian Creek coming in from the right. During dry periods this side stream may be the last reliable source of water for the next 12 miles.

Beyond the mouth of Indian Creek the trail continues up Lanphier Canyon for less than 0.5 mile before climbing out of the canyon's bottom along its north side. In the next mile it traverses a hilly terrace before dropping back to the canyon bottom. The forest cover along this portion of the trail ranges from a pinyon–juniper mix on the dryer slopes to ponderosa pine and white fir in the better protected areas. After following the creek for another 0.5 mile the trail crosses to the right of the stream and climbs steeply for less than a mile before reaching the Cow Flat Trail. From the trailhead to this junction, the route gains about 1,800 feet in 5.6 miles.

Keeping right on the Cow Flat Trail, the hike continues through stands of ponderosa pine for 2.2 miles to Campbell Flat, where it then turns right onto the WS Lake Trail. From this junction the route runs west for nearly 3 miles along the top of the Mogollon Rim. Dropping off rather severely to the south, the Rim forms a grand escarpment from which many expansive views are afforded. Forests here include stands of ponderosa pine and Gambel oak, plus some firs and aspens. Although

135

the trail along this section dips and climbs between 7,400 and 7,700 feet, the grades are mostly easy.

At the head of the Largo Creek drainage two trails drop north into the canyon. The first, the Little Blue Trail, crosses the WS Lake Trail 2.5 miles west of Campbell Flat. The second, the Largo Trail, branches off to the right 0.3 mile farther at a saddle situated just below Bear Mountain. Although this is the return route to the trailhead, be sure to continue on for another mile to the Bear Mountain Lookout. From the Largo Trail turnoff, the WS Lake Trail climbs steeply through a series of switchbacks before meeting the top end of the Sawmill Trail. Turn left here and continue another 0.25 mile to the summit.

The best view from the well-forested, 8,550-foot summit of Bear Mountain is from the fire tower, which is staffed in the summer. It is permissible to climb up to the observation decking to enjoy the scenery. If the facility is closed, it is still possible to take in the 360-degree panorama from the steps below. From this vantage point you can see deep into neighboring New Mexico, south to the Pinaleno Mountains, and north across the forested ridges of the White Mountains. If you decide to camp in the area, keep in mind that the nearest source of water is Bear Spring, which is 2.4 miles beyond the lookout and 1,500 feet lower.

Upon returning to the head of the Largo Trail, turn left to complete the last 5.6 miles of the hike. Dropping some 2,000 feet in all, this trail follows normally dry Largo Creek for much of the way. Two springs, Maple and Dutch Oven, do provide reliable sources of water about halfway down. About 4 miles into the drainage the trail leaves the canyon bottom to gain a ridge to the right. Crossing a small ridge, it then drops into Lanphier Canyon. From here it is 0.5 mile back to the trailhead.

Water is usually available in Lanphier Canyon and along Largo Creek, but not on top of the Mogollon Rim or Bear Mountain. As always, any surface water should be treated before consuming. Watch for lightning on the higher ridges. Although this hike can be completed in 2 days, it may be better to allow 3 days, given the rugged nature and grand beauty of the route.

53   BEAR WALLOW

Distance: 15.2 miles round trip
Difficulty: moderate
Hiking time: 10 hours
Elevation: 8,700 to 6,700 feet
Management: Apache–Sitgreaves NF

Wilderness status: Bear Wallow WA
Season: May to October
USGS maps: Baldy Hill, Hoodoo Knoll

Named for the large number of bear wallows that settlers found here in the late 1800s, the Bear Wallow Wilderness Area encompasses a pristine drainage system, complete with productive trout streams and virgin stands of timber. Running adjacent to Bear Wallow Creek, the

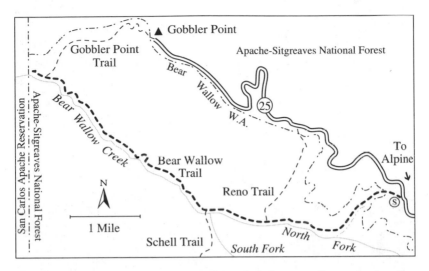

7.6-mile Bear Wallow Trail provides a handy route for exploring the length of the wilderness.

Drive 28 miles south from Alpine on US Highway 191 (formerly 180/666) to Forest Road 25. Turn west and drive another 3.1 miles to a signed trailhead on the left.

For the first 1.5 miles the trail drops south at a gentle to moderate grade along a small side drainage. Intermittent for most of the way, water eventually surfaces in this draw as it nears the perennial North Fork of Bear Wallow Creek. Along this first leg of the hike, take note of the diverse mix of trees. In addition to some rather mature ponderosa pine, these broken stands of timber include Douglas fir, Engelmann spruce, Colorado blue spruce, and quaking aspen. The Bear Wallow Wilderness boasts one of the last remaining virgin conifer forests in the state.

Upon reaching the North Fork of Bear Wallow Creek, the trail continues downstream along the right side of the creek among stands of timber and across occasional small meadows. Although the scenery is mostly restricted to the immediate forest, there is a pleasant countenance to this riparian bottomland. Alder, ash, willow, Mexican locust, bracken fern, and poison ivy are just a few of the plant species that grow along the canyon bottom. And, true to the creek's name, you may indeed stumble across places where black bears have rolled in boggy areas to cool off and escape from bothersome insects. Besides its healthy population of bears, the wilderness is also home to deer, elk, mountain lion, and wild turkey.

As the trail continues westward, it sticks close to the creek, crossing it more than a dozen times. In the quieter pools you will likely spot small schools of Apache trout, a species officially listed as threatened. Over the years the U.S. Forest Service and Arizona Fish and Game have been working to establish a healthy population of the fish in

Virgin forestlands within the Bear Wallow Wilderness

Bear Wallow Creek. In 1979 a fish barrier was built to prevent the more common rainbow trout from diluting the genetic stock. Flooding four years later opened up the barrier, allowing an influx of rainbow. The structure has since been repaired and efforts to establish the Apache trout have begun again.

About 1 mile beyond where the Bear Wallow Trail joins the North Fork, the route reaches the lower end of the Reno Trail, which climbs 1.9 miles north out of the drainage. A second side trail and the junction of the north and south forks of Bear Wallow Creek are reached 3.5 miles from the trailhead. Climbing south to the Mogollon Rim from this point, the 2.8-mile Schell Trail accesses some broad views that are absent along Bear Wallow Creek below. At mile 6.6 is the fish barrier mentioned above, and at 7.1 miles the 2.7-mile Gobbler Point Trail takes off for the north rim of the drainage.

From the Gobbler Point Trail junction, the Bear Wallow Trail runs for an additional 0.5 mile to a fence marking the boundary between the Apache–Sitgreaves National Forest and San Carlos Apache Reservation. The boundary is the turnaround point for this hike, as a permit from the tribe is needed to venture any farther.

Water is plentiful along the way, but be sure to treat it before drinking. The hike to the San Carlos Reservation boundary makes for a wonderful overnight trip, although a shorter day hike is also possible by turning back where you please.

54 SQUAW PEAK

Distance: 2.4 miles round trip
Difficulty: strenuous
Hiking time: 2 hours
Elevation: 1,400 to 2,608 feet

Management: City of Phoenix
Wilderness status: none
Season: October to May
USGS map: North Phoenix

Because Squaw Peak rises in the midst of Arizona's largest metropolitan area, the trail to the top sees extremely heavy use, especially on weekends and in the evenings. It is, however, a worthwhile hike for anyone visiting Phoenix. The views of the surrounding city are outstanding, especially at sunset.

Located in Squaw Peak Park, 9 miles northeast of downtown Phoenix, the trailhead is reached by driving north on 24th Street to Lincoln Drive. Turn left onto Lincoln and follow it to Squaw Peak Drive. Turn right here and drive 0.5 mile to the signed trailhead.

Although steep and rocky, the trail is well used and very easy to find. At the start it switchbacks north through the desert foothills of the peak. After 0.5 mile it intersects the Squaw Peak Circumference

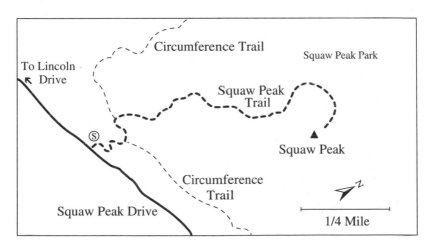

View from the Squaw Peak Trail

Trail. Nearly 4 miles long, the Circumference Trail circles the peak, accessing a variety of vistas along the way. Keeping right at this junction, the Squaw Peak Trail continues to climb northward along a moderate to strenuous ridge. The surrounding desert terrain includes impressive saguaro cactus, palo verde trees, barrel cactus, and cholla. Geologically speaking, Squaw Peak consists mostly of Precambrian schist.

Upon reaching the peak's southwest ridge the trail steepens as it continues to climb up the back face of the mountain. All along this hike it is possible to take in an ever-changing view of the city below. Although urban development virtually engulfs the peak, this panorama is nevertheless spectacular. Also of interest is the parade of city dwellers who stroll, hike, or jog up the mountain. As you approach the jagged summit, choose your footing well. Armed with a little knowledge about Phoenix and the surrounding Valley of the Sun, you can pick out a variety of distant landmarks including South Mountain, the Sierra Estrellas, the White Tank Mountains, the McDowell Mountains, and the Superstitions.

Although Squaw Peak can conceivably be hiked any time of the year, the summer months are unbearably hot. Bring plenty of drinking water and watch for lightning storms.

55 HIDDEN VALLEY

Distance: 4 miles round trip
Difficulty: easy
Hiking time: 3 hours
Elevation: 2,360 to 1,950 feet

Management: City of Phoenix
Wilderness status: none
Season: October to May
USGS map: Lone Butte

More than 16,000 acres in size, Phoenix's South Mountain Park is touted as the largest city park in the world. Included in it are 40 miles of hiking trails. One of the more interesting routes is a 2-mile stretch of the National Trail that leads to Hidden Valley. Situated high above the city, this secluded basin atop South Mountain's east end promises interesting views all around plus a wonderful selection of desert flora.

From downtown Phoenix, South Mountain Park is reached by following Central Avenue south to the park entry gate. From the gate drive 2 miles and then turn left onto the Summit Road. Turn right in another 3.4 miles and drive to the Buena Vista Lookout at road's end (6.5 miles from the gate). There is no entry fee for South Mountain Park.

From the Buena Vista Lookout, the National Trail (a National Recreation Trail that traverses South Mountain Park from end to end) skirts northeast along a ridge for the first 0.5 mile before crossing over into a shallow valley. Passing through lower Sonoran desert typical of the Phoenix area, you'll see scattered saguaro, barrel, cholla, and hedgehog cactus, as well as ocotillo and palo verde trees. Spring flowers include brittlebush, globe mallow, and Mexican golden poppy. Scenic vistas from the trail take in much of Phoenix and the Salt River Valley, as well as the Estrella Mountains to the west and the Casa Grande area to the south.

The route crosses into a second small valley 1 mile from the trailhead, and 1.5 miles into the hike a sign indicates the turnoff for Hidden Valley. Turn right at the sign to drop through Fatman Pass—a very narrow passage through some large boulders—and into Hidden

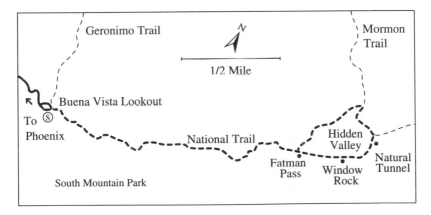

On the hike in Hidden Valley

Valley itself. Hidden Valley is a shallow and isolated drainage that parallels the main National Trail. Beyond Fatman Pass the trail follows along the wash bottom before encountering Window Rock and the Natural Tunnel—two more passageways through boulders in the streambed. At Window Rock the rocks are slippery from the wear of countless hikers.

Just beyond the Natural Tunnel, the Hidden Valley spur trail reconnects with the National Trail, which will take you back to the Buena Vista Lookout. A right turn at this intersection leads 1.5 miles to Pima Canyon in the park's eastern end.

The National Trail is popular among mountain bicyclists, so be wary of them. Water is not available along the hike to Hidden Valley, so bring plenty. Rattlesnakes are common in South Mountain Park and lightning can pose a hazard during thunderstorms. Because this hike falls within the Phoenix Mountains Preserve system, everything (rocks, plants, artifacts, and so on) is protected by law.

56 ROCK KNOB

Distance: 6 miles round trip
Difficulty: moderate
Hiking time: 3 hours
Elevation: 1,550 to 2,900 feet

Management: Maricopa County
Wilderness status: none
Season: October to May
USGS map: White Mountains

Embracing several tracts of mountainous terrain in and around Phoenix, the Maricopa County park system provides locals and visitors alike with easy access to outstanding desert wildlands. This network of county parks is one of the most extensive anywhere, and the largest of its eleven units is 26,337-acre White Tank Regional Park, with 25 miles of hiking trails. The Rock Knob Trail promises outstanding scenery and more.

Drive 15 miles west from Peoria (a northwest suburb of Phoenix) on Olive Avenue. Rising at the end of this road, the White Tank Mountains separate the Phoenix Basin from the Hassayampa Plain to the west. Follow signs to the Canyon Loop picnic area.

The hike to Rock Knob begins by following either the Waterfall Trail or the Mesquite Springs Trail, both of which have trailheads in the vicinity of the Canyon Loop picnic area. The Waterfall Trail is often crowded because it provides casual strollers with an easy hike to a secluded waterfall. It is nevertheless a good place to begin. Not only is the waterfall itself worth a visit when it is flowing, but many prehistoric petroglyphs are etched into boulders along this trail. Created by the Hohokom Indians between A.D. 500 and 1100, these fine examples of rock art provide a fascinating insight into the prehistoric past of these desert basins.

After making the very easy 1-mile hike to the waterfall, head back toward the trailhead to find a spur trail that climbs up the hillside to the north. Difficult to find, this turnoff is marked by a small rock cairn about 0.25 mile before the waterfall. Between this turnoff and the ridge top above, the trail climbs about 500 feet; it starts out as overgrown and rocky, but becomes more distinct on top. Along the ridge, the route heads west to dip in and out of rolling terrain. The surrounding desert is characterized by scattered stands of saguaro cactus, as well as cholla, ocotillo, and palo verde trees. Spring flowers include an abundance of brittlebush.

Within 1.75 miles of the trailhead the route encounters a small basin in which the Mesquite Springs and Waterfall trails connect. Marked

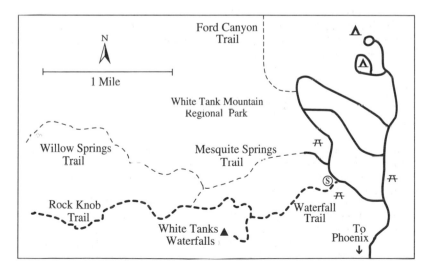

Hohokom petroglyphs along the Waterfall Trail

by signs, this junction allows for an alternate return route via the Willow Spring Trail. The walk down to the Willow Spring trailhead is about 1 mile, plus another 0.3 mile of road back to the start of the Waterfall Trail.

Continuing west from this junction is the Rock Knob Trail. After traversing another basin the route climbs steeply up the far hillside before ending at a small saddle shortly beyond. From the top the view takes in both the surrounding White Tank Mountains and the vast agricultural lands of the Phoenix area to the east. Not far to the west is a mountaintop crowded with radio towers. When you return to the Waterfall–Mesquite Springs–Rock Knob trail junction, take either the Mesquite Springs Trail or the Waterfall Trail back to the trailhead.

Do not attempt this hike in the summer, when temperatures are very high. Bring plenty of drinking water no matter what time of the year you go, and don't expect to find any shade along the route. Watch for rattlesnakes along the way.

57 WIND CAVE

Distance: 3.2 miles round trip
Difficulty: moderate
Hiking time: 2 hours
Elevation: 2,000 to 2,800 feet

Management: Maricopa County
Wilderness status: none
Season: October to May
USGS map: Apache Junction

Like White Tank Mountain Regional Park, the Usery Mountain Recreation Area is part of the Maricopa County park system. Situated at the foot of Pass Mountain on the eastern end of the Phoenix metropolitan area, the recreation area serves as a prelude to the expansive

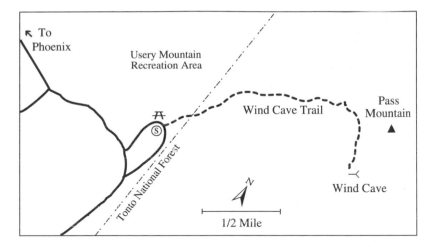

Superstition Mountains, which rise to the east. A short but excellent hike within the Usery Mountain Recreation Area is the Wind Cave Trail.

Drive 4.8 miles north on Ellsworth Road (this road turns into Usery Pass Road at McPhillips Road) from Apache Junction. An entry fee is charged for the park. Follow signs to the picnic area.

Beginning along the picnic area loop road, the Wind Cave Trail runs for 100 yards before crossing a boundary fence into the Tonto National Forest. From there it steadily ascends for the next 1.5 miles. As the route winds through lower Sonoran desert terrain typical of this part of Arizona, trailside plants include saguaro and barrel cactus, ocotillo, palo verde, creosote bush, and brittlebush. Deer, gray fox, coyote, javelina, and jackrabbits are known residents of the area, as are cactus wrens, Gambel quail, roadrunners, and Gila woodpeckers.

Cactus growing beside the Wind Cave Trail

As the trail draws closer to the cliffs that line the summit of Pass Mountain, it becomes noticeably steeper. Wind Cave, actually a shallow alcove that has been carved out mostly by wind, is visible at the base of these cliffs to the right. Composed of volcanic tuff, this rock has a yellowish tint to it. In the cave itself, faint seeps provide enough water for a few hanging plants. Wind Cave has a fantastic view of the Phoenix Valley: the White Tank Mountains, South Mountain, and the city of Phoenix itself are all visible.

Although the trail is well maintained, it is steep in places, so wear sturdy shoes. Take plenty of drinking water and do not attempt the hike in the heat of the summer. Watch for rattlesnakes.

58 RAINBOW VALLEY

Distance: 12.5 miles round trip
Difficulty: moderate
Hiking time: 7 hours
Elevation: 900 to 1,400 feet
Management: Maricopa County

Wilderness status: none
Season: October to May
USGS maps: Avondale SE,
   Avondale SW

The Estrella Mountain Regional Park is another of Maricopa County's large wilderness parks. Situated southwest of Phoenix, the Estrella Mountain unit completes the unique system of desert preserves that rings Arizona's largest metropolitan area. Designed to set aside large tracts of land for public use, the park system features extensive networks of hiking trails. One of several backcountry routes that crisscross Estrella Mountain Regional Park, the Rainbow Valley Trail offers hikers spectacular views and a nice look at the surrounding lower Sonoran desert environment. This description follows most of the lengthy Rainbow Valley Trail, along with a segment of the Pack Saddle Historical Trail.

Drive west from Phoenix on Interstate 10 to the Estrella Parkway. Turn south and continue past State Highway 85 to West Vineyard Avenue; turn left and drive east to the park entrance. Turn left just inside the park onto Casey Abbot Drive North. The start of the Rainbow Valley Trail is located at the Rodeo Arena. From the park entrance it is 1.9 miles to the trailhead.

Following the 18.7-mile Rainbow Valley Trail counterclockwise, this hike begins by heading north from the trailhead. In approximately 0.75 mile the route bends west to pass just south of the park's amphitheater and picnic areas. A number of short side trails connect the Rainbow Valley Trail with these facilities, but signs indicate the way at most intersections. Stay on the Rainbow Valley Trail, which eventually heads south into the heart of the park's backcountry. Within the first 1.5 miles of the hike the route climbs and drops a bit as it dips into washes and traverses rocky rises. The going is not too difficult, however, and the vistas include a distant view of Phoenix to the east.

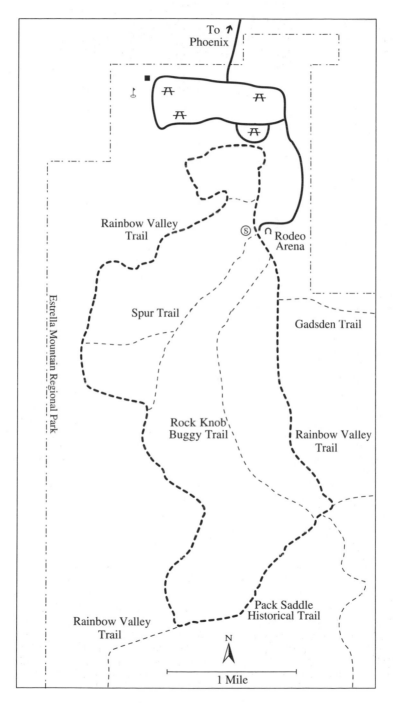

Old saguaro cactus in the Estrella Mountain Regional Park

At 1.75 miles the Rainbow Valley Trail connects with the west end of the 0.25-mile Rainbow Valley Connector Trail. The east end of this trail begins just north of the Rodeo Arena trailhead; using this short-cut will shave 1.25 miles off the hike. Beyond the Connector Trail, the Rainbow Valley Trail heads southwest for a little more than 2 miles to its next junction, with a fork of the Spur Trail. In this stretch the trail tops a number of low rises and ridges before dropping into a wash area. Upon reaching the north branch of the Spur Trail the route stays right and then ascends a small pass before reaching the main fork of the Spur Trail about 5 miles from the trailhead. It is possible to turn left on the Spur Trail and follow it 1.7 miles back to the trailhead.

Continuing south from the Spur Trail, the Rainbow Valley Trail covers another 2.5 miles before reaching the next major junction—that with the Pack Saddle Historical Trail. While the Rainbow Valley Trail continues west and then south from this point to enter the broad Rainbow Valley, this hike description turns left onto the Pack Saddle Trail to cut 6 miles of mostly flat, uneventful hiking off the trip. From this junction follow the Pack Saddle Trail northeast for 1.6 miles to where it reconnects with the Rainbow Valley Trail. Following an old jeep road, this section of the hike heads up a wash for part of the way as it cuts across the northern end of Rainbow Valley. Just before it rejoins the Rainbow Valley Trail, the Pack Saddle Trail intersects with the south end of the Rock Knob Buggy Trail.

Upon reaching the Rainbow Valley Trail turn left and continue north for 3.5 miles to return to the Rodeo Arena trailhead. Along this section the route intersects the Gadsden Trail, which loops through the northeast quarter of the park. Unlike the segment of the hike that follows the Pack Saddle Historical Trail, this final leg mostly follows a foot trail.

Water is not available along this hike, so be sure to fill your canteens before setting out. Because this route traverses very arid and mostly shadeless terrain, do not attempt it on hot days. Watch for rattlesnakes and flash flooding during heavy rainstorms.

59 CAVE CREEK

Distance: 8 miles	Wilderness status: none
Difficulty: moderate	Season: year-round
Hiking time: 5 hours	USGS maps: Humboldt Moun-
Elevation: 3,400 to 4,080 feet	tain, New River Mesa
Management: Tonto NF	

With 31 miles of backcountry trails, the Cave Creek Trail System offers a variety of hiking terrain. Located in the Tonto National Forest just north of Carefree, this network of hiking routes encounters pristine desert and riparian communities within a short distance of downtown Phoenix. A nice day hike here follows Cave Creek west from the vicinity of the Seven Springs Picnic Grounds for a few miles before returning via the desert foothills to the south.

Drive east from Carefree on the Cave Creek Road for 6 miles to the Tonto National Forest boundary. From this point continue another 12 miles on the same route, which is now Forest Road 24. This good gravel road is passable to all vehicles. The developed trailhead and parking area are just north of the Seven Springs picnic grounds and CCC campground.

This hike begins by following the Cave Creek Trail to a junction with the Skunk Tank Trail. Bordering perennial Cave Creek, this first segment of the hike is rated easy as the grade drops about 400 feet in 3 miles. Along the way the trail is easy to find because it never leaves the canyon bottom. The chief attraction is the wonderful ribbon of riparian vegetation that grows adjacent to the creek. Arizona sycamore make up the bulk of the deciduous tree species, but ash, alder, and

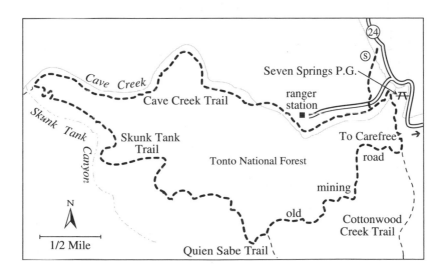

Riparian growth along Cave Creek

Arizona walnut are also represented. As is the case with most riparian areas in the state, the Cave Creek corridor is also home to a variety of birds and mammals.

At the junction of the Cave Creek and Skunk Tank trails, the hike turns left to follow the 4.8-mile Skunk Tank Trail back to the trailhead. It is possible to continue farther along the Cave Creek route. After following the stream bottom for another 2.5 miles, the trail eventually climbs away from the creek to cross the adjacent desert hills. The 10.5-mile Cave Creek Trail ends at a trailhead on the Spur Cross Road (Forest Road 48) north of the town of Cave Creek.

The most difficult section of the hike occurs shortly after you turn onto the Skunk Tank Trail. Climbing 1,000 feet in the next 1.5 miles, the trail makes several switchbacks to gain a ridge just east of the Skunk Tank drainage. As the route climbs away from Cave Creek, it leaves behind the leafy riparian community and instead encounters such lower Sonoran plants as saguaro and cholla cactus, ocotillo, palo verde trees, and a variety of desert grasses. As it approaches the Seven Springs area, the hike returns to a forest of scattered juniper trees.

Near its halfway mark, the Skunk Tank Trail connects with the north end of the 2.6-mile Quien Sabe Trail. A footpath up to this point, the Skunk Tank route now takes up an old mining road, which it follows for the rest of the way to the trailhead. Because it drops about 600 feet over the next 3 miles or so, this section of the hike is rated as easy. Upon reaching the end of the Skunk Tank Trail, turn left onto the Cottonwood Creek Trail and continue another 0.5 mile to the trailhead.

Although water is available in Cave Creek, the Forest Service advises against drinking it. It is best to pack all that you will need beforehand. Although this hike can be completed year-round, summers typically mean very hot temperatures. If you are planning a summer hike here, you may want stick to the Cave Creek Trail, where shade is a bit more prevalent.

60 PERALTA TRAIL

Distance: 4.5 miles round trip
Difficulty: moderate
Hiking time: 3 hours
Elevation: 2,400 to 3,766 feet
Management: Tonto NF

Wilderness status: Superstition WA
Season: October to May
USGS map: Weavers Needle

Few, if any, mountain ranges of the American West have stirred the imagination like the Superstitions. Rising east of Apache Junction in a great jumble of volcanic rock, these mountains have earned what geologists say is an erroneous reputation as an area rich in gold. At the center of this mistaken identity is the legend of the Lost Dutchman's Mine. And the Peralta Trail evokes that legend in no uncertain terms. Although it is one of the more heavily used trails in the state, the Peralta Trail offers an introduction to the 159,700-acre Superstition Wilderness that should not be missed.

Drive 8.5 miles southeast of Apache Junction on US Highway 60-89, and turn east at the well-marked turnoff for the Peralta trailhead. Follow this good gravel road for 8 miles to its end. Although a large parking area is provided at the trailhead, it may be necessary to use auxiliary parking nearby.

Two different trails are accessed from the Peralta trailhead. The Dutchman's Trail heads east toward Miner's Needle, while the Peralta Trail heads northwest along its namesake canyon, climbing 1,300 feet in 2.25 miles before reaching Fremont Saddle. Although easy to follow, this trail has been eroded down to bedrock in places and includes a few steep pitches.

The view to the north from Fremont Saddle is one of the most spectacular in the state, for towering 1,000 feet above a wilderness of rock is the Weavers Needle. As the most identifiable landmark within the Superstitions, this volcanic plug is indicative of the fiery origins of

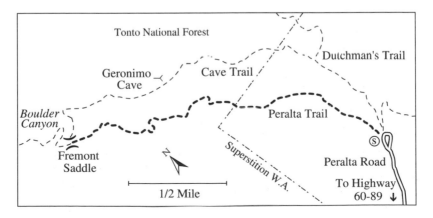

these mountains. Erupting between 15 million and 35 million years ago, five volcanoes deposited thick layers of ash across the region. Today, most of the range consists of well-weathered tuff, a rock that geologists contend does not produce much in the way of precious metals. Nevertheless, the legends persist. Don Miguel Peralta reportedly discovered a prodigious lode of gold in 1845. A few decades later, Jacob Waltz, a German immigrant whom locals called the "Dutchman," supposedly rediscovered Peralta's mine. Although Waltz never revealed the exact whereabouts of the mine, stories claim that it lies within the shadow of Weavers Needle. Since Waltz's death in 1891, the Lost Dutchman's Mine has eluded hundreds of would-be prospectors.

From Fremont Saddle the Peralta Trail drops north into Boulder Canyon for several miles before connecting with the Dutchman's Trail. Because the saddle commands the best views, however, it is a good place for day hikers to turn around. If you are prepared for a very rugged route (too rugged to be called a trail), you could return to the trailhead via the Cave Trail. Branching east from Fremont Saddle, the Cave Trail skirts along the ridge top that bounds Peralta Canyon to the east. Not maintained, this route is not only difficult to find, it is also dangerous in spots due to drop-offs and a very steep descent down smooth bedrock. While this route is strictly for parties of sure-footed adventurers (don't attempt it alone), it does provide a scenic and seldom-used alternative to the main trail. It is named for a shallow cave along the way.

Although a stream occasionally flows through Peralta Canyon, it is best to bring your own drinking water. Avoid this hike in the summer because of very hot temperatures. Watch for rattlesnakes throughout the hike and be forewarned that this trail receives exceptionally high use, especially on weekends. Plan on 3 hours to complete this hike, longer if you return on the Cave Trail.

61   BLACK MESA

Distance: 8 miles
Difficulty: easy
Hiking time: 4 hours
Elevation: 2,300 to 2,750 feet
Management: Tonto NF

Wilderness status: Superstition WA
Season: October to May
USGS map: Goldfield

Another popular trailhead in the Superstition Mountains is the First Water trailhead. From here the 18-mile Dutchman's Trail heads south toward its southern terminus at the Peralta trailhead. The Second Water Trail starts near here as well. Combining segments of these two routes with the entire length of the Black Mesa Trail makes a wonderful loop across the relatively gentle northern slope of the range.

Drive 5 miles north from Apache Junction on State Highway 88 (the Apache Trail). Turn right just past the Lost Dutchman State Park and follow Forest Road 78 for 2.6 miles. Camping is prohibited along this graded road.

To begin the hike, follow the Dutchman's Trail for 0.25 mile to the first junction. Turn right and continue southeast on the Dutchman's Trail for another 3 miles. A favorite among horse packers, the Dutchman's Trail does receive heavy use. Within 2 miles the trail climbs an easy 350 feet to Parker Pass. Expansive views are possible in all directions from this high point.

From Parker Pass the trail drops into Boulder Basin, where it connects with the southeastern end of the Black Mesa Trail. Three miles long, the Black Mesa Trail climbs about 400 feet before traversing an interesting basin on top of Black Mesa. Up to this point the desert plant life has been mostly a mix of saguaro cactus and palo verde trees, but across much of the mesa top is a thick forest of cholla cactus. Look for bird nests that are carefully nestled among the thorny branches. There's also a nice view of Weavers Needle.

After dropping off the north end of Black Mesa, the trail enters Garden Valley—a basin of scattered cholla forests, saguaro cactus, palo verde, and ocotillo. Springtime often brings colorful displays of Mexican golden poppies, brittlebush, and Indian paintbrush. The Black Mesa Trail ends at the junction with the Second Water Trail in Garden Valley. From this junction it is 1.5 miles back to the Dutchman's Trail and then another 0.25 mile to the trailhead. Crossing the First Water

The Rogers Canyon Cliff Dwellings

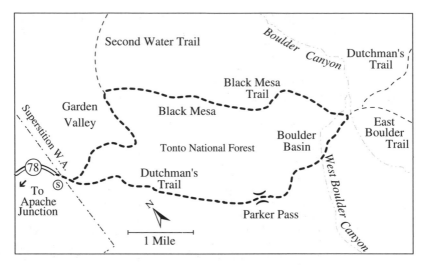

Creek drainage, this segment of the hike encounters some interesting washes and rock outcrops along the way.

Be sure to bring plenty of drinking water—this hike traverses some hot desert terrain. Avoid this hike in the summer and be wary of rattlesnakes.

62 ROGERS CANYON

Distance: 9 miles round trip
Difficulty: moderate
Hiking time: 5 hours
Elevation: 4,883 to 3,700 feet
Management: Tonto NF

Wilderness status: Superstition WA
Season: September to June
USGS map: Iron Mountain

Because access requires a 4WD vehicle, the hike into Rogers Canyon is a pleasurable alternative to the more crowded trails of the Superstitions. But the hike has other attributes, including interesting topography, a nice riparian ecosystem, and a well-preserved prehistoric cliff dwelling.

From Florence Junction drive 2 miles east on US Highway 60 to the Queen Valley Road. Turn left and drive another 2 miles to the Hewitt Station Road (Forest Road 357). Turn right here, follow this gravel road for 3 miles to Forest Road 172 (a sign points the way), turn left, and follow the road for 19 miles to Forest Road 172A. Follow this route for another 4 miles to the Rogers Trough trailhead. Although Forest Road 172 crosses several washes and is rough in spots, it is passable to high-clearance 2WDs when dry. The last 4 miles along Forest Road 172A are very steep and washed out.

Located at the head of Rogers Canyon, the Rogers Trough trailhead directly accesses the Reavis Ranch Trail. From the parking area, follow this route north as it drops easily into the Rogers Creek drainage. Within a short distance the West Pinto Trail branches off to the right; approximately 1.25 miles from the trailhead a second trail junction marks the start of the Rogers Canyon Trail. By staying right you can follow the Reavis Ranch Trail for 14 additional miles to a trailhead along the Apache Trail on the north end of the wilderness. To continue down Rogers Canyon, however, turn left and parallel the stream northward.

Unlike the lower west end of the Superstition Mountains, this corner of the range is high enough to support thick stands of Arizona white oak, Emory oak, manzanita brush, and alligator juniper. Thanks to the substantial amount of water that flows through this drainage in the winter and spring, the canyon bottom includes white-barked Arizona sycamore, Arizona walnut, and velvet ash trees. A few isolated pines also grow in the higher terrain.

About 3 miles from the trailhead (and 1.75 miles from the Reavis Ranch Trail junction) Rogers Canyon gets really interesting. Outcrops of volcanic tuff gain enough stature to become soaring cliff walls. The canyon bottom narrows and inviting pools of water alternate with noisy cascades and waterfalls. This is prime terrain for mule deer, javelina, coyote, mountain lion, and other species common to the Superstitions.

Trail signs on the Black Mesa hike

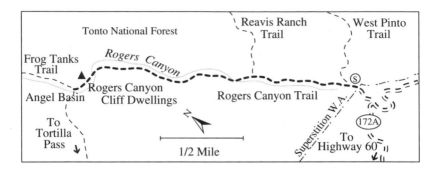

A little more than 4 miles from the trailhead, the drainage angles west and the Rogers Canyon Cliff Dwellings come into view. Tucked away in a sheltered cave, many rooms of this ruin are well preserved. Archaeologists attribute these structures to the Salado Indians, who inhabited the mountains north and east of Phoenix more than 700 years ago. Like the Anasazi, Hohokom, and other prehistoric groups of the Southwest, the Salado made pottery, grew crops, and built elaborate homes. These ruins and all associated artifacts are protected by law and should not be disturbed in any way.

Less than 0.5 mile beyond the cliff dwellings, the Rogers Canyon Trail enters Angel Basin—a meadow area where three drainages join together. The turnaround point for this hike, Angel Basin is very scenic and a great place to camp. The Frog Tanks Trail continues downstream to Fish Creek, while the Rogers Canyon Trail turns up a side drainage and climbs to Tortilla Pass. At the pass it meets the JF Trail, which is accessed by the Woodbury trailhead. Because the Woodbury trailhead can be reached by driving 2WD Forest Road 172, the JF Trail offers alternative access to lower Rogers Canyon for those without a 4WD vehicle.

Short stretches of the Rogers Canyon Trail may be hard to follow, especially where the stream has washed it out. Summers may be too hot for hiking this trail. Be sure to bring plenty of water. It is not always available in Rogers Canyon.

63 REAVIS RANCH

Distance: 20 miles round trip
Difficulty: moderate
Hiking time: 2 days
Elevation: 3,260 to 4,900 feet
Management: Tonto NF

Wilderness status: Superstition WA
Season: year-round
USGS maps: Pinyon Mountain, Iron Mountain

This nice multiday hike in the Superstitions pays a visit to the old Reavis Ranch in the eastern half of the wilderness. Quite remote and surrounded by beautiful scenery, this former homestead was the residence of Elisha Reavis for nearly twenty-five years during the late nineteenth century. Known as the "Hermit of the Superstitions," Reavis occasionally showed up in town to sell the vegetables and fruit he grew along Reavis Creek.

Drive 28 miles northeast of Apache Junction on State Highway 88. Turn right on Forest Road 212 (the Reavis Ranch Road) and drive 3 miles to the road's end and the Reavis trailhead. Portions of Forest Road 212 may require a high-clearance vehicle.

Because it follows an old road for the entire 10 miles to the ranch, the Reavis Trail is not difficult to find. For the first 3 miles or so it ascends gently along a ridge from which the scenery is excellent. Included are views of Apache Lake, Four Peaks, and the Mazatzal Wilderness Area. Trailside plant species include shrub live oak, century plants, sotol, and a variety of yuccas. Approximately 4 miles from the trailhead the route begins traversing the east face of Castle Dome (elevation 5,308 feet). Here you start to see thicker stands of pinyon pine, juniper, and taller oaks.

South of Castle Dome the Reavis Trail passes through a small saddle just prior to reaching Windy Pass. From this high point be sure to take in the view of Fish Creek Canyon, Weavers Needle, and the rest of the western portion of the Superstition Mountains. Traveling east from Windy Pass, the route encounters another saddle before dropping slightly to where it intersects the Frog Tanks Trail, 8 miles from the trailhead. Beyond, the Reavis Trail eventually bends southward to parallel Reavis Creek, which runs along the drainage bottom to the left. The trail soon encounters the west end of the Reavis Gap Trail

A sotol plant growing next to the Reavis Ranch Trail

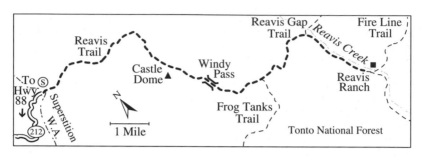

and shortly after passes an apple orchard and some antiquated farm machinery. This is Reavis Ranch.

A cabin at the ranch (not built by Reavis, but rather by cattlemen some years after his death) may serve as overnight shelter, if you so desire. There are, however, many suitable campsites nearby. While Reavis Creek typically flows only in late winter and spring, it nevertheless supports some shady groves of Arizona sycamore. Ponderosa pines are also scattered about the surrounding valley. The apples, which ripen in the fall, are a big draw for backpackers. Given the serene beauty of the surrounding landscape, it is not hard to understand why Reavis secluded himself here for all those years.

Water is only available after the winter rains—typically from February to April. At other times of the year you will need to carry your own. Summers bring high temperatures in all parts of the Superstition Mountains. Watch for rattlesnakes and be wary of lightning on exposed ridges. While this hike can be completed in 2 days, 3 days would allow for further explorations into the eastern reach of the range.

64 MAZATZAL PEAK

Distance: 17 miles
Difficulty: strenuous
Hiking time: 2 days
Elevation: 4,200 to 6,500 feet

Management: Tonto NF
Wilderness status: Mazatzal WA
Season: March to November
USGS map: Mazatzal Peak

At 205,500 acres, the Mazatzal is one of the largest wilderness areas in the state. Encompassing the Mazatzal Mountains, it ranges in elevation from 2,100 feet along the Verde River in the west to the 7,903-foot summit of Mazatzal Peak in the east. The premier, and consequently most popular, hike in this expansive parcel of pristine terrain follows the Barnhardt, Mazatzal Crest, and Y Bar Basin trails around Mazatzal Peak.

From Payson drive 14.5 miles south on State Highway 87 to the signed turnoff for the Barnhardt trailhead, along the eastern front of the range. Turn right onto Forest Road 419 and drive west for nearly 5 miles to its end. Although rocky, the road is passable to most vehicles.

Three trails take off from the trailhead; this hike begins by following the Barnhardt Trail, which starts at the west end of the parking area. Heading west up an easy but rocky grade, the Barnhardt Trail reaches the wilderness boundary within the first 0.5 mile. It then begins climbing more moderately along the precipitous south face of Barnhardt Canyon. Vegetation along this lower portion of the hike includes Arizona white and Emory oaks, two species of juniper, century plants, sotol, and nolina.

Near the 1.5-mile mark the Barnhardt Trail begins climbing up the south wall of the canyon it has been following through a series of moderate to strenuously steep switchbacks. This ascent continues as the route eventually angles west again. Side drainages along the way shelter velvet ash, Arizona walnut, sycamore, and ponderosa pine. Flowing streams are also found in some of these drainages after the rainy season.

Approximately 5 miles from the start, the Barnhardt Trail intersects the east end of the Sandy Saddle Trail. After keeping left at this junction, the route then climbs along a mostly gentle grade for another 1.2 miles before reaching Barnhardt Saddle and the Mazatzal Divide Trail. Nearly 30 miles long, this major north–south route stretches across the entire eastern end of the wilderness. Although the hike turns left here to follow the Mazatzal Divide Trail south, you may want to follow the Divide Trail to the right for about a mile to Chilson Spring. With a reliable source of water and several suitable sites, this abandoned cowboy camp is an ideal place for camping.

From Barnhardt Saddle the hike follows the Mazatzal Divide Trail south across sometimes grassy and sometimes forested west-facing

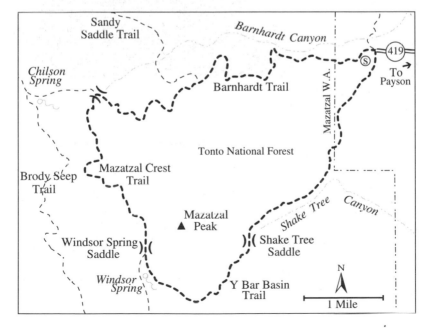

On the Barnhardt Trail

slopes. The trail may be overgrown in this section, but it is never too
difficult to follow. As with Barnhardt Saddle, the views along this section take in the western half of the Mazatzal Wilderness and the Verde
River Valley.

About 1.5 miles from Barnhardt Saddle the route reaches the turnoff
for the Brody Seep Trail. Approximately 1 mile to the west, this spring
does not flow year-round. The hike then continues south below the impressive west face of Mazatzal Peak. Consisting mostly of shale and
rhyolite, these spectacular cliffs have withstood the effects of erosion
quite well.

As the Mazatzal Divide Trail passes Mazatzal Peak, it climbs
slightly before reaching Windsor Spring Saddle. At 6,500 feet, this is

the high point of the hike. It is also 9.5 miles from the start of the hike. Vistas from the saddle take in the Tonto Basin and the Sierra Ancha Range to the east. Although Windsor Spring is intermittent at best, some suitable spots nearby make this a nice place to camp.

From Windsor Spring Saddle the Mazatzal Divide Trail continues south along the crest of the range. This hike, however, bears left onto the Y Bar Basin Trail (also known as the Shake Tree Trail). After dropping into the secluded Y Bar Basin (a reliable source of water is found here) the route turns northeast to climb about 1 mile to Shake Tree Saddle. From this point the trail descends among shady ponderosa pines into the upper end of Shake Tree Canyon. The route follows this drainage for a little over a mile, then continues to contour northeast while the canyon turns abruptly south. From here it is another 4 miles or so to the Barnhardt trailhead. From Windsor Spring Saddle, the Y Bar Basin Trail descends about 2,500 feet in 7.5 miles.

Although no water sources are 100 percent reliable along this hike, Barnhardt Creek, Chilson Spring, and Y Bar Tanks are your best bets. Check with the Forest Service before setting out and be sure to treat all surface water before drinking. Watch for lightning in the higher terrain.

$\underline{65}$ CITY CREEK

Distance: 18 miles round trip
Difficulty: strenuous
Hiking time: 2 days
Elevation: 3,400 to 6,700 feet

Management: Tonto NF
Wilderness status: Mazatzal WA
Season: March to November
USGS map: North Peak

Traversing the entire length of the eastern Mazatzal Wilderness is the Mazatzal Divide Trail. From the City Creek Trailhead west of Payson, this 29-mile route heads south to roughly parallel the City

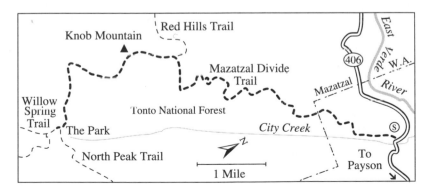

Creek drainage before crossing over into the Wet Bottom Creek Basin. Following the first 9 miles of the Mazatzal Divide Trail, this hike turns around at the head of City Creek in an area known as The Park.

To approach the City Creek trailhead from Payson, drive west on Main Street, which soon turns into the East Verde River Road (Forest Road 406). Follow the occasionally steep and often difficult dirt road (it may require a 4WD after a rain) for 11 miles to a small parking area just past a major switchback. Parking is on the right side of the road; the trail takes off to the left.

After crossing intermittent City Creek, the Mazatzal Divide Trail follows the creek bottom for the first mile or so before climbing away to the west. The grades become steeper and switchbacks become numerous as the route heads up a ravine. In addition, since the trail receives relatively little use, it is often overgrown and may be hard to follow in places. The Mazatzal Wilderness boundary is crossed a little over 1 mile from the trailhead. A small saddle that overlooks the country to the north is topped after 2.5 miles. Included in this view is the East Verde River and Polles Mesa.

Beyond this saddle, the Mazatzal Divide Trail continues to switchback up a mostly moderate grade along the divide west of City Creek Canyon. Because vegetation along this stretch includes various species of desert oaks, manzanita, mountain mahogany, and only scattered juniper trees, shade is at a premium. Upon nearing the end of this lengthy climb the trail bends westward to follow a ridge from which nice views of the City Creek drainage open up. Across the drainage is North Peak (elevation 7,449 feet), a landmark that has been visible all along the route. Less than 0.5 mile farther, the east end of the Red Hills Trail branches off to the right. Keep left at this junction and follow the Mazatzal Divide Trail south for about 1 mile to reach the high point of the hike, 6,700-foot Knob Mountain. In nearly 7 miles the route has climbed 3,300 feet.

From Knob Mountain the Mazatzal Divide Trail drops about 700 feet in 1 mile before reaching a side drainage of City Creek. It then traverses for another mile to the head of the canyon before crossing into the Wet Bottom Creek drainage. Upon doing so it enters a nicely forested area of tall ponderosa pines. Known as The Park, this is the turnaround point for the hike. Several suitable camping spots are located here and two trails that branch off in different directions allow for further explorations. The first trail is the 3.5-mile North Peak Trail, which heads east to a remote trailhead in the Rye Creek drainage. A short distance beyond this turnoff is the upper end of the 16-mile-long Willow Spring Trail, which traverses the wilderness to reach the Sheep Bridge trailhead on the Verde River. Water is sometimes available in Pete's Pond, a short distance west of The Park.

Because water is not usually found along much of this hike, be sure to pack plenty. If you plan to spend the night, check with the Forest Service first on water availability at Pete's Pond. Watch for lightning along exposed portions of this hike.

66 FOUR PEAKS

Distance: 8 miles round trip
Difficulty: moderate
Hiking time: 6 hours
Elevation: 5,700 to 6,100 feet
Management: Tonto NF

Wilderness status: Four Peaks WA
Season: May to October
USGS map: Four Peaks

Rising abruptly to 7,657 feet from desert elevations of less than 2,000 feet, Four Peaks is a well-known landmark throughout central Arizona. Actually forming the southern end of the Mazatzal Mountains, these rugged summits require technical skills to climb. An easy to moderately difficult trail does access the eastern slope of the massif, however, allowing for an up-close look at the peaks. Interestingly, the Four Peaks Wilderness contains one of the greatest concentrations of black bears in Arizona.

This hike follows the Four Peaks Trail, which begins at the Lone Pine Saddle trailhead. To reach Lone Pine Saddle, drive north from Mesa on State Highway 87 for 21 miles to the Four Peaks Road (Forest Road 143), just past the Desert Vista pull-off. Turn right and continue east for 20 miles to the Mazatzal Divide. Turn right here on Forest Road 648 and continue 1.4 miles to the road's end. High-clearance 2WD vehicles are required from the turnoff on Highway 87 to the trailhead.

From Lone Pine Saddle the Four Peaks Trail heads south for about 1 mile to where it intersects the Amethyst Trail. Three miles long, this side route eventually accesses the privately owned Amethyst Mine just west of the peaks. Beyond this first junction the route continues to be well defined and easy to follow. Grades are mostly easy with a few

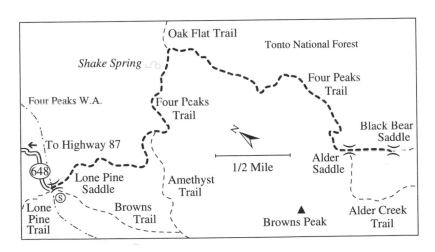

Browns Peak in the Four Peaks Wilderness

moderately steep pitches. The shady stands of ponderosa pine along the way are an added bonus. A variety of oaks grow beneath this over-story, and an occasional break in the timber provides views of Theodore Roosevelt Lake to the east.

Within the second mile of the hike, the route drops about 500 feet into a drainage where it encounters Shake Spring. It then intersects the upper end of the Oak Flat Trail. This 1.5-mile trail climbs up from the Oak Flat trailhead to the east, offering an alternate route to this point. After staying right at the junction, the Four Peaks Trail contin-ues south for another mile in which it climbs a moderate grade and then skirts around the east end of Browns Peak, the highest of the four peaks. The rugged face of the peak above consists mostly of Precam-brian shale and quartzite. Magnificent views of the Tonto Basin open to the east.

After reaching the high point of the hike just below Browns Peak, the trail descends into a canyon where it joins the upper end of the Al-der Creek Trail. A lengthy backpacking trip could drop down Alder Creek to the Cane Spring trailhead, then follow the Cane Spring and Soldier Camp trails back up to a point within a few road miles of the Lone Pine trailhead. Beyond the Alder Creek–Four Peaks trail junc-tion, the Four Peaks Trail descends a mostly moderate grade before reaching Black Bear Saddle. Situated along the ridge between the Four Peaks and Buckhorn Mountain, Black Bear Saddle is the turn-around point for this hike. The Four Peaks Trail does continue for an-other 5.5 miles before reaching the end of Forest Road 429. Beyond Black Bear Saddle, however, the trail is difficult to follow in places and the grades become more difficult. Retrace the 4 miles of trail just hiked to return to your car.

Because springs in the Four Peaks area are not always reliable, it is best to bring all the water you will need. If you need to fill your can-teen in the field, be sure to boil or treat the water before drinking. Watch for lightning in the exposed higher terrain. Take all necessary precautions when storing food for the night—this is bear country.

67 PICACHO PEAK

Distance: 4 miles round trip
Difficulty: strenuous
Hiking time: 4 hours
Elevation: 2,000 to 3,374 feet

Management: Picacho Peak SP
Wilderness status: none
Season: October to May
USGS map: Newman Park

Probably serving as an important landmark for as long as humans have inhabited this part of the Southwest, Picacho Peak is one of the more challenging short hikes in the state. First built by the CCC in 1933 and then improved by Explorer Scouts in 1972, the Hunter Trail reaches the top of this jagged peak in only 2 miles. Although not recommended for children under fourteen or inexperienced hikers of any sort, this route offers rewards that few other hikes in the state can.

The Hunter Trail is located in Picacho Peak State Park, which lies along Interstate 10 (at Exit 219) between Phoenix and Tucson. Follow the signs into the park from the highway, then turn left onto Barrett Loop Road, 0.2 mile beyond the park entrance. A fee is collected for entering the park.

From the trailhead the route climbs quickly through a desert community of saguaro, cholla, palo verde, and ocotillo. From this angle Picacho Peak seems like an unapproachable stone fortress, and yet, after climbing through a series of switchbacks (many of which include cable handholds), the trail reaches the base of some cliffs high above. A bit farther—approximately 1 mile from the start—the route reaches a saddle just west of the summit.

Although blessed with wonderful views, this saddle is only the halfway point of the hike. From here the trail drops quite severely down the back side of the mountain (a pair of cable handrails provides much-

Looking north from Picacho Peak

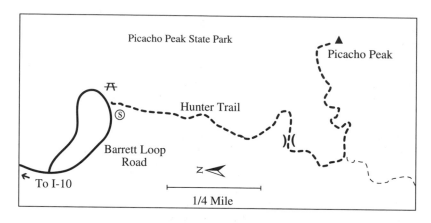

needed assistance along this stretch), which loses much of the 900 feet it has just gained. Not until reaching the 2,500-foot level does the trail again turn uphill to head for the summit. At this point a trail junction is reached at which the Hunter Trail keeps left. It then climbs very steeply (900 feet in about 0.5 mile) to arrive at the top. Again, cable handholds provide assistance along the steeper stretches.

Because the summit is mostly barren and cliffs drop straight down to the desert floor below, the views are superb. Interstate 10 cuts an arrow-straight path close to the base of the peak. It was in this area that Arizona's only Civil War battle took place in April 1862. The newly completed Central Arizona Project Canal can be seen running along the base of the Picacho Mountains to the north. The Santa Catalina and Rincon mountains rise in the vicinity of Tucson to the southeast. Telescope-studded Kitt Peak looms to the south and countless desert mountain ranges march farther south into Mexico.

Bring plenty of drinking water, sturdy hiking boots, and gloves. Avoid this hike during the summer months when daytime temperatures can reach above 100 degrees Fahrenheit. Be prepared for loose footing and precipitous drop-offs.

68 WASSON PEAK

Distance: 9 miles round trip
Difficulty: strenuous
Hiking time: 6 hours
Elevation: 2,850 to 4,687 feet

Management: Saguaro NM
Wilderness status: Saguaro WA
Season: October to May
USGS map: Avra

Divided into east and west units, the Saguaro National Monument encompasses tracts of desert mountain terrain on either side of Tucson. Saguaro National Monument West takes in the Tucson Mountains, the highest summit of which is Wasson Peak (elevation 4,687

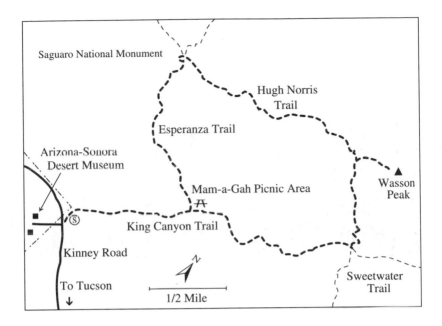

Saguaro National Monument

Hugh Norris Trail

Esperanza Trail

Arizona-Sonora Desert Museum

Mam-a-Gah Picnic Area

Wasson Peak

King Canyon Trail

Kinney Road

To Tucson

N

1/2 Mile

Sweetwater Trail

feet). Providing the shortest access to the top is the King Canyon Trail.

To reach the western unit of the Saguaro National Monument, drive west from Tucson on Speedway, which eventually turns into the Gates Pass Road (closed to oversize vehicles, such as RVs). Turn right on Kinney Road after crossing over Gates Pass and continue for another 2 miles to the Arizona–Sonora Desert Museum. The King Canyon trailhead is located directly across the road from the museum entrance.

For the first 0.9 mile, the trail follows an old mining road along the bottom of King Canyon to the backcountry Mam-a-Gah Picnic Area. Keep right at the picnic area to follow the King Canyon Trail for another 1.4 miles to the top of a ridge to the east. This section of the route starts out as a foot trail but follows an old road as it draws closer to the ridge. The grade is moderately steep along this section. Upon reaching the ridge, the trail intersects with the Sweetwater Trail, which approaches from the east. After staying left at this junction the King Canyon Trail then climbs north for 0.9 mile through a series of steep switchbacks. Nearly half of the hike's 1,800 feet of elevation gain is completed along this stretch. At the next trail junction, a right turn leads 0.3 mile to the summit of Wasson Peak, while the left-hand fork provides the return route.

The view from the top of Wasson Peak is spectacular. Tucson spreads out to the east, as do the Santa Catalina and Rincon mountains. Mount Wrightson is visible toward Mexico and Kitt Peak, with its collection of telescopes, rises to the west. Both military and commercial aircraft use nearby air space while making their approach to the airport in Tucson. While the noise can be disturbing, from Wasson it seems as if you are almost at eye level with the pilots.

View from the summit of Wasson Peak

It is possible to take an alternate route when returning to the trailhead. Rather than walking back down the south-running ridge, turn right a short distance from the summit and follow the Hugh Norris Trail west for 1.9 miles to where it intersects the Esperanza Trail. Springtime along this stretch of the route reveals a plethora of wildflowers, including lupine and Mexican golden poppies. Other species of flora found along the entire hike include palo verde, barrel cactus, cholla, and, of course, saguaro. Keep left on the Esperanza Trail and continue southeast for 1.4 miles to the Mam-a-Gah Picnic Area. From there it is 0.9 mile to the trailhead.

Avoid this hike in the summer, when temperatures can be quite hot. Bring plenty of water, for none is found along the way. Be wary of lightning along exposed ridges and mountaintops. Watch for rattlesnakes.

69   TANQUE VERDE RIDGE

Distance: 30.8 miles round trip
Difficulty: strenuous
Hiking time: 4 days
Elevation: 3,100 to 8,000 feet
Management: Saguaro NM

Wilderness status: Saguaro WA
Season: year-round
USGS maps: Tanque Verde
   Peak, Mica Mountain

Rising from the saguaro cactus forests that grow east of Tucson, the Rincon Mountains climb through six biotic communities—from desert scrub to mixed conifer forest—before topping out at 8,666 feet. A hike through this array of climatic zones can be compared to traveling from Mexico to Canada within the span of a few miles. By combining the Tanque Verde Ridge and Cow Head Saddle trails, such a dramatic climb is possible.

The entire hike is located within the eastern unit of the Saguaro National Monument. Drive east from downtown Tucson on Broadway. Bear right onto the Old Spanish Trail and follow it to the monument entrance. The Tanque Verde Ridge Trail begins at the Javelina Picnic Area, a little more than 1 mile beyond the visitor center. Be sure to obtain a permit before heading out overnight. This may be done by calling the monument at (602) 296-8576 and then picking up the permit at the visitor center by noon on the day of the hike.

For the first mile the Tanque Verde Ridge Trail traverses along an easy grade across desert terrain typical of the Tucson area. Saguaro cactus, cholla cactus, ocotillo, and palo verde trees are plentiful in number, as are desert marigolds and other colorful bloomers in the springtime. This desert ecosystem is also home to javelina, coyotes, rattlesnakes, and a variety of birds.

At the 1-mile mark the trail reaches the toe of Tanque Verde Ridge, along which it climbs for the next several miles. Grades along the ridge range from easy to strenuous, although most are moderate. Because little or no shade exists along this first stretch of the hike, count on extremely hot temperatures from May to September. You may even want to plan on starting out early in the morning to beat the heat. Additionally, in areas where the trail crosses bare bedrock, attention should be paid so as not to lose the way.

Around the 4,000-foot level the saguaro cactus thin out as bear grass and sotol become more prevalent. Attesting to the plant's adaptability to cooler environments, ocotillo are still plentiful. Closer to the 5,000-foot level, the first alligator junipers are encountered, and as the trail climbs a little bit higher, this species of tree is joined by others—Mexican pinyon, manzanita, and Arizona white oak to name three. Through this stunted forest, the trail climbs and drops over a few ridges before reaching the Juniper Basin backcountry campground. Because National Park Service regulations restrict camping to only two campgrounds along the entire Tanque Verde Ridge hike, you may want to plan on spending the first night at Juniper Basin. Otherwise you will have to travel all the way (15.4 miles) to Manning Camp to reach the second alternative. Juniper Basin features three individual sites, an outhouse, and fire pits. Water is available seasonally, but do not count on it unless you check first at the visitor center.

Nearly 7 miles from the trailhead, Juniper Basin is just shy of the halfway mark. At 6,000 feet, however, it is well above the median elevation of the route. From here the trail climbs northeast along a ridge toward nearby Tanque Verde Peak. Topping out near the 7,049-foot summit, the trail then drops eastward along a ridgeline toward Cow Head Saddle. From this high point be sure to take in the sweeping vistas. To the south rise the Whetstone, Santa Rita, and Huachuca mountains. Tucson spreads out far below to the west and Mount Lemmon occupies the northern horizon.

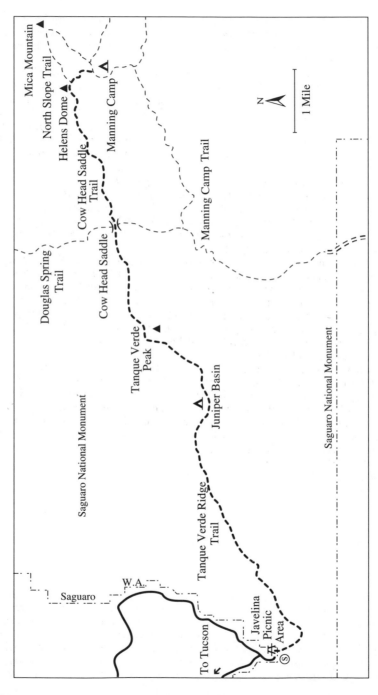

From Tanque Verde Peak it is 2.5 miles to the next landmark, Cow Head Saddle. Because the saddle is nearly 1,000 feet lower than the peak, expect moderate to steep descents, and a respectable climb on the way out. Whereas ponderosa pines haunted a few sheltered locales below, they become more prevalent along this stretch. At the saddle the Tanque Verde Ridge Trail connects with the 8.3-mile Douglas Spring Trail, which begins in the monument's northwest corner. This trail provides a shorter route to this point. Continuing eastward from the signed junction, the hike now takes up the Cow Head Saddle Trail, which climbs toward Helens Dome, 3.3 trail miles away. The grades along this stretch are mostly moderate, although some are strenuous. On the southeastern flank of Helens Dome the North Slope Trail comes in from Italian Spring to the northeast. Keep right at this junction and continue 0.6 mile to Manning Camp (elevation 8,000 feet). Situated among tall ponderosa pines, Manning Camp features a backcountry campground with six sites and a year-round supply of water. A nearby log cabin was built in 1905 as a summer home by Levi Manning. It now houses backcountry operations.

With a layover day at Manning Camp it is possible to explore the network of trails that spread east across the upper reaches of the Rincon Mountains. Of particular interest is 8,666-foot Mica Mountain, the high point of the range. To reach the summit from Manning Camp, head northeast for 1.4 miles on the Mica Mountain Trail.

To return to the trailhead, retrace the Cow Head and Tanque Verde Ridge trails to the Javelina Picnic Area. With the exception of the climb from Cow Head Saddle to Tanque Verde Peak, the going is mostly downhill.

All water from sources along this hike should be treated. A permit is needed for overnight travel. Also, check with monument personnel about the weather conditions before setting out. Snow may preclude hiking up high in the winter. Watch for lightning on exposed ridges.

70   SEVEN FALLS

Distance: 4.8 miles round trip
Difficulty: easy
Hiking time: 3 hours
Elevation: 2,800 to 3,300 feet
Management: Coronado NF

Wilderness status: Pusch Ridge WA
Season: year-round
USGS map: Sabino Canyon

Surrounded by soaring canyon walls, Seven Falls is one of the more alluring wonders of the Santa Catalina Mountains. Dropping through a staircase of pools, the cool water of Bear Creek tempts hikers to linger a bit. Because it is short and easy, this hike is quite popular. But regardless of the crowds, Seven Falls is a destination well worth visiting.

Currently, the hike to Seven Falls begins at the Lower Bear Picnic Area, a 10-minute ride on the Bear Canyon shuttle (a fee is charged)

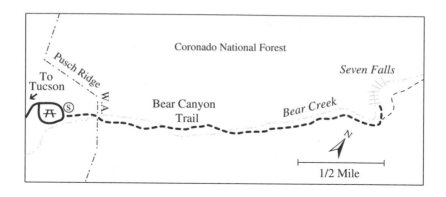

from the Sabino Canyon Visitor Center. To reach the visitor center drive north on Sabino Canyon Road in northeast Tucson. The shuttle may eventually be shut down because of bad road conditions. If this occurs, you will need to add an extra 1.7 miles each way to the hike.

From the trailhead the route follows along the level canyon bottom for about 1.5 miles. Growing here are stands of giant saguaro cactus, along with other lower Sonoran flora such as palo verde, cholla, prickly pear cactus, mesquite, and brittlebush. Cottonwood and sycamore trees intermittently shade the creek bottom. Shortly into the hike the first of seven stream crossings is encountered. Although Bear Creek is

One of several pools of water at Seven Falls

easy to cross at most times of the year, heavy rains and melting snow occasionally swell the flow considerably. Flash floods are also a possibility. For current conditions, check with the staff at the Sabino Canyon Visitor Center before heading out.

After 1.5 miles the trail climbs out of the canyon bottom along the west wall. After making one long switchback it then traverses along a contour a couple of hundred feet above the canyon bottom. This climb is initially moderate in difficulty, but it soon levels off. At 2.2 miles the trail arrives at a signed junction where a left turn leads 0.2 mile to Seven Falls. The trail to the right eventually climbs over into Sabino Basin.

Although the falls at Seven Falls are often reduced to a trickle (and are sometimes dried up completely), the pools are usually filled with clear, cool water. Care should be taken when entering them because of the slippery bottoms and hidden obstructions. Similarly, caution should be used when climbing to each successive pool. Whether you swim or not, it is hard not to linger for a bit at this beautiful little oasis.

Because all water in Bear Creek should be treated before consumption, it is best to pack in all that you will need. Temperatures can reach well above the century mark in the summer months. Flash floods are a possibility, especially in the summer monsoon season. Keep in mind that the Coronado National Forest does not encourage swimming in the creek.

71 SABINO CANYON

Distance: 8.2 miles round trip
Difficulty: moderate
Hiking time: 5 hours
Elevation: 3,330 to 3,900 feet
Management: Coronado NF

Wilderness status: Pusch Ridge WA
Season: year-round
USGS map: Sabino Canyon

Of all the drainages along the Santa Catalina's front range, Sabino Canyon is by far the most popular. Accessed by a narrow paved road that extends 3.8 miles upstream, it attracts countless folks who come to stroll, jog, bicycle, or ride a shuttle bus through this scenic desert canyon. From road's end, however, the Sabino Canyon Trail ventures beyond the crowds and noise to reveal a rugged and beautiful wilderness. An ideal destination for day hikers along this route is Hutch's Pool.

Drive 4 miles north on the Sabino Canyon Road from the Tanque Verde Road in Tucson to the Sabino Canyon Visitor Center. The size of the parking lot here is indicative of the amount of use this area receives. To access the trailhead, ride the shuttle bus (tickets can be purchased just prior to the trip) to the road's end. It is possible to bypass the shuttle ride by hiking an additional 4.7 miles (each way) on the Phoneline Trail, which contours along the canyon's east face.

For the first 0.5 mile the Sabino Canyon Trail climbs through some

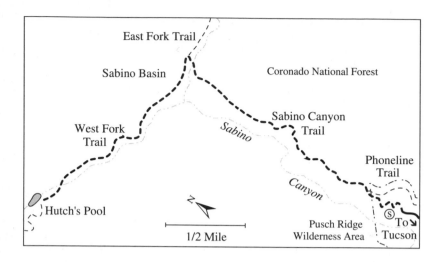

East Fork Trail

Sabino Basin

Coronado National Forest

West Fork Trail

Sabino

Sabino Canyon Trail

Phoneline Trail

Hutch's Pool

1/2 Mile

Pusch Ridge Wilderness Area

To Tucson

short switchbacks to connect with the end of the Phoneline Trail. Turning left at this junction, the Sabino Canyon Trail continues upstream along the canyon's east side. Although dipping occasionally, the next 2 miles follow a mostly easy grade. Be sure to enjoy the spectacular views of Sabino Canyon along the way.

About 2.5 miles from the trailhead the route drops easily into Sabino Basin. An open area where several canyons converge, Sabino Basin is quite beautiful. Just prior to the first stream crossing, a trail junction is reached. Branching to the right, the East Fork Trail eventually drops into Bear Canyon; a left turn onto the West Fork Trail leads to Hutch's Pool. Although intermittent, this stream can prove difficult to cross during periods of high runoff.

Beyond the crossing the hike follows the open bottom of Sabino Basin. Typified by grasslands interspersed with sotol, agave, manzanita, and stands of oak, Sabino Basin lies at the boundary between two ecological life zones. You may note a few saguaros growing among rocky areas of the basin. These stragglers mark the upper limit of the lower Sonoran life zone. The grassland community that now prevails is indicative of the upper Sonoran zone. In addition, a fine riparian community of sycamores, cottonwoods, and other deciduous trees grows along the streambed.

About 1.3 miles from the trail junction, the route makes a second stream crossing (this one may be more difficult during periods of high water), after which it follows the left bank of the creek for another 0.3 mile to Hutch's Pool. Along the way a nice glade of tall Arizona cypress is encountered. Situated in an elongated, rock-rimmed basin, Hutch's Pool is quite scenic but it does receive a lot of use. The Coronado National Forest suggests that overnight visitors not camp in the vicinity of the pool.

Although this hike can be completed year-round, summers often bring hot temperatures to all of Sabino Canyon. High water (typical

Hutch's Pool

during the monsoon season in the summer and after periods of snow-melt in the winter) may make stream crossings impossible. Be sure to treat any surface water before drinking. Because this is within a desert bighorn sheep management area, dogs are not allowed.

72 FINGER ROCK CANYON

Distance: 10 miles round trip
Difficulty: strenuous
Hiking time: 6 hours
Elevation: 3,100 to 7,255 feet
Management: Coronado NF

Wilderness status: Pusch Ridge WA
Season: year-round
USGS maps: Tucson North, Oro Valley

The Finger Rock Trail offers the quickest access to Mount Kimball—the top of the Santa Catalinas' broken front range. This steep and rugged route reveals some interesting geological formations, and provides some particularly spectacular vistas of Tucson and beyond.

The Finger Rock trailhead lies at the end of Alvernon Way, 1 mile north of Tucson's Skyline Drive. Skyline can be accessed from either Ina Road or Swan Road. From the parking area the route heads up the hill behind the iron "bighorn sheep" sign.

For the first 1.1 miles the trail climbs easily up the bottom of Finger

Rock Canyon, along which is found a wonderful example of the lower Sonoran desert. Dominated by giant saguaro cactus, this plant community includes sotol, ocotillo, patches of prickly pear cactus, and yucca. Wildflowers include penstemon, groundsel, and brittlebush. A variety of riparian plant species also grow along the streambed.

At the 1.1-mile mark, the trail reaches Finger Rock Spring. Beyond this point it begins a long and difficult ascent along the rugged southeast face of the canyon. Steep and rocky for the next 2 miles, this section includes a few switchbacks plus areas of loose rock. There are also some precipitous drop-offs. Despite its ruggedness, however, the route does open up to views that become more spectacular the higher up it climbs. For the first few miles Finger Rock is visible along the high skyline to the north. And then, as the canyon deepens, the city of Tucson is nicely framed by sheer rock walls. You may also get a chance to observe some desert bighorn sheep because the canyon beyond Finger Rock Spring has been designated as a bighorn management area.

After 3 miles and 2,500 feet of climbing, a short side trail leads to a notch that opens up to an even broader view of the city. Beyond the notch, the trail passes among thick stands of oak and juniper as it traverses around the head of the canyon. At the 4.5-mile mark a saddle is reached. Here, keep left at the junction of the Finger Rock and Pima Canyon trails to continue another 0.5 mile to the top of Mount Kimball. Beyond the summit, the Pima Canyon Trail continues southwest, eventually dropping into its namesake drainage.

Some exposure and slick bedrock is encountered. Dangerous electri-

Looking down on Tucson from the Finger Rock Canyon hike

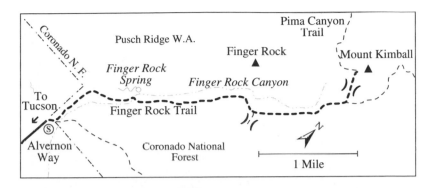

cal storms can crop up quite suddenly, so watch for lightning in the exposed higher terrain. Do not expect to find water in the drier months, and watch for rattlesnakes. While this is considered a year-round hike, summers usher in temperatures over 100 degrees Fahrenheit and winters may see the upper end of the trail snow-covered for short periods of time. Dogs are not permitted on this trail.

73 PIMA CANYON

Distance: 14.2 miles round trip
Difficulty: strenuous
Hiking time: 8 hours
Elevation: 2,900 to 7,255 feet
Management: Coronado NF

Wilderness status: Pusch Ridge WA
Season: year-round
USGS maps: Tucson North, Oro Valley

A popular hike among locals, Pima Canyon offers a varied experience within a few minutes of Tucson. The canyon skirts below rugged Pusch Ridge before approaching Mount Kimball. Despite its impressive vertical gain, the first half of the Pima Canyon Trail is an easy and pleasant hike. By following the 7.1-mile route the entire way, however, you will wind up on top of Mount Kimball.

From Tucson, take the Oracle Highway to Magee Road, turn east, and drive 1.5 miles to the road's end. A small parking area is provided, although this quickly fills up on weekends. Plans for a new trailhead are in the works because of a resort being built nearby.

For the first 0.25 mile the Pima Canyon Trail crosses private land, after which it reaches the national forest boundary. It then continues to skirt along the foot of the mountains as it heads east toward the mouth of Pima Canyon. All along this section and well into the canyon itself, the route encounters beautiful stands of saguaro cactus, palo verde, ocotillo, sotol, agave, and other desert species. Open views of the city spread out to the right.

About 1 mile from the trailhead the route encounters the canyon

Saguaro cactus in Pima Canyon

bottom, which it then follows for the next 3 miles. Although it crosses the streambed on several occasions, the trail is not difficult to follow. While the stream in Pima Canyon is intermittent at best, it is enough to support cottonwoods and other riparian species of plants. Providing a dramatic contrast to the surrounding desert hillsides, Pima Canyon's riparian community is a favorite destination among bird-watchers, especially in the winter months. Deer and javelina inhabit the canyon, as do desert bighorn sheep. Like Finger Rock Canyon, Pima Canyon is included in a bighorn sheep management area.

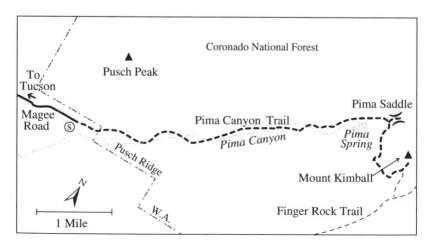

After following an easy grade for 4 miles, the Pima Canyon Trail finally climbs more arduous grades as it approaches Pima Saddle at the head of the drainage. Expect switchbacks, some loose rocks, and moderate to strenuous ascents along this 1.6-mile stretch. Some route finding may also be necessary. Within 0.5 mile of the saddle the trail passes Pima Spring, a usually reliable source of water. Be sure to treat it beforehand, however.

Situated at about 6,300 feet, Pima Saddle is 3,400 feet higher than the trailhead. Just before it reaches the saddle, the Pima Canyon Trail veers south and continues for another 1.5 miles to the summit of Mount Kimball. A short side trail to the left accesses the saddle. Within this final segment the trail switchbacks several times to gain the last 1,000 feet of the climb. Again, trail conditions include steep pitches and loose rock.

Bring plenty of water. Expect hot temperatures in the summer and occasionally cold conditions higher up in the winter. Watch for rattlesnakes in the deserts and lightning up high. Dogs are prohibited along this trail because it enters a desert bighorn sheep management area.

74 ROMERO CANYON

Distance: 14.4 miles round trip
Difficulty: strenuous
Hiking time: 10 hours
Elevations: 2,800 to 6,100 feet
Management: Coronado NF

Wilderness status: Pusch Ridge WA
Season: year-round
USGS maps: Mount Lemmon, Oro Valley

Like other routes in the Santa Catalina Mountains, the Romero Canyon Trail begins at the base of the range but eventually climbs to its upper reaches. The canyon itself is quite rugged and beautiful, and a surprising variety of flora is encountered.

Drive 5 miles north of the Tucson city limits on US Highway 89 to Catalina State Park. Enter the park (a fee is charged) and drive to the day-use area. The trail begins near the information board at road's end.

For the first 1.1 miles the Romero Canyon Trail follows an old roadbed across relatively level terrain. Beyond a point that overlooks the Montrose Canyon drainage the route passes through the boundary fence of the Coronado National Forest before taking up a narrow foot

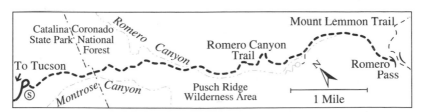

A hiker on the Romero Canyon Trail

trail. Climbing steeply, the route occasionally switchbacks as it gains the rugged north face of Montrose Canyon. Traversing a lot of rocky terrain, the trail is rough in places but easy to follow. Along the way saguaro cactus, ocotillo, and palo verde trees abound. Spring often brings a plethora of wildflowers along this stretch of trail, including brittlebush and paperflower. It is also possible to spot coyotes, desert bighorn sheep, javelinas, and perhaps even an elusive mountain lion along this hike.

Approximately 2.5 miles from the trailhead, the route passes through a small notch before dropping into Romero Canyon proper. As the trail approaches this high point a nice vista of Pusch Ridge opens up to the south. Forming the dramatic southwest facade of the Santa Catalina Range, the Pusch Ridge consists mostly of Catalina Gneiss, a hard Precambrian rock banded with veins of white quartz.

Nearly 3 miles from the trailhead the trail reaches the bottom of Romero Canyon. Just downstream from this point are several pools that occasionally have water in them. Here you can also get a close-up look at the riparian plant life that grows along drainages like Romero Canyon. Veritable jungles compared to the sparse lower Sonoran desert ecosystem, these verdant communities include sycamore, cottonwood, velvet ash, cattails, and other water-loving flora.

Continuing up Romero Canyon, the trail soon enters a narrow section of canyon where it ascends a series of switchbacks along the drainage's north wall. Gaining 800 feet in less than a mile, this stretch is steep, but it is followed by a gentler traverse high above the canyon bottom. About 5 miles from the trailhead the route drops back down to the canyon bottom, where a short spur trail runs downstream to Romero Spring. The spring is unreliable in the drier months, so don't count on always finding water here.

Beyond Romero Spring, it is another 2 miles and 1,300 vertical feet to the top of 6,100-foot Romero Pass. At first following the main branch of Romero Canyon, the trail takes up a steep side tributary for the last mile. At the pass itself, the Romero Canyon Trail connects with the Mount Lemmon and West Fork trails. The Mount Lemmon Trail continues north to the summit of the range. At this elevation, pinyon pine, alligator juniper, Arizona white oak, and even ponderosa pine replace the desert flora that grows below.

Be sure to bring plenty of drinking water because streams along the route are not always flowing and are not potable without treatment. Be wary of rattlesnakes and watch for lightning in the higher terrain. Dogs are prohibited along this trail.

75 GREEN MOUNTAIN

Distance: 7.8 miles round trip
Difficulty: moderate
Hiking time: 5 hours
Elevation: 7,300 to 6,000 feet

Management: Coronado NF
Wilderness status: none
Season: April to November
USGS map: Bellota Ranch

Accessing some spectacular views along the Santa Catalina Range's east side, the Green Mountain Trail makes for a nice day hike.

From the turnoff on Tanque Verde Road in Tucson, drive 22 miles up the Catalina Highway to the San Pedro Vista. (The official name for the Catalina Highway is the Hitchcock Highway although locals often refer to it as the Mount Lemmon Highway.) The route begins on the right side of the vista's parking area.

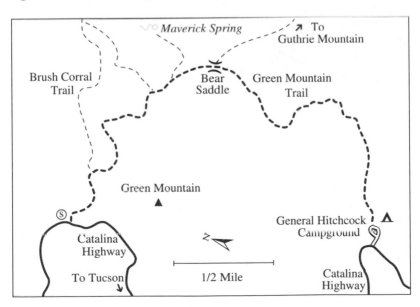

Rock outcrop near the start of the Green Mountain Trail

The route is somewhat confusing for the first 100 yards or so, thanks to a lot of foot traffic to a rock outcrop nearby. To find the start of the Green Mountain Trail, climb up the hill immediately to the southeast. Once on top, it is easy to pick up the actual trail. From this point the route begins contouring around the north side of Green Mountain. Passing through a comparatively lush forest of ponderosa pine and Douglas fir, this stretch is quite pleasant. About 0.25 mile from the trailhead is a junction with a side trail to the top of Green Mountain—keep left here. After descending one switchback, the Green Mountain

Trail reaches the start of the Brush Corral Trail, a rugged route that drops down the eastern side of the mountains. Keep right at the junction.

As it continues circling around its namesake peak, the Green Mountain Trail eventually enters drier terrain. This is reflected in the shorter stature of the surrounding forest: rather that towering pines and firs, the route is instead surrounded by oak, manzanita, yucca, bear grass, and only scattered ponderosa pine. After 1.5 miles the Green Mountain Trail reaches a junction with a spur to the Brush Corral route (keep right here); at 1.9 miles it reaches another side trail (keep right again), which leads to Maverick Spring. Located 0.4 mile away, the spring is usually flowing.

After 2.1 miles the Green Mountain Trail reaches 6,950-foot Bear Saddle. From this point a secondary route leads 1.2 miles to Guthrie Mountain, a summit with fine views of the San Pedro Valley to the east. From the saddle the Green Mountain Trail drops an additional 1.8 miles before ending at the General Hitchcock Campground. This easy descent leads mostly through ponderosa pine forest along a dry streambed.

With a shuttle this hike could end at the campground, making it 3.8 miles long. Without a shuttle, however, it is necessary to hike back up the Green Mountain Trail, a climb of 1,300 feet. Bring plenty of water, and watch for lightning during thunderstorms.

76   ASPEN LOOP

Distance: 3.7 miles
Difficulty: moderate
Hiking time: 3 hours
Elevation: 7,500 to 8,100 feet
Season: April to November

Management: Coronado NF
Wilderness status: Pusch Ridge
  WA
USGS map: Mount Lemmon

This pleasurable walk through a variety of high mountain forests is quite popular among local hikers. Do not be turned away by the crowds, however, as this is a short, easy hike that should not be missed.

From its intersection with Tanque Verde Road in northeastern Tucson, drive 30.5 miles north on the Catalina Highway (also known as the Hitchcock Highway and the Mount Lemmon Highway) to the Marshall Gulch picnic site, less than a mile south of Summerhaven. Upon reaching Summerhaven, drive a bit farther to the end of the road.

To take advantage of a more gradual climb, and to save the stands of aspen for last, this description begins by following the Marshall Gulch Trail, which takes off just to the right of the outhouse. Alternating between easy and moderate grades, the Marshall Gulch Trail climbs west from the picnic site. Blessed with an intermittent stream, this relatively lush drainage features towering firs, leafy bigtooth maple, and Arizona alder. Watch for small wildflowers, as well. Near the upper end of Marshall Gulch, as the topography opens up somewhat, the

Aspen along the Aspen Loop hike

forest includes more arid stands of ponderosa pine intermixed with
smaller firs and Gambel oak.

At 1.2 miles the Marshall Gulch Trail tops out on Marshall Saddle,
where it connects with other routes. The Wilderness of Rock Trail
continues west from the saddle, while the Aspen Trail runs north and
south. The Aspen Loop hike takes up the latter route by turning left.

From Marshall Saddle the Aspen Loop continues south along a dry
ridgeline forested by ponderosa pine, fir, and silverleaf oak. Watch for
possible viewpoints to the right of the trail. These vistas take in the

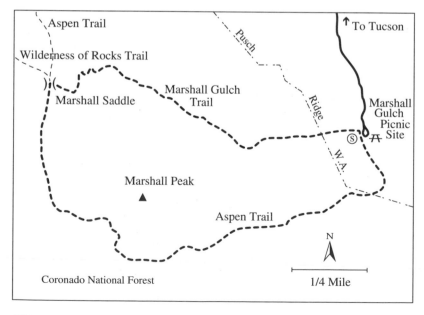

southern flank of the Santa Catalinas and the Tucson area beyond. Nearly 1 mile from the saddle, a faint trail branches off to the right. Keep left on the main trail, however, and continue on to where the trail switchbacks downhill.

As the trail bottoms out in this last mile of the hike, sporadic stands of aspen grow among thick evergreen forests. The tall, white-barked trees are being crowded out by the persistent pines and firs. Eventually, the deciduous trees will disappear altogether unless a forest fire or some other disturbance starts the ecological cycle over again. In the final 0.5 mile the trail contours along the upper reaches of Sabino Canyon. The Aspen Loop ends back at the Marshall Gulch picnic site.

Water is usually available along the Marshall Gulch Trail, although it should be treated. Watch for poison ivy, especially in and around the picnic area.

77   ORACLE RIDGE

Distance: 13 miles one way
Difficulty: strenuous
Hiking time: 2 days
Elevation: 7,800 to 4,700 feet
Management: Coronado NF

Wilderness status: none
Season: May to November
USGS maps: Mount Lemmon,
    Mount Bigelow, Oracle,
    Campo Bonito

From Mount Lemmon, two main ridges drop from the north side of the Santa Catalina Range toward the vicinity of Oracle. One of these, the Oracle Ridge, is accessed by trailheads on both ends. A hike down the spine of this prominent feature not only provides some spectacular views but also offers a fine lesson in the ecology of southeastern Arizona's mountain ranges.

This hike begins at the trail's upper end to take advantage of a gradual drop in elevation. From the Tanque Verde Road in northeastern Tucson, drive 29 miles north on the Catalina Highway (also known as the Hitchcock Highway and the Mount Lemmon Highway) to the Oracle Control Road (Forest Road 38). Turn right and drive 0.2 mile to a cattle guard. The signed trailhead is on the left.

Skirting along the west side of Oracle Ridge, the first mile of the trail is a pleasant and mostly level walk through shady ponderosa pine and Douglas fir forests. Upon reaching Stratton Saddle, however, the route takes up the crest of the ridge where a variety of smaller trees—oaks and mountain mahogany—and only scattered pines and firs grow. Some rather large alligator junipers are also found here. Thanks to this sparser vegetation, views on either side begin to open up. The Galiuro and Pinaleno mountain ranges are visible to the east, while the Reef of Rock formation and Samaniego Ridge constitute the western skyline. The well-forested north side of Mount Lemmon comes into view and you can even see the glass bubble of Biosphere II far below near Oracle.

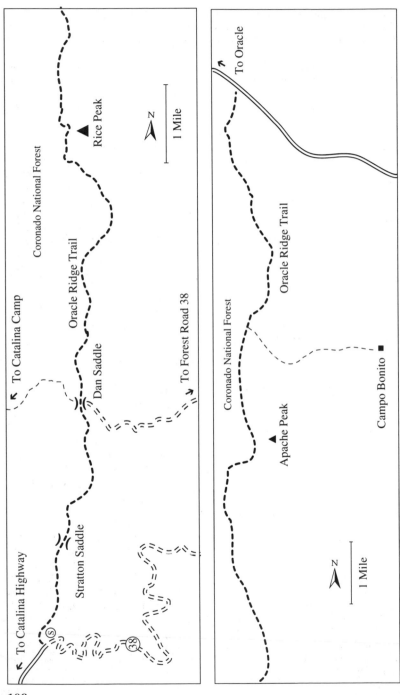

Looking west from Oracle Ridge

About 2 miles from the trailhead the Oracle Ridge Trail meets up with an old mining road, which it then descends for 0.5 mile to 6,900-foot Dan Saddle. Although this track accesses some old mining claims on the ridge's eastern slope, it has not been driven in years. At Dan Saddle the hike intersects a 4WD road that does see occasional use. To the right this road drops down to the Oracle Control Road (Forest Road 38) and to the left it accesses Catalina Camp, an abandoned mining camp. Although the search for gold began in these mountains in the nineteenth century, it was not until the Oracle Control Road was built in 1918 that ready access to this higher terrain was possible.

At the 2.5-mile mark, Dan Saddle offers a few camping spots. Beyond this point the Oracle Ridge Trail becomes less distinct as most hikers usually turn around here. To continue north on the trail, look for a faded footpath a couple of feet left of the cattle guard. Undoubtedly, the condition of this stretch of trail should improve because the newly designated trans-state Arizona Trail takes up the next 8.5 miles of the Oracle Ridge route.

From Dan Saddle the Oracle Ridge Trail climbs along the west side of the ridge as it heads toward Rice Peak. About 0.5 mile prior to the 7,577-foot summit the trail takes up another old mining road, which it then follows for nearly 2 miles. North of Rice Peak the route drops rather abruptly (about 1,000 feet in 1 mile) before leveling off again. The roadbed eventually turns east and a foot trail is once more followed.

About 9 miles from the start, the Oracle Ridge Trail skirts just west of Apache Peak (elevation 6,441 feet). And at 10 miles is a side trail to Campo Bonito, an old mining camp that lies a mile east of the ridge.

From this junction, the Oracle Ridge Trail continues north along the ridge, which by now is broader and less defined. In contrast to the tall timbers of its upper end, this last stretch of trail is typified by oaks, manzanita, and other desert shrubs. Shortly after crossing the national forest boundary, the Oracle Ridge Trail ends at a residential area just outside the town of Oracle.

Because no water is available along this 2-day hike, be sure to pack plenty—a gallon per person per day is a good rule of thumb. USGS maps are a good idea—parts of the trail may be difficult to find. Watch for lightning along most of this route. Because the Oracle Ridge trail traverses rugged and isolated terrain, it is best not to hike it alone.

78 BOG SPRINGS

Distance: 5 miles round trip
Difficulty: moderate
Hiking time: 4 hours
Elevation: 5,100 to 6,600 feet
Management: Coronado NF

Wilderness status: Mount Wrightson WA
Season: year-round
USGS map: Mount Wrightson

Nestled among the high summits of the Santa Rita Mountains south of Tucson, Madera Canyon is one of the premier bird-watching areas in the country. In all, more than 200 species of birds have been spotted here, many of which are considered rare north of the Mexico border. A primary reason for the canyon's attraction to birds is that it offers cool refuge from the desert heat in the summertime. Providing a wonderful introduction to the natural beauty of Madera Canyon is the hike to Bog and Kent springs.

The Bog Springs Trail begins in the Bog Springs Campground. Take Interstate 19 to the Continental exit just south of the retirement community of Green Valley. There is also a sign for Madera Canyon here.

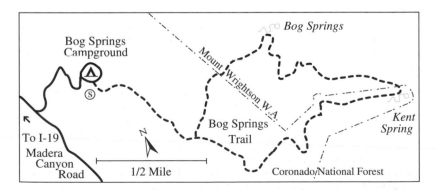

Old growth trees near Bog Springs

Drive southeast on a narrow paved road for 13 miles to Madera Canyon. Turn onto the road to the Bog Springs Campground and drive another 0.5 mile. The trail begins at site 13, but a few parking spaces are available at the upper end of the campground loop.

The Bog Springs Trail begins by climbing moderately along an old road (closed now) for 0.7 mile to a signed junction. The route then turns left to follow a foot trail for 0.8 mile to Bog Springs. This section climbs at a steeper pace as it approaches the spring. Along the first part of the hike a low-profile forest of alligator juniper, Mexican pinyon pine, Arizona white oak, silverleaf oak, and Emory oak predominates. Scattered yucca and sotol also grow here. In the vicinity of Bog Springs, a wonderful riparian community of stately sycamores and Arizona walnut trees is encountered.

It is in riparian areas such as that found at Bog Springs, and Kent Spring farther on, that you might spot some of the birds for which Madera Canyon is known. Topping the list for most birders is the elegant trogon. A relative of the quetzal, this colorful bird migrates here from Mexico in late spring and does not leave until summer's end. Of course, many other species of birds have enthusiasts scouting the treetops with binoculars from April to September. A variety of mammals, including white-tailed deer, black bears, and coatimundis, also frequent the area.

From Bog Springs (a good place to fill canteens) the trail continues south toward Kent Spring, 1.2 miles away. Climbing another 800 feet, this leg of the route is steep in places but does open up to some nice views of Madera Canyon and beyond. It also reveals a change in plant communities as taller Chihuahua pines become more common.

From Kent Spring the route drops quite rapidly for 1.6 miles before reaching the trail junction encountered earlier. Following an old road that has been closed to vehicles for some time, this part of the hike parallels a beautiful stream that tumbles through picturesque waterfalls and cascades. It is 0.7 mile from this junction back to the trailhead.

Although water is usually available at both Bog and Kent springs, check first with the Forest Service before setting out.

79   MOUNT WRIGHTSON

Distance: 11.7 miles round trip
Difficulty: strenuous
Hiking time: 8 hours
Elevation: 5,400 to 9,453 feet
Management: Coronado NF

Wilderness status: Mount
  Wrightson WA
Season: June to October
USGS map: Mount Wrightson

Towering above the surrounding desert floor, Mount Wrightson (elevation 9,453 feet) and the Santa Rita Mountains offer a superb example of what are often called "sky islands." By providing a considerably cooler and wetter climate, these desert ranges feature ecosystems that are strikingly different from those of the desert below. In addition to finding shady oak and pine forests, hikers will also discover a surprising selection of fauna. Madera Canyon, in which this hike begins, is world-renowned for the great number of birds that frequent its wooded environs. From March to September, birders flock to the canyon in droves with hopes of spotting an elegant trogon, Lucifer hummingbird, flammulated owl, or any of the dozens of other rare species that summer here. Just as these birds find refuge from the desert heat in the Santa Rita Mountains, so too will hikers who choose to head up Mount Wrightson.

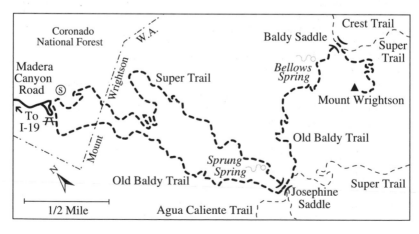

A hiker reads an interpretive sign on Mount Wrightson

This hike combines segments of two different trails that climb Mount Wrightson. The 8.1-mile Super Trail takes its time making the 4,000-foot ascent, while the 5.4-mile Old Baldy Trail makes a more direct assault. Both begin at the Roundup trailhead, which is at the end of the Madera Canyon Road (Forest Road 70). From Tucson, drive south on Interstate 19 to the Continental exit, where a sign points the way to Madera Canyon. Drive southeast on the paved route for 13 miles to the Roundup Picnic Area. Turn left here to find the developed trailhead.

Taking advantage of its mostly gentle ascent, this hike follows the Super Trail for the first 3.7 miles to Josephine Saddle. Climbing just over 1,600 feet, this leg of the hike first traverses through thickets of oaks (Arizona white, Emory, and silverleaf) and alligator juniper. As it nears the saddle, however, taller stands of pines (Apache and ponderosa, among others) are common. Sycamore, Arizona walnut, and wild grape also grow along streambeds. This leg of the Super Trail makes a few long switchbacks as it contours along the upper reaches of Madera Canyon, but it never really steepens beyond a moderate grade. Just short of Josephine Saddle the Super Trail reaches Sprung Spring, a developed water hole that is usually flowing.

At 7,080-foot Josephine Saddle, the Super Trail meets the Old Baldy Trail, which makes the climb to this point in 2.2 miles. A number of other trails take off from here as well. The Agua Caliente Trail continues west toward Agua Caliente Saddle and Rattlesnake Canyon, while the Josephine Canyon and Temporal Gulch trails drop into drainages to the south. Josephine Saddle features some suitable campsites, but it was also the scene of a rather tragic episode. In November 1958 three Boy Scouts perished here when they were caught by a sudden snow-storm. A memorial at the intersection of the Super and Old Baldy trails serves to remind hikers of the mishap.

From Josephine Saddle, the Super and Old Baldy trails continue as one for 0.2 mile to a junction. From here, the Super Trail loops around the south side of the summit to reach Baldy Saddle in 3.3 miles. The Old Baldy Trail, on the other hand, reaches the same point in only 1.8 miles by cutting across the steeper north face of the peak. Since both routes climb 1,800 feet, one offers moderate grades while the other is more strenuous. This hike description bears left on the Old Baldy Trail because of the more interesting plant communities found on the north face of the mountain.

Upon parting with the Super Trail, the Old Baldy Trail wastes little time in gaining elevation. Moderate and some strenuous grades can be expected, not to mention several switchbacks. The trail is well main-tained, however, and the footing is good. Soon, impressive cliffs that ring the summit above come into view. Open pine forests along the way are good places to spot white-tailed deer and even black bear. Farther on, the trail crosses small avalanche chutes in which are found small patches of aspen. Gambel oak is also plentiful here. The trail passes Bellows Spring and soon after tops Baldy Saddle. The Crest Trail runs north from Baldy Saddle, while the upper end of the Super Trail is found a short distance to the south. Baldy Saddle is open and scenic, and it features some nice campsites.

From Baldy Saddle it is a 0.9-mile, 600-foot climb to Mount Wright-son's summit. Keep right at the Super Trail junction and continue south. After passing among some stands of Douglas fir, the trail steep-ens and climbs through a few short switchbacks.

The treeless summit was, for the first half of this century, home to a fire lookout. Active until the 1950s, the structure was eventually re-moved and all that remains now is a concrete foundation and an inter-pretive sign. From the top you have a spectacular 360-degree view. To the north lies Tucson, Mount Lemmon, and the Rincon Mountains. Along the western skyline rises Baboquivari and Kitt peaks, while nearby Mount Hopkins features the Smithsonian Astrophysical Obser-vatory. To the east the Whetstone, Dragoon, and Chiricahua mountain ranges rise from the valley floor. Miller Peak and the Huachuca Moun-tains are visible to the southeast. The Patagonia Mountains march south toward Mexico, and stacking up on the horizon south of the border are seemingly countless other ranges, each impressive in its own respect.

Although the Super Trail offers a different perspective, the quickest way back down to the Roundup trailhead follows the Old Baldy Trail for its entire 5.4-mile length. The grade drop between Josephine Saddle and the parking lot is similar to that of the route's upper leg— that is, not too steep for a comfortable descent.

Water is usually available at Sprung and Bellows springs. Watch for lightning, especially on the summit, and sudden changes in weather during the spring, summer, and autumn months.

80 SYCAMORE CANYON

Distance: 10.6 miles round trip
Difficulty: moderate
Hiking time: 8 hours
Elevation: 4,000 to 3,500 feet

Management: Coronado NF
Wilderness status: Pajarita WA
Season: year-round
USGS map: Ruby

Situated adjacent to the U.S.–Mexico border, Sycamore Canyon is home to a variety of rare plants not commonly found in this country. The canyon itself is rugged and quite scenic, and the hiking route runs along the canyon bottom to a turnaround point at the border.

Take Interstate 19 to the Pena Blanca–Ruby Road exit, 3 miles north of Nogales. Turn west and drive 9 miles on the paved road to the Pena Blanca Recreation Area, then veer left onto Forest Road 39. Follow this for 8.8 miles to the signed turnoff for Sycamore Canyon. The trail starts at the road's end, 0.4 mile south.

At the trailhead a historical marker describes the crumbling adobe walls that lie just beyond the parking area. This was once the site of the John ("Hank") Bartlett and Henry ("Yank") Hewitt Ranch, established in the 1880s. Beyond these old foundations an actual trail heads south for a little way before it enters the canyon bottom. Beyond this point the route mostly follows the canyon bottom for the rest of the hike.

Although the first 1.25 miles are easy, with only shallow stream crossings to negotiate, a difficult passage is reached where the canyon bends to the right and its walls close ranks. After wading through some thigh-deep pools you encounter a much deeper pool that may require swimming in high water. It is possible to climb around to the right along the cliff face, but the rock is slick, especially with wet shoes. A second stretch of canyon bottom that requires some climbing is reached in 0.5 mile. Here again, deep pools can be avoided by climbing along the rock wall to the right. Beyond this point the hike alternates between areas where boulder hopping is necessary and places where the route simply follows the creek bed. A few short stretches of foot trail are also encountered.

Hiking difficulties notwithstanding, the natural history of Sycamore Canyon is unique, to say the least. The first few miles of the hike pass

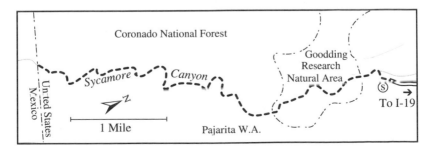

In Sycamore Canyon

through the Goodding Research Natural Area. Named after noted botanist Leslie N. Goodding, this 545-acre tract was established in 1970 to protect the many rare species of flora that grow in the canyon. Among them are the Goodding ash and a species of fern found only in the Himalaya, Mexico, and Sycamore Canyon. Birders will find this canyon to be rich in both numbers and variety. Watch for black phoebes, elegant trogons, green kingfishers, and beardless flycatchers, among other more common species. And Sycamore Canyon is home to the Tarahumara frog and the diminutive Sonora chub, both of which are rare in this country.

After slow going through the upper portion of the hike, the canyon opens up as it nears the border. Here mesquite is the dominate plant type in the canyon bottom and saguaro cactus grows along the hillsides. Eventually, 5.3 miles from the trailhead, a barbed wire fence stretched across the canyon marks the international boundary and the turnaround point for the hike.

While the canyon lies within the Pajarito Wilderness Area, camping is not permitted in the Goodding Research Natural Area. Hiking is possible all year long, but be wary of flash floods, especially during the summer months. Stream crossings may be chilly in the winter. All water should be treated before drinking. It is also a good idea not to hike alone because of the rugged nature of the hike.

ATASCOSA LOOKOUT

Distance: 5 miles round trip　　　**Management: Coronado NF**
Difficulty: strenuous　　　　　　**Wilderness status: none**
Hiking time: 3 hours　　　　　　**Season: year-round**
Elevation: 4,700 to 6,249 feet　　**USGS map: Ruby**

Although short and steep, the hike up to the Atascosa Lookout is well worth the effort. This 6,249-foot vantage point commands a view as spectacular as any found in southern Arizona, and the elevation change makes for an interesting array of plant types.

The Atascosa Trail begins west of the Pena Blanca Recreation Area. To reach the trailhead, turn off Interstate 19 at the Pena Blanca–Ruby exit, about 3 miles north of Nogales. Follow the paved road west to Pena Blanca Lake and then keep left onto Forest Road 39. Follow this graveled route for 4.8 miles to a small parking area on the left side of the road. Marked by only a small, brown trail sign, the Atascosa Trail takes off on the north side of the road.

Because the Atascosa Trail is not regularly maintained, it is rocky and overgrown in places. This, compounded with some steep grades, makes for a strenuous hike. Within the first 0.25 mile the route switchbacks up through a hillside of ocotillo, agave, sotol, and a variety of grasses. Nearly a mile from the trailhead the route tops a small saddle, where it passes through a gate. The trail continues north from here across the head of a drainage that drops off to the east. Beyond the saddle, trees become more common as Mexican pinyon pine, Mexican blue oak, and Emory oak all find suitable habitat here.

After 2 miles the trail passes beneath a soaring buttress of lichen-covered rock. It then makes a switchback just below the lookout to gain a ridge that extends south from the summit. The last 100 yards or so climb a rocky area on the west face of the mountain.

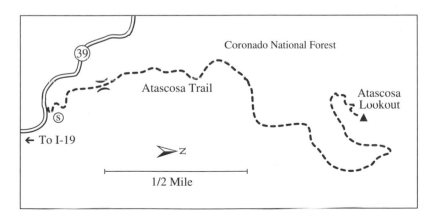

View from Atascosa Lookout

On top is an abandoned fire lookout that is mostly intact. A nearby outhouse clings rather precariously to the cliff's edge. And the 360-degree views are outstanding. Directly north is Atascosa Peak (elevation 6,422 feet), the actual high point of its namesake range. It is possible to make out Sycamore Canyon to the southwest and Pena Blanca Lake to the east. The border town of Nogales is visible to the southeast. To the distant north and northeast rise the Santa Rita, Santa Catalina, and Rincon mountain ranges. Baboquivari and Kitt peaks highlight the western skyline. And marching deep into Mexico are a variety of mountain ranges.

Bring plenty of water—none is available along the way. Watch for rattlesnakes and be extra wary of lightning.

82   MILLER PEAK

Distance: 9.8 miles round trip
Difficulty: strenuous
Hiking time: 7 hours
Elevation: 6,500 to 9,466 feet
Management: Coronado NF

Wilderness status: Miller Peak WA
Season: May to October
USGS maps: Miller Peak, Montezuma Pass

At nearly 9,500 feet, Miller Peak strikes an imposing profile along the skyline just west of Sierra Vista. As the high point of the Huachuca Mountains, this summit commands one of the more memorable views in the state. Not only can you see every major mountain range in southeastern Arizona from the top, but you can peer deep into Mexico as well. Several trails access the top of Miller Peak; this description follows the Crest Trail north from Montezuma Pass.

Follow State Highway 92 south from Sierra Vista for 20 miles to the Montezuma Pass Road (also known as the Coronado Memorial

Highway). Turn right and drive into the Coronado National Memorial. Continue past the visitor center along the winding gravel road to Montezuma Pass. Parking is available at the interpretive pull-off on top of the pass. The trail begins across the road to the north.

From Montezuma Pass the Crest Trail begins climbing among open, south-facing slopes. The vegetation here includes Mexican pinyon pine, Arizona white oak, mountain mahogany, cholla cactus, bear grass, and a variety of true grasses. Grades are mostly moderate. About 1.5 miles in, the route comes upon some old mine shafts and tailings. Such mines are often unstable and should not be entered. Beyond the mines, the Crest Trail continues to gain elevation—a fact that is supported by changes in vegetation. As you climb higher, you begin to see not only alligator juniper, silverleaf oak, Gambel oak, and manzanita growing at trailside, but also Douglas fir and limber pine in several sheltered locations.

After climbing steadily for 2.6 miles the trail reaches the crest of the mountain range, along which the route continues northward. Alternately climbing and dipping, and then climbing again, the route opens up to many fine views on both sides of the ridge. After 1.4 miles of this traverse, the Crest Trail reaches the top end of the Ash Canyon Trail (also known as the Lutz Canyon Trail), which climbs up from the east. A bit farther a trail drops to the west for a short distance to Bond Spring and then on to Ida Canyon below. In the 0.7 mile beyond this trail junction, the Crest Trail continues north, climbing among some interesting cliffs. In addition to the before-mentioned Douglas fir and Gambel oak, watch for scattered patches of aspen. They add a lot of color to the hike in the fall. Upon reaching the west slope of Miller Peak 4.4 miles from the trailhead, turn right at the final trail junction and hike 0.5 mile to the top.

Once the site of a fire lookout, the summit of Miller Peak today features little more than a crumbling concrete foundation. The wonderful 360-degree view from the top, however, takes in such distant peaks as Mount Wrightson, Mount Lemmon, the Rincons, Baboquivari, Cochise Stronghold, and the Chiricahuas. Many other mountain ranges poke up above the deserts of Mexico to the south. The expansive grasslands of the San Rafael Valley lie to the west, while the town of Sierra Vista sits at the foot of the Huachucas to the east. Also of interest is the

View from the summit of Miller Peak

giant balloon that hovers over nearby Fort Huachuca. Fitted with advanced radar equipment, this tethered eye in the sky assists in drug smuggling interdiction. It actually floats higher than the summit of Miller Peak.

Water is not available along this hike, although Bond Spring, a reliable water source, is not too far off the trail. Because of the hike's overall climb of nearly 3,000 feet it is rated as strenuous. Watch for lightning during thunderstorms.

LUTZ CANYON

Distance: 3.8 miles round trip
Difficulty: moderate
Hiking time: 3 hours
Elevation: 5,700 to 6,500 feet
Management: Coronado NF

Wilderness status: Miller Peak WA
Season: year-round
USGS map: Miller Peak

Steep and rugged, the Huachuca Mountains are sliced by several impressive canyons, many of which make for wonderful day hikes. One such drainage is Lutz Canyon on the range's southeastern face.

Drive 12 miles south of Sierra Vista on State Highway 92 to the Ash Canyon Road. Turn right and drive 1.6 miles to the signed turnoff for Lutz Canyon. Turn right and drive 0.6 mile to the trailhead at road's end. The last 0.5 mile of the drive may require a high-clearance 2WD.

Tracing an old mining road for its entire 1.9-mile length, the Lutz Canyon Trail is easy to follow. At the start the trail climbs along a moderately steep grade, but it soon becomes strenuous and remains so for much of the way. Along the entire hike, the trail is shrouded by thick forests of Arizona white, Emory, and silverleaf oak. A few alligator junipers and Mexican pinyon pines also grow at the lower elevations. Along the route's upper end the trail runs adjacent to a drainage bottom where small stands of Douglas fir are found. A few of these trees are quite large. White-tailed deer and javelina frequent these ubiquitous forests, and signs of black bear are plentiful.

Almost 2 miles from the start, the Lutz Canyon Trail reaches the destination of this hike—an old mine site that includes tunnels, tailing piles, and a variety of old machinery. Beginning in the late 1870s, Lutz Canyon, like many other canyons in the Huachucas, was abuzz with

Old mine machinery in Lutz Canyon

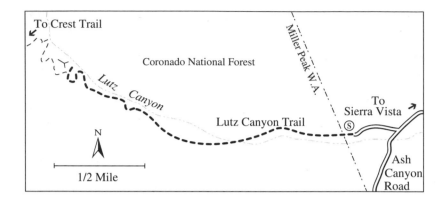

the sounds of picks, shovels, and crusher engines. Gold was the chief draw, but other minerals were found as well. Although they were active into this century, these mines eventually closed and the remains have since turned into antiquated relics.

The route continues past the mine in the form of a narrow trail that is severely overgrown. Another mine tunnel is found up above, and the trail eventually connects with the Crest Trail south of Miller Peak. If you do not mind the constant tug of thorny brush at your legs, you may consider continuing on beyond the first mine.

Water is not available in Lutz Canyon. As with any open mine shaft, entering the tunnels can be hazardous.

RAMSEY CANYON

Distance: 2 miles round trip
Difficulty: moderate
Hiking time: 2 hours
Elevation: 5,400 to 6,200 feet
Management: The Nature
  Conservancy, Coronado NF

Wilderness status: Miller Peak
  WA
Season: year-round
USGS map: Miller Peak

World renowned for its hummingbirds, Ramsey Canyon is one of Arizona's best-known birding areas. From April to September this 300-acre preserve is visited by more than a dozen different species of hummingbirds. Of course, the wonders of Ramsey Canyon are not restricted to birds. Blessed with a perennially flowing creek, the drainage supports both a lush riparian ecosystem and several species of animals besides birds. A short excursion, this hike explores the different faces of Ramsey Canyon and the surrounding Huachuca Mountains.

Drive 6 miles south of Sierra Vista on State Highway 92 to the Ramsey Canyon Road. Turn right and drive 3.5 miles to the road's end.

Hikers must pick up a trail pass at the visitor center. Because The Nature Conservancy restricts the number of daily visitors, it is best to visit the preserve on a weekday. Weekend visits require reservations because of the canyon's popularity. A small cash donation is requested from nonmembers of The Nature Conservancy.

Beginning in front of the visitor center, this hike first follows a dirt road along the canyon bottom for 0.5 mile. Closed to most traffic, this road accesses several rustic cabins that The Nature Conservancy rents out on a nightly basis. Call (602) 378-2785 for reservations. Along this stretch the preserve's riparian plant life can be enjoyed. Paramount are the giant Arizona sycamores, which have obviously benefited from the nearby gurgling stream. Other species of deciduous trees include Arizona walnut, bigtooth maple, and willow. Among this leafy overstory it is possible to spot not only several different species of hummingbirds but a variety of other birds, as well. The painted redstart, yellow-eyed junco, sulfur-bellied flycatcher, and elegant trogon are but a few.

Along the first 0.5 mile you can also see the remains of several old buildings, most of which have fallen into disrepair. After being settled at the turn of the century, 280 acres of the canyon bottom came under the ownership of N. C. Bledsoe, a doctor from nearby Bisbee. Safeguarding the natural beauty of the area, Bledsoe removed several structures left behind by the earlier homesteaders. Upon Bledsoe's death in 1974 the land was donated to The Nature Conservancy.

In the second 0.5 mile of the hike, the Ramsey Canyon Trail climbs 600 feet up the drainage's south face. Growing on this semiarid slope

Old cabin in Ramsey Canyon

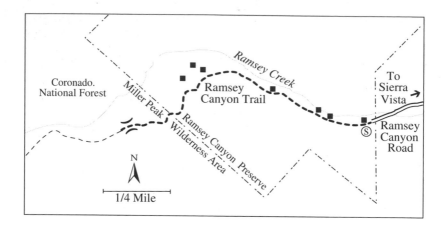

are Mexican pinyon pine, manzanita, ponderosa pine, and a variety of oaks—including Emory, silverleaf, Arizona white, and Gambel. The Nature Conservancy has identified eight different species of oak that grow in the canyon.

Soon after crossing into the Coronado National Forest the trail reaches a small saddle that serves as the turnaround point for the hike. Upon reaching this high point be sure to scramble out on the rocks to the right. This viewpoint overlooks much of the canyon below. By continuing up the trail beyond this saddle it is possible to access a network of trails that explore the adjacent Miller Peak Wilderness.

Gaining 800 feet in 1 mile, this hike is moderate in difficulty. Because the creek water must be treated, it is best to fill up a canteen at the visitor center. The Nature Conservancy regulations prohibit pets, firearms, and livestock within the preserve.

85 JOE'S CANYON

Distance: 7 miles round trip
Difficulty: moderate
Hiking time: 4 hours
Elevation: 5,300 to 6,800 feet
Management: Coronado National Memorial

Wilderness status: none
Season: year-round
USGS map: Montezuma Pass

When Coronado marched into what would become the American Southwest in 1540, it marked an important, and sometimes tragic, episode in American history. For the first time the tradition-bound Native Americans of the Southwest came in contact with European settlers. The National Park Service has established the Coronado National Memorial along a scenic stretch of the Arizona–Mexico border. Climbing

Looking into Mexico from the Joe's Canyon Trail

to a high ridge overlooking both sides of the international boundary is the Joe's Canyon Trail.

Drive south from Sierra Vista on State Highway 92 for 16 miles to the Montezuma Canyon Road (also known as the Coronado Memorial Highway). Turn west and drive 5 miles to the memorial's visitor center. Park here and find the trail's start next to the turnoff for a picnic area across the road.

The first 0.5 mile of the Joe's Canyon Trail crosses a burn area that spread across much of the Coronado National Memorial in 1988. Here, as on the ridge top above, blackened skeletons of trees are scattered about along with lush grasses, occasional clumps of bear grass (a member of the lily family), yucca, and sotol. Beyond the burn area the trail switchbacks up the right side of a small draw, within which an

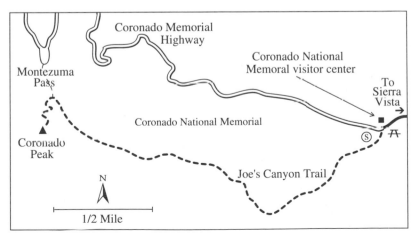

untorched section of forest includes Arizona white oak, blackjack oak, Mexican pinyon pine, and alligator juniper.

After climbing for 1.25 miles the trail tops out on an open ridgeline, which it then follows to the west. All along the ridge the views in all directions are impressive. To the south stretches Mexico, with its isolated *ranchitas* and alluring mountain ranges. To the north rises the bulk of the Huachuca Mountains—Ash Peak, Montezuma Peak, and the tip of the range's high point, Miller Peak. And eastward lies the San Pedro River Valley, the route Coronado probably followed on his 1540 expedition.

Because most of the hike's 1,500-foot climb is completed in the first 1.25 miles, the rest of the walk to Coronado Peak (visible to the west) is a pleasurable stroll with only moderate changes in the grade. At 6,864 feet, Coronado Peak offers a fine vantage point above the San Rafael Valley to the west of the memorial. Sprawling across this wide open area are some beautiful grasslands and remote ranches. Beyond the valley rise the Patagonia Mountains and, some 80 miles distant, Baboquivari Peak on the Tohono O'odham Indian Reservation is visible. The summit of Coronado Peak is connected to Montezuma Pass (which can be reached from the memorial's visitor center via a gravel road) by a 0.5-mile interpretive trail.

Bring drinking water, as none is found along this trail. Watch for lightning. Pets are not permitted on trails in the national memorial.

86 SAN PEDRO RIVER

Distance: 2.5 miles round trip
Difficulty: easy
Hiking time: 2 hours
Elevation: 4,100 to 4,000 feet

Management: BLM
Wilderness status: none
Season: year-round
USGS map: Fairbank

In an arid state such as Arizona the importance of riparian areas cannot be overstated. Water, especially that which flows year-round, provides not only suitable growing conditions for various species of trees, shrubs, and plants, but also supports a variety of wildlife. The San Pedro River is a good example. Flowing north out of Mexico toward its eventual rendezvous with the Gila River at Winkelman, the San Pedro forms a 100-mile-long greenbelt in southeastern Arizona. Nearly 40 miles of the river—from the border to St. David—is included in the San Pedro Riparian National Conservation Area (NCA). Established in 1988 by an act of Congress, this 57,000-acre parcel of land is managed by the BLM. This hike begins at the Charleston Road and travels downstream (north) to the Narrows.

Drive southwest on Charleston Road from Tombstone toward Sierra Vista for 8.5 miles, to the Charleston Road crossing. A large parking area is provided on the left side of the road just before the bridge. Walk underneath the bridge to reach the riverbed.

The San Pedro River

No established trail is followed, but none is needed because the route simply continues down the riverbed. Some parts of the flood plain may prove too thick with undergrowth for easy walking, and river crossings usually require wading.

Providing shade for much of the way are impressive stands of Fremont cottonwoods and willow trees. Ash, netleaf hackberry, soapberry, and Arizona walnut also grow here, but with less frequency. Tracks along the muddy riverbank may include those of white-tailed and mule deer, ringtail cats, javelina, bobcats, and even mountain lions. Bird life along the San Pedro is especially abundant: some 350 species either inhabit or at least visit the area. These include the vermilion flycatcher, the mourning dove, the yellow-billed cuckoo, and more than two dozen

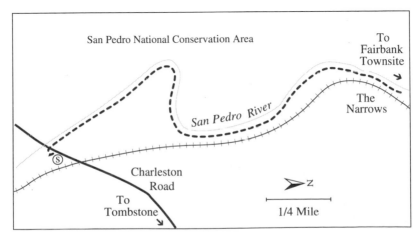

different species of raptors. So plentiful are birds in the San Pedro Riparian NCA that it is rated as one of the best birding areas in the country.

At 1.25 miles the route reaches the Narrows, where the San Pedro passes between two low hills. At this point this hike turns back. It is possible, however, to hike another 7 miles to the next crossing, at the Fairbank Townsite. Here, where State Highway 82 crosses the San Pedro, is the BLM's headquarters for the San Pedro Riparian NCA. Visitors may pick up additional information, including maps. Overnight camping is allowed but a permit must first be obtained. A camping fee is also charged. Five crossing areas offer access to different sections of the NCA.

Bring plenty of drinking water—the river is not fit for consumption. Hot temperatures may persist in the summer. Do not attempt this hike in periods of very high water.

87 COCHISE TRAIL

Distance: 6 miles round trip	Management: Coronado NF
Difficulty: moderate	Wilderness status: none
Hiking time: 4 hours	Season: year-round
Elevation: 4,900 to 6,000 feet	USGS map: Pearce

Named for the famed Apache chief, Cochise Stronghold is an alluring and mysterious place. Ringed by salmon-tinted granite domes and faces, this wilderness of rock provided safe haven for Cochise during the twelve years that he and his warriors fought the U.S. Army. Never surrendering, Cochise agreed to peace only in exchange for land in 1872. Cochise died on June 8, 1874, and he was buried somewhere among the rocks of the Stronghold by friends. To this day, no one is sure where, though. Circling south from a Forest Service campground to Stronghold Divide, the Cochise Trail offers a wonderful look at this memorable locale.

Located on the east side of the Dragoon Mountains (named after the U.S. Cavalry Dragoons), East Cochise Stronghold is reached by driving south from Interstate 10 on US Highway 191 (formerly 180/666) to Sun Sites. Turn west at the sign for the stronghold and drive 9 miles on a graded gravel road. The trailhead is located in the Cochise Stronghold Campground. The Cochise Trail actually begins at the end of a short nature trail that is easy to follow.

For the first mile the route climbs up a gentle grade along a canyon bottom. Thick woodlands of Mexican pinyon pine, Arizona white oak, alligator juniper, and manzanita persist. A few sycamores also grow in the creek bottom. After 0.5 mile the trail cuts through some rocky terrain where it scrambles a bit among large boulders. These colorful granite formations are often clad with lichens, which add wisps of green to the pink rock. With literally thousands of nooks, crannies, and

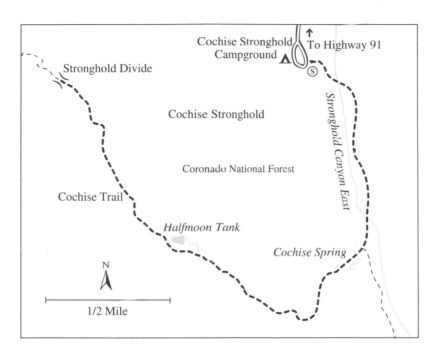

Cochise Stronghold Campground

To Highway 91

Stronghold Divide

Cochise Stronghold

Stronghold Canyon East

Coronado National Forest

Cochise Trail

Halfmoon Tank

Cochise Spring

N

1/2 Mile

The Cochise Stronghold is a wonderful collection of rocks.

crevices here, it is easy to understand how Cochise's body has lain undisturbed for more than a century.

After 1 mile the trail passes Cochise Spring and then climbs moderately through a few switchbacks for 0.75 mile to Halfmoon Tank. Complete with cattails, this small stock pond is an important source of water for wildlife in the area. Beyond the tank, the trail generally levels off before reaching Stronghold Divide, 3 miles from the trailhead. Because this saddle lies behind the rocky facade that towers over the campground it offers a very different view of the picturesque stronghold. Beyond the divide, the trail continues down Stronghold Canyon West for another 1.75 miles to the end of a 4WD road. The divide, however, makes a logical turnaround point for the hike.

Bring drinking water on this hike. Cochise Spring is not always flowing, and water from Halfmoon Tank must be treated. Watch for lightning during thunderstorms. Expect hot temperatures in the summer.

88 HEART OF ROCKS

Distance: 7.1 miles round trip
Difficulty: moderate
Hiking time: 5 hours
Elevation: 5,400 to 6,860 feet
Management: Chiricahua NM

Wilderness status: Chiricahua
WA
Season: year-round
USGS maps: Cochise Head,
Rustler Park

Revealing some of the most interesting geological formations that Chiricahua National Monument has to offer is the Heart of Rocks area. Punch and Judy, Pinnacle Balanced Rock, and Duck on a Rock are but three of several aptly named formations found within this vast garden of naturally created statuary. In reaching the Heart of Rocks, this hike also reveals some interesting plant communities within Rhyolite and Sarah Deming canyons.

Drive about 30 miles southeast from Willcox on State Highway 186.

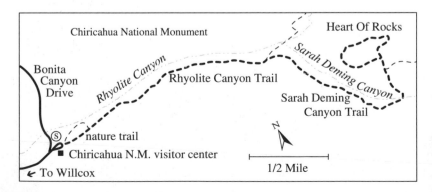

Turn east onto State Highway 181 and continue another 4 miles to the monument entrance. This hike begins at the Chiricahua National Monument visitor center, about 1 mile farther.

Beginning at the east end of the parking lot, the first 0.25 mile of the route follows a nature trail along the level bottom of Rhyolite Canyon. This is a good chance to identify some of the flora of the area thanks to interpretive signs along the way. Although the stream is intermittent in this canyon, there is still enough groundwater to support a generous overstory of Apache and Chihuahua pines, Arizona cypress, alligator juniper, and several oaks—Emory, silverleaf, and Arizona white, to name a few.

After branching right from the nature trail, the route continues up the Rhyolite Canyon Trail. Rhyolite is the volcanic rock of which the monument's formations are made. Geologists believe that it originated as ash from a fiery volcanic explosion 25 million years ago. Eroding at different rates, countless hoodoos of many shapes and sizes resulted. The first of these come into view as the Rhyolite Canyon Trail climbs out of the canyon bottom along the south side of the drainage. Well maintained, this trail is a breeze to follow, despite its mostly moderate grade.

After following the Rhyolite Canyon Trail for 1.5 miles, the route then turns right up Sarah Deming Canyon. Continuing on for a little over a mile, this leg of the hike climbs an easy to moderate grade. Along the way some rather stately Apache pine forests and a few gigantic Arizona cypress add to the scenery, as do more rock formations. Shortly after crossing the drainage bottom the trail begins to climb a series of short switchbacks as it gains the north face of the canyon.

Rock formations in the Heart of Rocks area

Upon passing some impressive stone spires the trail reaches a saddle of sorts and a trail junction, 3.1 miles from the trailhead. The right-hand route continues east toward Totem Canyon and Inspiration Point. A short distance to the left is a trail register and a sign marking the start of the 0.9-mile Heart of Rocks Trail.

Although you can follow this loop trail in either direction, this description turns left at the trail register to trace it clockwise. After climbing a short distance, the trail reaches Pinnacle Balanced Rock, a massive totem precariously balanced on the left side of the trail. Beyond this impressive formation are others, including Camel's Head, Thor's Hammer, Punch and Judy, Duck on a Rock, and the Kissing Rocks. The Heart of Rocks Trail also provides spectacular views of the rugged north end of the Chiricahua Mountains. Of particular prominence is Cochise Head, a large face of rock that rises northeast of the monument. Also, take note of the vegetation in the Heart of Rocks area. In comparison to the canyon bottom below, this drier basin supports diminutive Apache pines, Mexican pinyon pines, stunted oaks, small Arizona cypress, and manzanita bushes. Upon finishing the Heart of Rocks loop, return to the trailhead by retracing the Sarah Deming Canyon and Rhyolite Canyon trails.

Water is not available along this hike, so bring plenty. Summers may see temperatures in the 90s, while winter snowfall may make the trail difficult to follow. Watch for lightning in exposed terrain.

89 ECHO CANYON

Distance: 3.5 miles
Difficulty: moderate
Hiking time: 3 hours
Elevation: 6,780 to 6,330 feet
Management: Chiricahua NM

Wilderness status: Chiricahua WA
Season: year-round
USGS map: Cochise Head

Winding through a stunning collection of strange rock formations, the loop hike through Echo Canyon offers a short yet memorable introduction to the wonders of the Chiricahua National Monument. Add to this lesson in geology some fine vistas and a fascinating variety of plant life and you have a great hike. Constructed by the Civilian Conservation Corps in 1936 and 1937, the Echo Canyon Trail has that sturdy, comfortable feel that most CCC projects possess.

Drive 30 miles southeast from Willcox on State Highway 186. Turn east onto State Highway 181 and continue for another 4 miles to the monument entrance. This hike begins at the Echo Canyon Trail Parking Area, 5.5 miles past the Chiricahua National Monument visitor center on the Bonita Canyon Drive.

Shortly after starting out this hike reaches the first of four trail junctions along the way. Turn right onto the Echo Canyon Trail, which begins winding among lichen-covered rocks and pinnacles. After 0.5

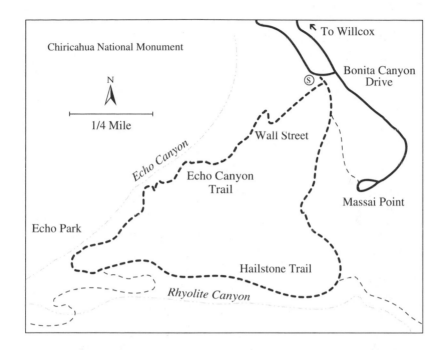

mile the grade drops slightly and the trail enters an area known as "Wall Street." Crowded in by towering columns of rock, this stretch of the hike reveals several secretive grottos and passageways. Although these passageways may be inviting places to explore, it is imperative to be extra cautious because of dangerous drop-offs.

About 1 mile from the trailhead, the route descends some short switchbacks into Echo Canyon. Following a mostly moderately steep grade, the trail soon reaches the canyon bottom. Whereas Mexican pinyon pine, oaks, manzanita, and other low-profile trees grow among the rock formations above, the availability of groundwater in this drainage bottom allows for towering Apache pine, Douglas fir, and Arizona cypress. This shady area is known as Echo Park.

After 1.6 miles, the route reaches a second junction. The trail to the right leads down Rhyolite Canyon to the visitor center. Turn left and head back to the Echo Canyon trailhead by way of the Hailstone Trail. Climbing easily along the arid south-facing wall of Rhyolite Canyon for 0.8 mile, this section of the hike passes among pinyon and juniper forests.

At a third trail junction near the upper end of Rhyolite Canyon, keep left to follow a shallow drainage for 0.7 mile. This section of the hike climbs along an easy grade that is partially shaded by pines. At the final trail junction the route keeps left again and continues another 0.2 mile to the trailhead. A right turn here leads 0.2 mile to Massai Point and the end of the Bonita Canyon Drive. From this vista it is possible to look out over most of the monument.

The "Wall Street" section of the Echo Canyon hike

Be sure to bring plenty of drinking water—none is found along the Echo Canyon hike. Ice and snow may be encountered in the winter. Watch for lightning and precipitous terrain in the higher areas.

90 CHIRICAHUA PEAK

Distance: 10 miles round trip
Difficulty: moderate
Hiking time: 6 hours
Elevation: 8,400 to 9,796 feet
Management: Coronado NF

Wilderness status: Chiricahua WA
Season: May to October
USGS maps: Rustler Park, Chiricahua Peak

Topping out at nearly 10,000 feet, the Chiricahuas are the second-highest mountain range in southeastern Arizona. Despite their lofty status, however, reaching the summit is a relatively simple task, thanks to the Crest Trail. In just 5 miles of mostly easy grades this hike will put you on top of 9,796-foot Chiricahua Peak.

From Douglas drive 35 miles north on US Highway 191 (formerly

180/666) to State Highway 181. Turn east on Highway 181 and drive 26 miles, following the signs for Chiricahua National Monument. Just before entering the monument, keep right on the graveled Pinery Canyon Road (Forest Road 42) and continue 12 miles to Onion Saddle and the turnoff for Rustler Park. From this junction drive 3 miles south to the upper loop of Rustler Park Campground.

After traveling a short distance west from the trailhead, the route bears left to take up the Crest Trail heading south along the gentle, tree-covered crest of the range. At 1.5 miles the route reaches Bootlegger Saddle, where the Rock Creek Trail climbs up from the west. Some fine views are afforded from nearby rock outcrops. The Crest Trail continues from the saddle for another mile before reaching a major intersection of trails. One spur trail leads 0.7 mile north to the end of the 4WD Long Park Road, which is now closed to vehicles. Another trail heads east from this point for 1.9 miles to scenic Centella Point. And still another route climbs to the top of nearby Flys Peak (elevation 9,666 feet).

Continuing south, the Crest Trail covers another 0.6 mile before connecting with the upper end of the Saulsbury Trail, a popular route that begins at Turkey Creek. In another 0.3 mile the Crest Trail crosses a small opening known as Round Park. Such breaks in the forest cover are rare along the higher portions of the Chiricahua range. A 0.2-mile spur trail turns left shortly beyond Round Park to find Booger Spring, which, like most springs in the area, is usually flowing.

From Round Park, the Crest Trail continues for 0.7 mile to Cima Park, where the Greenhouse Trail drops off to the east. In another 0.2 mile the trail arrives at a junction with the upper end of the Mormon Ridge Trail. Following that is the turnoff for Anita Park, which, complete with a spring and some old-growth conifers, makes for a nice overnight spot. Be sure to camp among the trees and not in the fragile meadow. A short distance farther, the Crest Trail reaches Junction

Impressive forests grow beside the trail to Chiricahua Peak.

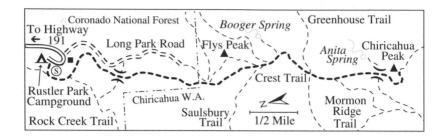

Saddle and a final crossroad of routes. It is not difficult to find the well-marked trail that makes the moderate 0.5-mile climb to the top of Chiricahua Peak, although it actually branches off a short distance beyond Junction Saddle. Because the summit is shrouded in thick forest cover, the only indications that you are standing on top of the range are a sign and a geological marker.

Despite the lack of views from Chiricahua Peak, this hike provides other highlights. Of primary interest is the changing forest cover encountered all along the route. Starting out among stands of Chihuahua and Apache pines—both of which are Mexican species—the hike soon encounters timber more typical of latitudes to the north. In addition to ponderosa pine and Douglas fir, the Crest Trail also passes among beautiful stands of Engelmann spruce. Chiricahua Peak, in fact, marks the southernmost extent of the species in North America. Several stands of aspen also shade the trail, making a colorful canopy in the fall.

Two different springs within a mile of the Crest Trail—Booger and Anita—usually provide adequate drinking water. Overnight hikers should take precautions appropriate for camping in bear country. Lightning may be hazardous during summer thunderstorms.

91 POLE BRIDGE CANYON

Distance: 4.8 miles round trip
Difficulty: strenuous
Hiking time: 3 hours
Elevation: 6,200 to 8,000 feet
Management: Coronado NF

Wilderness status: Chiricahua WA
Season: May to November
USGS map: Chiricahua Peak

Located in the southernmost corner of the state, the Chiricahua Mountains are home to a number of plants and animals not normally found in the United States. Fauna usually associated with Mexico's Sierra Madre, such as the Apache fox squirrel and the Mexican chickadee, are often spotted in the Chiricahuas. Tree species such as the Chihuahua pine grow here, as well. The Pole Bridge Research Natural Area was designated to protect a sampling of the Chiricahuas' unusual collection of flora and fauna. Encompassing a short yet steep

Old growth forest in Pole Bridge Canyon

drainage, the area is accessed by the Pole Bridge Trail.

Pole Bridge Canyon is reached by driving up the Turkey Creek drainage on the west slope of Chiricahua Peak. From Douglas drive approximately 35 miles north on US Highway 191 (formerly 180/666) to the turnoff for Chiricahua National Monument. Drive east on State

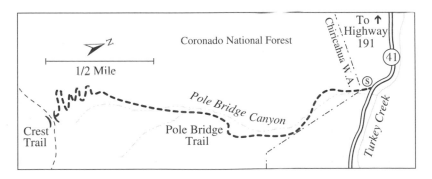

Highway 181 for 12 miles to where the road turns 90 degrees north. Follow Forest Road 41 east for 9.8 miles to the signed start of the Pole Bridge Trail. The trail follows a small canyon south from the road.

For the first 0.75 mile the trail climbs up the canyon bottom along a mostly easy grade. Although normally dry, some small pools of water may surface along the streambed. Completely forested, this leg of the hike encounters a varied mix of oaks (Emory and silverleaf), ponderosa pine, and Chihuahua pine. Also noteworthy are a few very large alligator junipers.

Nearing the 1-mile mark, the trail steepens as the first of several switchbacks is reached. Beyond this point the route ascends a moderate to strenuous grade as it climbs 1,400 feet in the next 1.5 miles. During this gain in elevation you begin to see a change in forest type. Although pines are still plentiful, Douglas fir is now more common. Gambel oak becomes the prominent species of deciduous tree, although silverleaf oak is still present. And ferns find suitable habitat on the open forest floor.

As the trail nears a saddle on the ridge that separates Pole Bridge Canyon from Long John Canyon to the south, the terrain becomes sufficiently steep to allow for limited vistas through the upper branches of trees growing below. In a few places you can glimpse the overall ruggedness of the west side of the Chiricahua Mountains, and the nearly ubiquitous timber that covers it. On the saddle the Pole Bridge Trail connects with the Long John Trail, which runs in both directions along the ridge top. A right turn eventually leads south to Long John Canyon, while a left turn continues 1.4 miles east to Johnson Peak. Although this hike turns around here at the saddle, be sure to walk 50 yards east for a nice view into the southwestern quarter of the Chiricahua range.

Because water is not always available in Pole Bridge Canyon, be sure to bring all that you will require.

92   FORT BOWIE

Distance: 3 miles round trip	**Management: Fort Bowie NHS**
Difficulty: easy	**Wilderness status: none**
Hiking time: 3 hours	**Season: year-round**
Elevation: 4,700 to 5,152 feet	**USGS map: Cochise Head**

Situated in Apache Pass, Fort Bowie played an integral role in the conquest and settlement of the American West. A visit to this national historic site today will reveal the complete story. To better protect the delicate antiquities of the site, the facility is accessed by a 3-mile round trip interpretive trail.

The hike to Fort Bowie begins along the graveled Apache Pass Road that runs south from the town of Bowie on Interstate 10 to State Highway 186. The signed trailhead is 13 miles south of Bowie and 8 miles northeast of Highway 186.

Before starting out be sure to read the interpretive signs at the trailhead. One describes how the Apache Pass area lies on the border of two distinct biomes—the Sonoran and Chihuahuan deserts—and how plant and animal species of both are represented here. This lesson in natural history is continued all along the hike in the form of small signs that identify numerous plants, including ocotillo, cane cholla, Palmer agave, soaptree yucca, saltbush, desert sumac, alligator juniper, scrub live oak, and Arizona walnut. Other plants that are plentiful in numbers are mesquite, sotol, and prickly pear cactus.

A second sign begins an interesting historical narrative that is continued along the entire hike. Originally the domain of the Chiricahua Apache Indians, Apache Pass proved to be of strategic interest to settlers because of Apache Spring—the only reliable source of water for dozens of miles. In 1854, a survey party explored the pass in search of a route for the Southern Pacific Railroad; the line was eventually built to the north. And in 1858 the famous Butterfield Overland Trail, a stage route between St. Louis and San Francisco, crossed the pass for three years before a conflict between the Apache chief Cochise and the Army arose. Shutting down the stage line, this disagreement led to a decade of warfare and the establishment of Fort Bowie. It was not until Cochise agreed to live peacefully in exchange for a 3,000-square-mile reservation that the disagreement was settled.

In the years that followed, conditions on the reservation deteriorated and discontent grew. In 1876, two years after Cochise's death, the Chiracahua Reservation was closed and its occupants were moved north to the San Carlos Reservation. After fleeing to Mexico, breakaway bands renewed fighting with the whites. Best known of these factions was a group led by Geronimo. Fort Bowie became headquarters for the lengthy campaign to quash Geronimo's resistance, and it was not until 1886 that he finally succumbed. His surrender brought an end to this nation's Indian wars and opened up settlement of the region. Eight years later, Fort Bowie was officially closed.

Today, the hike to Fort Bowie reveals many reminders of this chap-

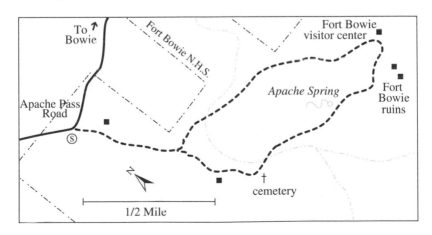

The remains of historic Fort Bowie

ter in American history. A stone foundation recalls a station along the Butterfield Overland Trail. The post cemetery reflected the ferocity of the times. Many grave markers simply read: UNKNOWN. KILLED BY INDIANS. The graves of the soldiers were moved to the National Cemetery in San Francisco in 1895, but one wooden marker left behind is that of Little Robe, a son of Geronimo. The adobe foundation of the Chiricahua Indian Agency hints at the spirit of cooperation that existed during the first years of the Chiricahua Reservation. A recreated Apache wickiup nearby offers a glimpse of what life was like for these mostly nomadic people. And much-coveted Apache Spring still gurgles at trailside near the fort itself.

Winding easily through the desert hills of Apache Pass, the trail reaches Fort Bowie in 1.5 miles. The ruins of the original Fort Bowie are located on a hill just south of the spring, while the second, much larger, fort is situated on the flats east of the spring. Included in the complex were such structures as corrals and stables, a general store, a hospital and school, officers' quarters, infantry barracks, a mess hall, and much more. As part of the national historic site, a small ranger station at the fort site offers an interesting display of old photos and relics. Books are for sale and a ranger is on hand to answer questions. Drinking water is also available.

From the fort site the route returns to the trailhead via a different, more scenic route that climbs a hill behind the ranger station. From this high point it is possible to look down upon Fort Bowie and much of the rest of the hike. After dropping off the ridge the route soon rejoins the incoming trail shortly after crossing a dry wash.

Although water is available at the ranger station, it is wise to bring along a canteen anyway. Watch for rattlesnakes (they have the right-of-way here) and be prepared for temperatures above 100 degrees Fahrenheit in the summer. Removal of any historic or natural items within a unit of the National Park Service is strictly prohibited. Metal detectors, shovels, and guns are also prohibited. And you are asked not to sit or climb on any walls or mounds.

93 BASS CANYON–HOT SPRINGS LOOP

Distance: 3.5 miles round trip
Difficulty: easy
Hiking time: 3 hours
Elevation: 4,000 to 4,200 feet
Management: The Nature
  Conservancy, BLM

Wilderness status: none
Season: year-round
USGS maps: Hookers Hot
  Springs, Soza Mesa

Jointly operated by the BLM, the Coronado National Forest, and The Nature Conservancy, the Muleshoe Ranch Cooperative Management Area encompasses 49,000 acres of pristine desert environments along the southern end of the Galiuro Mountains. Most critical are the riparian communities found along six perennial streams that flow through the area. Offering a good introduction to this unique preserve is the 3.5-mile Bass Canyon–Hot Springs Loop, which begins at the historic Muleshoe Ranch headquarters.

The ranch is situated in a remote area west of Willcox, and reaching it is in itself an adventure. From Willcox drive west on the Airport Road. Shortly after the airport the road turns to dirt and becomes the Cascabel Road. Fifteen miles from town, turn right at a sign for the Muleshoe Ranch. Continue for another 14 miles to the ranch. Although a bit rough toward the end, the drive is passable to most 2WD vehicles

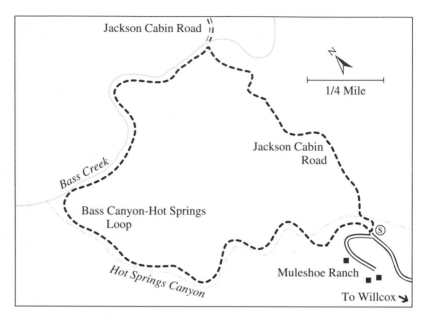

when dry. A day-use parking area is provided for hikers. It is requested that all visitors register at the turnoff for the Jackson Cabin Road.

The hike begins by following the 4WD Jackson Cabin Road 1 mile north to where it crosses Bass Creek. Topping a low ridge, this segment of the hike provides some good views of the surrounding topography. Where the road crosses Bass Creek, turn left at a small brown sign and follow the drainage downstream. For the next mile no actual trail exists, but because you follow the canyon bottom none is really needed.

Growing along Bass Creek are many beautiful stands of cottonwood and white-barked Arizona sycamore. The ground beneath these trees is often littered with deadfall, but the hiking is nevertheless easy. Like most riparian areas in southern Arizona, Bass Canyon is prime habitat for a variety of birds. More than 190 species regularly occur in the area, and several others have been sighted. Five different native species of fish inhabit the perennial waters of the creek, among them the Gila chub, the long-finned and speckled dace, and two varieties of sucker. Providing a stark contrast to the lush growth along the stream are the scattered saguaro cactus and ocotillo that grow among the surrounding hills. This lower Sonoran community serves as a reminder that this region of the state is mostly desert.

About a mile downstream from the Jackson Cabin Road, Bass Creek intersects Hot Springs Canyon, which in turn continues 12 miles west to the San Pedro River. The hiking route turns left to follow Hot Springs Wash 1.5 miles upstream to the ranch headquarters. Here again, no real trail is found—you simply follow the wash bottom.

Upon completing the hike be sure to visit the ranch itself. Established

Riparian growth along Bass Creek

more than a century ago, Muleshoe Ranch enjoys a colorful past. In 1862, army troops utilized the hot springs at the site. The area was then homesteaded by Dr. Glendy King. Envisioning the commercial possibilities of the hot springs, King established a spa in the early 1880s. In August 1884 he was gunned down over a dispute with a neighbor. The ranch changed hands several times before The Nature Conservancy purchased it in 1982. Many of the old adobe buildings have since been converted into *casitas,* which can be rented from the Conservancy; call (602) 384-2626 for information. A camping area and visitor center are also provided.

Although Bass Creek is almost always flowing, it is best to bring your own water. Expect very hot temperatures in the summer. Watch for flash flooding in the washes. Be wary of rattlesnakes throughout the hike. Keep in mind that the hot springs are open to *casita* guests only.

94   ARCADIA TRAIL

Distance: 10.2 miles round trip
Difficulty: moderate
Hiking time: 7 hours
Elevation: 6,700 to 9,500 feet

Management: Coronado NF
Wilderness status: none
Season: May to October
USGS map: Mount Graham

Topped by 10,717-foot Mount Graham, the Pinaleno Mountains are the highest of southeastern Arizona's sky islands. Surrounded by arid basins, this mountain range rises decisively near the town of Safford. In so doing it provides a dramatic shift in climatic conditions, which in

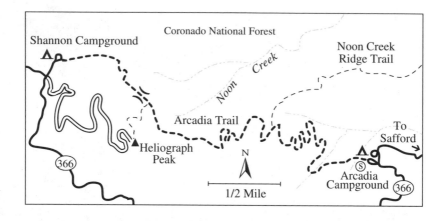

turn supports flora remarkably different from that of the desert below. A hike along the Arcadia National Recreation Trail reveals much about the range's biological countenance.

Because this route description includes the return hike to your car, it begins at the trail's lower end at the Arcadia Campground. From Safford drive 9 miles south on US Highway 191 (formerly 180/666) to the turnoff for State Highway 366. Follow it west for 11.4 miles to the group reservation picnic area, just past the Arcadia Campground. The trail takes off from the back end of the facility.

Within the first 0.5 mile the Arcadia Trail climbs moderately up a few switchbacks before leveling off to cross a drainage bottom. In contrast to the open ponderosa pine forest that first shades the trail, this ravine features a relatively lush collection of bigtooth maple, Arizona walnut, Gambel oak, limber pine, and several large Douglas fir. Upon crossing the normally dry streambed the trail begins to climb again as it bends around an east-facing slope. For the next 3.5 miles the route encounters a generally arid mix of scattered ponderosa pine and desert oak.

Climbing over 1,000 feet in the next 1.5 miles, the Arcadia Trail follows a long series of switchbacks before connecting with the upper end of the Noon Creek Ridge Trail. At this point you are 2 miles into the hike. After keeping left at the junction, the route continues to climb up a moderate to steep grade through additional switchbacks as it heads toward Heliograph Peak. Some nice views to the north and east come into play all along this leg of the hike.

About 4 miles from the trailhead, the Arcadia Trail connects with a 1-mile spur trail that leads to the summit of Heliograph Peak (elevation 10,022 feet). It then tops out on a small saddle that serves as the high point of the hike. Some nice vistas are possible from a rock outcropping to the right. Beyond the saddle the trail drops down a few easy switchbacks beneath a towering mix of quaking aspen and Engelmann spruce. Engelmann spruce are a rarity in southern Arizona because only a few mountains are high enough in elevation to support them. In the last 0.5 mile the Arcadia Trail is mostly level as it heads

Old growth timber along the Arcadia Trail

west through stands of Douglas fir and Engelmann spruce. After 5.1 miles the trail ends at the Shannon Campground (elevation 9,100 feet). The return to your car is easier, as you now descend the same 2,800 vertical feet just climbed. With a car shuttle it is possible to follow the Arcadia Trail in only one direction. If you choose this option, keep in mind that it is easier to follow the route downhill, in the opposite direction of this description. Shannon Campground lies 10 miles beyond Arcadia Campground via a good paved road.

Bring drinking water on this hike—none exists along the way. Watch for lightning and changing weather conditions.

95 ARAVAIPA CANYON

Distance: 11 miles one way
Difficulty: easy
Hiking time: 2 days
Elevation: 3,000 to 3,200 feet
Management: BLM

Wilderness status: Aravaipa
**   Canyon WA**
Season: year-round
USGS maps: Brandenburg
**   Mountain, Booger Canyon**

Thanks to perennial Aravaipa Creek, Aravaipa Canyon features one of the most diverse riparian communities in the state. Add soaring canyon walls and a smattering of historical sites to its wonderful collection of flora and fauna, and you have a truly memorable hike.

Eleven miles in length, Aravaipa Canyon may be accessed from

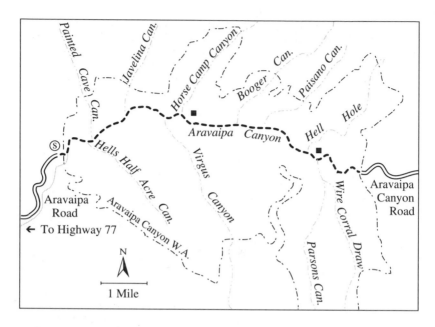

either end. Because the eastern side is remote, this hike description begins at the mouth of the canyon to the west. To reach the western trailhead, drive 11 miles south from Winkelman on State Highway 77 to the Aravaipa Road. Turn east and drive 12 miles to the end of this partially paved and partially graded dirt road. A small parking area with some primitive facilities and a self-service fee station is provided. A fee of $1.50 per person per day is charged. Because the BLM limits the number of people in the canyon to fifty per day, you must obtain a permit. To do so, contact the BLM, Safford District, 711 14th Avenue, Safford, AZ 85546; the phone number is (602) 428-4040.

Follow a short trail from the trailhead to the canyon bottom. Once in the canyon the hike follows Aravaipa Creek upstream. Although a few faint trails weave back and forth, it is best to simply follow the streambed. This means making numerous crossings. Because the creek is knee deep in most spots, it is impossible to keep your feet dry. Consider wearing old tennis shoes that you do not mind getting wet. Bring an extra pair to keep dry if you are staying overnight.

Although this description covers the length of the canyon, you can turn around wherever you wish. If you decide to hike the entire way, keep in mind that a 4-hour shuttle separates the two ends of the hike. Also, reaching the eastern trailhead entails driving nearly 50 miles of maintained gravel road. Day hikers who turn around sooner will still be well rewarded, as even an afternoon stroll of a few miles accesses some rather spectacular parts of the canyon.

It is possible to gain an appreciation for the natural history of the area along any stretch of Aravaipa Canyon. Thanks to the year-round flow of water, the canyon features stands of ash, cottonwood, sycamore, and willow. This lush vegetation provides a strong contrast to the collection of saguaro cactus, ocotillo, and such that grows along the rocky canyon walls. Javelina and mule deer are common in the canyon, as are coyotes and coatimundis. Desert bighorn sheep and mountain lions haunt the more remote areas. A variety of birds—more than 200 in all—have been spotted within the canyon, including Mexican species of songbirds and such endangered raptors as bald eagles and peregrine falcons.

While Aravaipa Canyon is rich in natural allure, it has also witnessed the coming and going of humans for countless centuries. The prehistoric Salado Indians utilized this natural route nearly a thousand years ago. More recently, the Apache Indians inhabited the canyon. Anglo settlers established small farms along the canyon bottom around the time of the Civil War. Remains of two homesteads are found near Horse Camp and Hell Hole canyons. In 1871 a growing conflict between the Apache and white settlers led to the Aravaipa Massacre, in which dozens of Indian men, women, and children were killed.

The entire canyon can be hiked in one very long day, but an overnight stay allows for the exploration of the many side drainages along the way. Be aware of the possibility of flash floods. Watch for rattlesnakes, especially if you end up scrambling around in rocky places. Creek water should be treated before drinking. Although this canyon may be visited year-round, summers often bring temperatures above the century mark. Conversely, stream crossings in the winter may be quite cold. Keep in mind that you may not enter the canyon without a permit. In addition, pets are prohibited and camping is limited to 2 nights in the canyon. For a complete list of regulations specific to Aravaipa Canyon, contact the BLM in Safford.

Aravaipa Creek

96 ESTES CANYON–BULL PASTURE

Distance: 4.1 miles round trip
Difficulty: moderate
Hiking time: 3 hours
Elevation: 2,400 to 3,400 feet
Management: Organ Pipe Cactus NM

Wilderness status: Organ Pipe WA
Season: October to April
USGS map: Mount Ajo

Situated along a remote stretch of the Arizona–Mexico border, Organ Pipe Cactus National Monument encompasses a vast parcel of pristine desert country. Included among the twenty-eight species of cactus that grow here is the organ pipe cactus. Although common in Mexico, this strangely beautiful succulent is rare in the United States. The Estes Canyon–Bull Pasture Trail passes some fine specimens as it climbs into the monument's primary mountain range, the Ajos.

After making the long drive to Organ Pipe Cactus National Monument from either Phoenix (go south on State Highway 85) or Tucson (go west on State Highway 86), it is best to stop at the visitor center

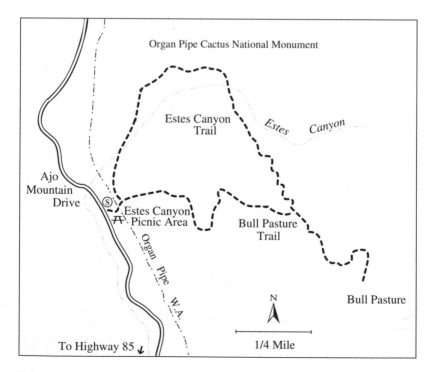

Organ pipe cactus on the hike to Bull Pasture

before heading out. There you can obtain up-to-date information on road conditions to the trailhead. From the visitor center, cross State Highway 85 to the Ajo Mountain Drive. Although passable to cars, this dirt road crosses washes that may become flooded during rainstorms, thereby closing the road. The trailhead is located about 10.5 miles in, at the Estes Canyon Picnic Area.

Just beyond the trail's start the route splits. The left-hand fork, the Estes Canyon Trail, winds gently up the bottom of Estes Canyon for 1.5 miles before ascending the canyon's south wall and reaching Bull Pasture at 2.3 miles. The right-hand fork climbs more directly to Bull Pasture. This route, known as the Bull Pasture Trail, makes the 800-foot climb in 1.8 miles. The two trails join 0.5 mile from the top, making for a nice loop hike. Whichever way you decide to go, there are steep grades to contend with, especially in the last 0.5 mile. The trail is often rough and rocky, so be sure to watch your footing. The way may also be indistinct in places.

Bull Pasture, a broad, V-shaped basin surrounded by the rugged Ajo Mountains, is quite scenic. The Ajos resulted from volcanic eruptions 14 million to 22 million years ago, and the alternating deposits of ash and lava left behind range in color from ocher to deep red. Lichen adds a tint of yellow and green to many rock faces. Ranchers Bill and Birdie Miller once utilized this natural closure to winter their cattle. Today, grasslands interspersed with saguaro cactus and ocotillo cover much of the basin. While the cows are gone, wildlife species include coyote, javelina, desert bighorn sheep, and mountain lion.

Once at Bull Pasture, be sure to scramble up the rocky ridge to the west. From here you get excellent views of the basin and range topography that typifies southern Arizona and neighboring Mexico. From

227

the summit of 4,808-foot Mount Ajo (the high point of the monument) just east of Bull Pasture, a clear day will provide a glimpse of the Gulf of California, some 70 miles to the southwest. Although no established trail climbs Mount Ajo, it is possible to pick your way up a ridge leading north to the peak.

Bring plenty of drinking water because temperatures can get quite hot along this trail. Do not attempt the hike in the summer. Watch for rattlesnakes throughout the hike and be wary of lightning during thunderstorms.

97   VICTORIA MINE

Distance: 4.5 miles round trip
Difficulty: easy
Hiking time: 3 hours
Elevation: 1,700 to 1,600 feet
Management: Organ Pipe Cactus NM

Wilderness status: Organ Pipe WA
Season: October to April
USGS map: Lukeville

An easy hike, the trail to the old Victoria Mine offers a wonderful look at both the natural and human history of Organ Pipe Cactus National Monument.

Drive to Organ Pipe Cactus National Monument from either Phoenix (go south on State Highway 85) or Tucson (go west on State Highway 86). The hike begins at the south end of the monument's only

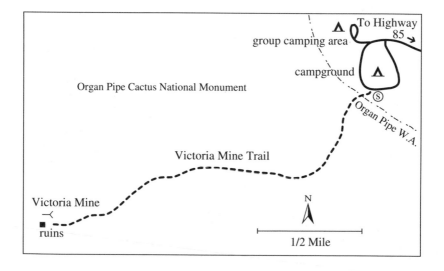

Old mine machinery at Victoria Mine

campground. Parking is provided for a few vehicles at the amphitheater on the west end of the campground loop; additional space may be found at the group camping area to the north.

Traveling southwest across gently rolling terrain, the Victoria Mine Trail is mostly level and easy to follow. Some loose rocks are present and you will have to watch for thorny brush along the way. Traversing a topography commonly referred to as bajada, the route crosses a large alluvial fan of eroded gravel and sands. In this section of the monument, the bajada is home to a mix of saguaro, cholla, ocotillo, and palo verde trees. Although a few organ pipe cactus do grow in this mostly flat topography, they much prefer the well-drained soils of south-facing hillsides.

Upon reaching the base of the Sonoyta Mountains, the trail ends at the Victoria Mine. Established in the 1880s by a prospector from California, the mine was first sold to a Mexican by the name of Cipriano Ortega, who then sold it to Mikul G. Levy in 1899. The Sonoyta Mountains, unlike most other ranges in the monument, consist of heavily mineralized granite, which produced some gold and silver. Today, the hillsides surrounding the mine are riddled with vertical mine shafts, some of which are fenced off. The masonry foundation of Levy's circa-1900 store still stands and pieces of machinery are strewn about. Extreme caution should be used around the mines, and keep in mind that it is unlawful to disturb or remove artifacts and relics of any kind.

Be sure to bring plenty of drinking water and watch out for rattlesnakes. Do not attempt this hike in the summer; temperatures have been known to reach 120 degrees Fahrenheit.

98 PALM CANYON

Distance: 1.5 miles round trip
Difficulty: easy
Hiking time: 1 hour
Elevation: 2,100 to 2,500 feet
Management: Kofa NWR

Wilderness status: Kofa Refuge
WA
Season: year-round
USGS map: Palm Canyon

The short hike into Palm Canyon reveals one of nature's more alluring surprises. Tucked into a narrow abyss of the Kofa Mountains is a grove of naturally occurring palm trees. These, along with a few others in other secretive canyons of the Kofa range, are possibly the only palms native to Arizona.

Located off US Highway 95 between Yuma and Quartzite in the southwestern corner of the state, Palm Canyon is part of the sprawling Kofa National Wildlife Refuge. Drive either 18 miles south from Quartzite or 63 miles north from Yuma to the signed turnoff for the canyon. Follow this dirt road 9 miles east to the base of the imposing Kofa Mountains. This road is passable to all vehicles.

From the parking area at road's end an established trail leads into the high-walled canyon before you. It is only 0.75 mile to a sign that points north into a narrow side canyon. Growing in the upper reaches of this canyon are four dozen or so California fan palms. It is possible to scramble up to the trees for a closer look. Sitting among the palms and listening to their fronds rustle in the cool breeze imparts a marvelous appreciation of these venerable trees.

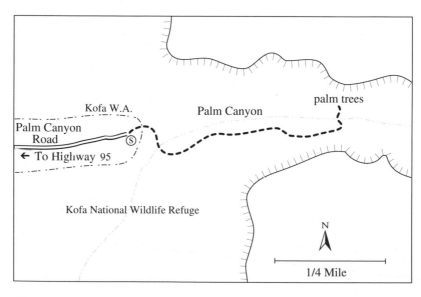

Palms growing in Palm Canyon

Two different theories explain the presence of these palms. One says that they were left over from the last ice age, when the environment was not so hot and dry. The other suggests that their seeds were transported via the digestive tracts of birds or coyotes. In either case, protected from direct sun and supplied with adequate moisture, these palms have been able to survive for many years. As precarious as their existence is, a fire in 1954 and thoughtless people etching their initials in the bark have not deterred them to any great degree.

In addition to the palms, other plants found in Palm Canyon include the green-barked palo verde, ironwood, the rare Kofa Mountain barberry bush, and nolina—a plant that is sometimes mistaken for young palm trees. Desert bighorn sheep are frequently spotted in Palm Canyon. The entire 665,400-acre refuge, in fact, is home to about 1,000 sheep. Coyotes are common. Desert kit fox also live here, as do desert tortoises.

After enjoying the palm trees you may want to venture farther up the canyon. Although no trail exists, it is not too difficult to scramble up along the boulders and scree slopes that litter the canyon bottom. The hike eventually leads to a rugged basin above. Look back down the canyon to gain a good feel for the ruggedness of these mountains. The Kofas consist mostly of rhyolite, a volcanic rock. The name "Kofa" is an acronym adopted from the King of Arizona Mine in the southern end of the range.

Bring drinking water—none is found along the way. Because this is one of the hottest regions of the state, hiking Palm Canyon in the summer should be restricted to the cooler times of the day. Watch out for rattlesnakes and flash floods.

99
HUALAPAI MOUNTAIN PARK

Distance: 4.3 miles round trip
Difficulty: moderate
Hiking time: 3 hours
Elevation: 6,814 to 7,600 feet
Management: Mohave County Parks

Wilderness status: none
Season: May to October
USGS map: Hualapai Peak

Rising rather abruptly above Kingman, the Hualapai Mountains offer a welcome contrast to the arid desert basins below. Topping the 8,000-foot level, the upper reaches of this range feature cool forests and a variety of wildlife. A pleasurable hike across this mountain terrain follows the Potato Patch Loop in Hualapai Mountain Park, which is owned and operated by Mohave County.

In Kingman, turn south onto Hualapai Mountain Road from Andy Devine Drive and continue 12 miles to the park entrance. Drive another 0.7 mile to the Hualapai trailhead. Keep right at each of the several forks in the road between the park entrance and the trailhead. A very small parking area is provided.

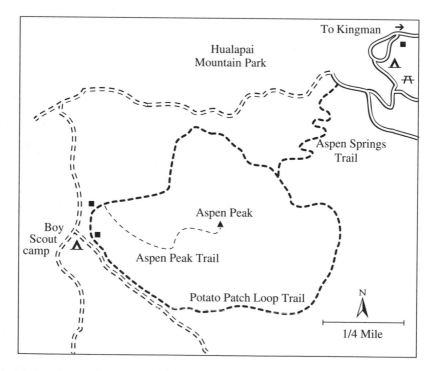

Originally constructed in 1937 by the CCC and rebuilt in 1981 by the Youth Conservation Corps, the Hualapai Mountain Park trail system is well established and easy to follow. From the trailhead this hike first follows the Aspen Springs Trail for nearly a mile to where it connects with the northern end of the Potato Patch Loop Trail. Climbing along a mostly moderate grade, the Aspen Springs Trail switchbacks among stands of ponderosa pine and Gambel oak. As it nears the junction, however, Douglas fir and white fir become common. Some interesting outcrops of granite are encountered along the way, as well.

Upon reaching the Aspen Springs–Potato Patch junction, this hike turns right to follow the loop counterclockwise. Shortly beyond, vistas to the north open up as the trail continues to gain in elevation. The rocky summit of Aspen Peak also comes into view directly south. Near an interesting rock formation known as the Three Gossips, the trail encounters the first of several stands of aspen along the way. After passing beneath a power line about 0.5 mile from the junction, the Potato Patch Loop Trail levels off and reaches its highest point. In the 1.5 miles from the trailhead to here, the hike gains about 800 feet.

The trail then drops slightly into a broad and scenic basin characterized by ponderosa pine and scattered aspens. The summit of Hayden Peak (elevation 8,390 feet) with its array of radio towers rises to the south, while Aspen Peak (elevation 8,239 feet) lies directly east. Within a short distance the trail joins a dirt road, which it follows to the left for 100 yards or so. At a signed left turn the route takes up a foot trail again as it enters a rustic Boy Scout camp. A side trail branches off from here to access the summit of Aspen Peak, 0.6 mile away. Shortly after, the route reaches a second road and turns left to

On the Aspen Springs Trail in Hualapai Mountain Park

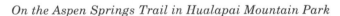

follow it for 25 yards or so before turning left again onto another road. Although this turn is not signed, you will know the way because it passes a large concrete block building. The trail follows this road through a string of established campsites (still part of the scout camp) for 0.3 mile to where a foot trail turns left into the brush. This turn is signed.

Beyond this point, the Potato Patch Loop Trail climbs briefly as it skirts around Aspen Peak's south-facing slope. Drier than the opposite side of the mountain, this section of trail encounters open ponderosa pine and Gambel oak forests, along with some manzanita. This is a good area to spot mule deer or elk, both of which inhabit the Hualapai Mountains. You will also get an unobstructed view of nearby Hualapai Peak. At 8,417 feet, this is the highest summit in the range. As with Hayden and Aspen peaks, pines, firs, and aspens grow on Hualapai Peak's rocky and jagged facade.

Eventually, the Potato Patch Loop Trail rounds the eastern side of Aspen Peak to complete the circle. Along this section of trail several vistas take in the broad valley to the east and the Aquarius Mountains beyond. Return to the trailhead via the Aspen Springs Trail.

Although water may be available at the Boy Scout camp, there are no other reliable sources along the Potato Patch Loop Trail. Watch for lightning in exposed areas, especially during summer thunderstorms.

¡OO ARIZONA HOT SPRINGS

Distance: 5.8 miles round trip
Difficulty: moderate
Hiking time: 4 hours
Elevation: 1,600 to 700 feet

Management: Lake Mead NRA
Wilderness status: none
Season: October to May
USGS map: Ringbolt Rapids

Although quite rugged and wholly inhospitable during the warmer months of the year, the Lake Mead National Recreation Area is not

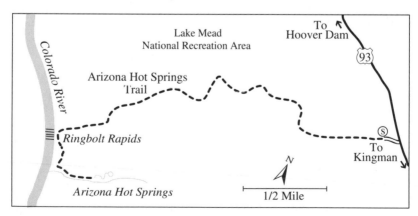

An old ladder accesses the Arizona Hot Springs.

without its interesting backcountry excursions. One such hike leads nearly 3 miles to the Colorado River and the Arizona Hot Springs.

From Kingman, drive north on US Highway 93 for 66.8 miles to a graveled left turn. A parking area and trail sign are located at road's end a short distance to the west. If you are approaching from the north the trailhead turnoff is 4.2 miles south of Hoover Dam.

From the trailhead the route drops moderately along an obvious trail toward the head of a narrow canyon visible to the west. Within 0.5 mile it takes up a sandy wash bottom, which in turn leads into what is known as White Rock Canyon. Interestingly, this canyon cuts through dark red and even black volcanic rock. The name originated with a large boulder of granite that washed down from the nearby Black Mountains some time ago. Once inside White Rock Canyon the trail follows the gentle canyon floor the rest of the way to the Colorado River. Except for loose sand and gravel in the wash, the going is easy along this stretch.

Despite the extreme climate of this desert environment, a variety of plants do manage to survive here. A partial list includes Mormon tea, rabbitbrush, desert fir, indigobush, desert tobacco, globe mallow, and rock daisy. Some animals are able to eke out a living here, as well. Most impressive are the desert bighorn sheep, which favor the rugged walls of White Rock and other nearby canyons.

After 2.2 miles the route reaches the Colorado River and Ringbolt Rapids. With Hoover Dam only a few miles upstream and the upper end of Lake Mohave just around the bend to the south, this short section of free-flowing water is an anomaly along the lower Colorado. From the mouth of White Rock Canyon a rugged trail continues downstream for another 0.7 mile before reaching the next side canyon to the south. This section of the hike passes among thickets of tamarisk as it climbs up and over rugged outcrops of rock. Watch your footing along the way.

Upon reaching the bottom of the next canyon south, turn left and follow the narrow drainage upstream. Although the hot springs are located less than 0.25 mile away, getting to them involves scrambling up some small drop-offs and climbing a 20-foot ladder. Producing 400 gallons of water per minute, the hot springs range in temperature from 85 to 120 degrees. Heated deep below the ground, where it comes in contact with molten rock, this water contains a variety of minerals. According to the Park Service it also contains *Naegleria fowleri,* a microorganism that can cause infection and even death. They suggest that you avoid splashing or submerging your head in the water because it can enter the body through the nasal passages. Before heading back to the trailhead, be sure to visit the beautiful little beach at the mouth of the hot springs canyon.

Because temperatures can reach 120 degrees Fahrenheit in the summer, do not attempt this hike between May and September. During the rest of the year you still need to bring plenty of drinking water. A hat is also a good idea. Watch for rattlesnakes and be aware of the possibility of flash floods during heavy showers.

Index

About the author

Scott S. Warren has lived in the Southwest for the last 20 years. He has spent much of that time in Arizona exploring its many different natural areas. "What I really love about hiking in Arizona is the incredible variety of terrain and plant life," Warren says. "From cactus forests and canyon bottoms to lush forests and high alpine summits, Arizona has it all." In addition to writing about the outdoors, Warren is also a photographer. He holds a bachelor of fine arts degree in photography from Utah State University and his images have appeared in *Audubon, Outside, Sierra, Travel & Leisure,* and various National Geographic publications.

THE MOUNTAINEERS, founded in 1906, is a nonprofit outdoor activity and conservation club, whose mission is "to explore, study, preserve, and enjoy the natural beauty of the outdoors...." Based in Seattle, Washington, the club is now the third-largest such organization in the United States, with 14,000 members and four branches throughout Washington State.

The Mountaineers sponsors both classes and year-round outdoor activities in the Pacific Northwest, which include hiking, mountain climbing, ski-touring, snowshoeing, bicycling, camping, kayaking and canoeing, nature study, sailing, and adventure travel. The club's conservation division supports environmental causes through educational activities, sponsoring legislation, and presenting informational programs. All club activities are led by skilled, experienced volunteers, who are dedicated to promoting safe and responsible enjoyment and preservation of the outdoors.

The Mountaineers Books, an active, nonprofit publishing program of the club, produces guidebooks, instructional texts, historical works, natural history guides, and works on environmental conservation. All books produced by The Mountaineers are aimed at fulfilling the club's mission.

If you would like to participate in these organized outdoor activities or the club's programs, consider a membership in The Mountaineers. For information and an application, write or call The Mountaineers, Club Headquarters, 300 Third Avenue West, Seattle, Washington 98119; (206) 284-6310.

Send or call for our catalog of more than 200 outdoor books:
The Mountaineers Books
1011 SW Klickitat Way, Suite 107
Seattle, WA 98134
1-800-553-4453